Also America's Test Kitchen Titles

Praise for America's Test Kitchen Titles

"The book is a great resource for beginner outdoor cooks or those who want to learn more about cooking al fresco. It covers gas and charcoal grills, flat-tops, fire pits and more, in the typical no-detail-is-too-small fashion that's an ATK hallmark."
MINNEAPOLIS STAR TRIBUNE ON *THE OUTDOOR COOK*

"Another winning cookbook from ATK. . .The folks at America's Test Kitchen apply their rigorous experiments to determine the facts about these pans."
BOOKLIST ON *COOK IT IN CAST IRON*

"Cooking inspiration: Enjoy 100 recipes, ranging from mini meatloaves to a whole chicken."
READERSDIGEST.COM ON *TOASTER OVEN PERFECTION*

"This book begins with a detailed buying guide, a critical summary of available sizes and attachments, and a list of clever food processor techniques. Easy and versatile dishes follow. . . Both new and veteran food processor owners will love this practical guide."
LIBRARY JOURNAL ON *FOOD PROCESSOR PERFECTION*

"A mood board for one's food board is served up in this excellent guide. . . This has instant classic written all over it."
PUBLISHERS WEEKLY (STARRED REVIEW) ON *BOARDS*

"If there's room in the budget for one multicooker/Instant Pot cookbook, make it this one."
BOOKLIST ON *MULTICOOKER PERFECTION*

"The book offers an impressive education for curious cake makers, new and experienced alike. A summation of 25 years of cake making at ATK, there are cakes for every taste."
THE WALL STREET JOURNAL ON *THE PERFECT CAKE*

"*The Perfect Cookie* . . . is, in a word, perfect. This is an important and substantial cookbook. . . If you love cookies, but have been a tad shy to bake them on your own, all your fears will be dissapated. This is one book you can use for years with magnificently happy results."
HUFFPOST ON *THE PERFECT COOKIE*

"The book's depth, breadth, and practicality makes it a must-have for seafood lovers."
PUBLISHER'S WEEKLY (STARRED REVIEW) ON *FOOLPROOF FISH*

"Another flawless entry in the America's Test Kitchen canon, *Bowls* guides readers of all culinary skill levels in composing one-bowl meals from a variety of cuisines."
BUZZFEED BOOKS ON *BOWLS*

"If you're one of the 30 million Americans with diabetes, *The Complete Diabetes Cookbook* by America's Test Kitchen belongs on your kitchen shelf."
PARADE.COM ON *THE COMPLETE DIABETES COOKBOOK*

"True to its name, this smart and endlessly enlightening cookbook is about as definitive as it's possible to get in the modern vegetarian realm."
MEN'S JOURNAL ON *THE COMPLETE VEGETARIAN COOKBOOK*

"The go-to gift book for newlyweds, small families, or empty nesters."
ORLANDO SENTINEL ON *THE COMPLETE COOKING FOR TWO COOKBOOK*

"An exhaustive but approachable primer for those looking for a 'flexible' diet. Chock-full of tips, you can dive into the science of plant-based cooking or just sit back and enjoy the 500 recipes."
MINNEAPOLIS STAR TRIBUNE ON *THE COMPLETE PLANT-BASED COOKBOOK*

"Reassuringly hefty and comprehensive, *The Complete Autumn and Winter Cookbook* by America's Test Kitchen has you covered with a seemingly endless array of seasonal fare. . . This overstuffed compendium is guaranteed to warm you from the inside out."
NPR ON *THE COMPLETE AUTUMN AND WINTER COOKBOOK*

Ultimate
AIR FRYER
PERFECTION

185 Remarkable Recipes for Everything You'll Want to Make

AMERICA'S TEST KITCHEN

Library of Congress Cataloging-in-Publication Data has been applied for.

ISBN 978-1-954210-84-4

America's Test Kitchen
21 Drydock Avenue, Boston, MA 02210

Printed in Canada
10 9 8 7 6 5 4 3 2 1

Distributed by Penguin Random House Publisher Services
Tel: 800.733.3000

Pictured on front cover: Pistachio-Crusted Salmon (page 172); Baked Eggs with Smoky Zucchini, Red Pepper, and Bread Hash (page 25); Steak Frites (page 102); Cheesecake (page 256); Beef-and-Bulgur Meatballs with Tahini-Yogurt Dipping Sauce (page 122); Roasted Chicken Sausages with Butternut Squash and Radicchio (page 84)

Pictured on back cover (clockwise from top left): Warm Chocolate Fudge Cakes (page 255); Roasted Broccoli (page 200); Red Curry Chicken Kebabs with Peanut Dipping Sauce (page 63); Roasted Fruit and Almond Butter Toast (page 33); Steak Tacos (page 109)

Editorial Director, Books ADAM KOWIT

Executive Food Editor DAN ZUCCARELLO

Deputy Food Editor STEPHANIE PIXLEY

Executive Managing Editor DEBRA HUDAK

Senior Editors NICOLE KONSTANTINAKOS, KAUMUDI MARATHÉ, AND SARA MAYER

Associate Editors AFTON CYRUS, LAWMAN JOHNSON, AND RUSSELL SELANDER

Test Cooks CAMILA CHAPARRO, JOSÉ MALDONADO, KATHERINE PERRY, AND DAVID YU

Digital Test Cook SAMANTHA BLOCK

Additional Recipe Development GARTH CLINGINGSMITH AND REBECCAH MARSTERS

Assistant Editors KELLY GAUTHIER AND EMILY RAHRAVAN

Design Director LINDSEY TIMKO CHANDLER

Deputy Art Director JANET TAYLOR

Associate Art Director ASHLEY TENN

Designer JEN KANAVOS HOFFMAN

Photography Director JULIE BOZZO COTE

Senior Photography Producer MEREDITH MULCAHY

Senior Staff Photographers STEVE KLISE AND DANIEL J. VAN ACKERE

Staff Photographer KEVIN WHITE

Additional Photography NINA GALLANT, JOSEPH KELLER, AND CARL TREMBLAY

Food Styling TARA BUSA, JOY HOWARD, CATRINE KELTY, CHANTAL LAMBETH, KENDRA MCKNIGHT, ASHLEY MOORE, CHRISTIE MORRISON, MARIE PIRAINO, ELLE SIMONE SCOTT, KENDRA SMITH, AND SALLY STAUB

Photoshoot Kitchen Team

Photo Team and Special Events Manager ALLISON BERKEY

Lead Test Cook ERIC HAESSLER

Test Cooks HANNAH FENTON, JACQUELINE GOCHENOUER, GINA MCCREADIE, AND JESSICA RUDOLPH

Assistant Test Cooks SARAH EWALD, HISHAM HASSAN, DEVON SHATKIN, AND CHRISTA WEST

Project Manager, Publishing Operations KATIE KIMMERER

Senior Print Production Specialist LAUREN ROBBINS

Production and Imaging Coordinator AMANDA YONG

Production and Imaging Specialists TRICIA NEUMYER AND DENNIS NOBLE

Copy Editors APRIL POOLE, JEFFREY SCHIER, AND RACHEL SCHOWALTER

Proofreader VICKI ROWLAND

Indexer ELIZABETH PARSON

Chief Creative Officer JACK BISHOP

Executive Editorial Directors JULIA COLLIN DAVISON AND BRIDGET LANCASTER

CONTENTS

WELCOME TO AMERICA'S TEST KITCHEN

This book has been tested, written, and edited by the folks at America's Test Kitchen, where curious cooks become confident cooks. Located in Boston's Seaport District in the historic Innovation and Design Building, it features 15,000 square feet of kitchen space including multiple photography and video studios. It is the home of *Cook's Illustrated* magazine and *Cook's Country* magazine and is the workday destination for more than 60 test cooks, editors, and cookware specialists. Our mission is to empower and inspire confidence, community, and creativity in the kitchen.

We start the process of testing a recipe with a complete lack of preconceptions, which means that we accept no claim, no technique, and no recipe at face value. We simply assemble as many variations as possible, test a half-dozen of the most promising, and taste the results blind. We then construct our own recipe and continue to test it, varying ingredients, techniques, and cooking times until we reach a consensus. As we like to say in the test kitchen, "We make the mistakes so you don't have to." The result, we hope, is the best version of a particular recipe, but we realize that only you can be the final judge of our success (or failure). We use the same rigorous approach when we test equipment and taste ingredients.

All of this would not be possible without a belief that good cooking, much like good music, is based on a foundation of objective technique. Some people like spicy foods and others don't, but there is a right way to sauté, there is a best way to cook a pot roast, and there are measurable scientific principles involved in producing perfectly beaten, stable egg whites. Our ultimate goal is to investigate the fundamental principles of cooking to give you the techniques, tools, and ingredients you need to become a better cook. It is as simple as that.

To see what goes on behind the scenes at America's Test Kitchen, check out our social media channels for kitchen snapshots, exclusive content, video tips, and much more. You can watch us work (in our actual test kitchen) by tuning in to *America's Test Kitchen* or *Cook's Country* on public television or on our websites. Listen to *Proof*, *Mystery Recipe*, and *The Walk-In* (AmericasTestKitchen.com/podcasts) to hear engaging, complex stories about people and food. Want to hone your cooking skills or finally learn how to bake—with an America's Test Kitchen test cook? Enroll in one of our online cooking classes.

However you choose to visit us, we welcome you into our kitchen, where you can stand by our side as we test our way to the best recipes in America.

facebook.com/AmericasTestKitchen

instagram.com/TestKitchen

youtube.com/AmericasTestKitchen

tiktok.com/TestKitchen

twitter.com/TestKitchen

pinterest.com/TestKitchen

AmericasTestKitchen.com

CooksIllustrated.com

CooksCountry.com

OnlineCookingSchool.com

Join our community of recipe testers

Our recipe testers provide valuable feedback on recipes under development by ensuring that they are foolproof in home kitchens. Help the America's Test Kitchen book team investigate the how and why behind successful recipes from your home kitchen.

AIR FRYER 2.0

INTRODUCTION

Air fryers continue to be all the rage, and for good reason. They cook food quickly and efficiently and have the ability to produce healthier fried foods. The air fryer earned a permanent place in our kitchen after we put it through its paces when developing our best-selling book *Air Fryer Perfection*. Since we first published that book, new and varied air fryers have come on the market, from toaster oven–air fryer hybrids to Instant Pot air fryer lids, and we've continued to test them all. Understanding exactly how they all work let us use this unique cooking method to our delicious advantage. *Ultimate Air Fryer Perfection* has been updated with all of our newest testing information covering a wider range of models and sizes.

So, we remain big fans of air fryers for their convenience, speed, and consistent results. Their benefits go well beyond frying. An air fryer is not a fryer at all. It's a mini convection oven that cooks food by circulating hot air around it with a fan. The genius of the method is that food cooked by convection can approach the crispiness of fried food while using far less oil (at least when cooked properly; you can also simply dry food out). But the intense hot air is also ideal for roasting and even allows us to prepare dishes we might otherwise cook on the grill. Viewed in this way, the air fryer is really appealing. We found that it could make dinner—a main and a side—with less mess and fuss (and in less time) than if we used our oven, so it was well worth the space on our counter.

The more we cooked and tasted, the more we liked the air fryer. Rosy steaks, juicy chicken, silky salmon, vibrant roasted vegetables, and even cheesecake all emerged from the basket and were eagerly devoured. Colleagues in the test kitchen couldn't believe what we cooked in the air fryer. The best part was the ease: There was no splattering, and the device could mostly be left alone. Our favorite model even turns itself off after the timer dings. Finicky dishes like bone-in chicken breasts became close to effortless thanks to the controlled temperature and timer, while delicate fish cooked to perfection. We also appreciated that when cooking for two people, the air fryer provided just the right amount of food. To cook for four people, many of the recipes in the book can be doubled if you have one of larger models of air fryer.

We made breakfast a priority and created recipes that include baked eggs, overnight grain bowls, and make-ahead vegetable-filled burritos. Since dinner is still the main event, we found fresh ways to deliver on the promise of creating a full meal using the air fryer. We air-grilled chicken skewers over vegetable skewers, perched sirloin steak over french fries for an easy steak frites, and roasted moist pieces of salmon over kimchi and broccoli, orchestrating the timing so everything finished together.

Want to cook a new version of spaghetti and meatballs in the air fryer? See pages 92, 121, and 155. Roast a whole chicken? See page 86. Air-fry juicy cheeseburgers (page 124), turkey burgers (page 89), and salmon burgers (page 180) (far less messy than using a skillet). Get fancy and roast boneless beef short ribs or lamb chops; they emerge rich and luscious. Knowing how well frozen food crisps up in the air fryer, we developed homemade takes on favorites such as chicken nuggets, fish sticks, and chocolate chip cookies that can be air-fried at a moment's notice.

Getting great results from the air fryer involves more than simply closing the basket and turning it on. Like all equipment, it benefits from the right techniques. Through exhaustive testing, we learned the secrets to producing air-fried chicken with a golden crust, brussels sprouts that tasted like they came out of a deep fryer, and french fries that raised the bar on what can be achieved without a pot of bubbling oil.

We incorporated all of the tips, discoveries, and secrets we learned in the test kitchen to create recipes that work in every air fryer, every time. In the following pages you'll learn how to cook crisp, evenly browned, and well-roasted food whether you've been air-frying for a while or are a complete novice. With *Ultimate Air Fryer Perfection*, you'll see why we now count the air fryer among our most well-loved appliances.

10 REASONS WE LOVE THE AIR FRYER

1 It produces real food Since it's essentially a small convection oven, the air fryer can cook many of the foods you might roast or bake with less fuss. The basket's perforated base helps food to cook evenly since air circulates on all sides.

2 Less-fat frying Yes, the air fryer's intended purpose holds true: Instead of quarts of oil, we can use just a small amount and achieve beautifully crisp results for french fries, chicken, fish, and more.

3 Set and (almost) forget Unlike stovetop cooking, air frying requires virtually no monitoring, thanks to its well-regulated temperature and automatic shutoff. Other than the occasional flip or toss, it does all the work, allowing you to focus on the rest of the meal.

4 Minimal mess The food basket is enclosed in the air fryer, and this translates into a clean kitchen—no splattering oil or multiple dirty pots and pans. Plus, the baskets are simple to clean—most are nonstick and dishwasher-safe.

5 No stove—or oven—needed On busy nights when we must convince ourselves to cook (even test cooks feel this way at times), not having to turn on the stove can be a blessing. And on hot nights, the air fryer keeps our kitchen from becoming a steam room.

6 It's fast The air fryer lets us skip past the common first step in cooking—heating fat in a pan or heating the oven or grill. This not only was convenient but also shaved valuable time off of our recipes.

7 Easy meals for kids The ability to crisp up a batch of chicken nuggets, bake a couple of hand pies, or roast carrots without embarking on a cooking project makes this a lifesaver for busy parents.

8 Ideal for two people When it's just the two of you eating (or you're cooking solo) and you don't want to make more than you need, the air fryer helps to prevent waste. Our recipes were made with standard air-fryer basket sizes in mind, and many yield two servings. (There are also instructions for how to double recipes to cook in larger models of air fryers.)

9 Your automated sous chef Cooking multiple dishes in the oven can be a juggling act. Hand a side dish over to the air fryer and free up valuable space.

10 Even results All of the previous benefits would amount to null if the air fryer's cooking results were spotty, but we continued to be surprised at how good the food tasted. The most common remark we heard at recipe tastings was, "I can't believe this came from an air fryer!"

TESTING AIR FRYERS

We cooked thousands of french fries and more than 50 pounds of chicken to answer one question: Which air fryer reigns supreme?

What You Need to Know

Despite their name, air fryers don't fry your food. They're essentially small convection ovens with powerful fans that circulate hot air around food to approximate the crisp and juicy results of deep frying. They require less oil—mere tablespoons, as opposed to quarts—and are less messy than deep frying. Air fryers are also marketed as a smaller and more convenient alternative to conventional ovens; they generally cook food quicker, shaving off 5 to 10 minutes from most recipes. They need to be preheated for only a few minutes, if at all, and they won't heat up your entire kitchen. Even people who already have a convection oven may appreciate the speed, convenience, and extra cooking space that these appliances offer. Throughout years of testing air fryers, we've concluded that even the best models can't achieve the perfect golden crispiness that deep frying offers, but some come impressively close. With a little finessing, some of our favorite oven and deep-fry recipes can work quite well in an air fryer.

We tested three styles of air fryers: drawer-style models with baskets that pull out from the front; flip-top models with lids that lift up from the top; and bigger, cube-shaped models with doors that swing open in the front and multiple racks inside like an oven. The oven-style models often include revolving rotisserie baskets or propeller-shaped auto-stir attachments, both of which automatically rotate to toss food around, supposedly for more-even heating and crisping. After testing air fryers with all sorts of innovations, we really liked a few newer models. Their large capacities, speedy cooking times, and simple controls impressed us.

What to Look For

Drawer-Style Models: No matter the size or capacity of the air fryers we tested, the best results came from those with drawer-style frying baskets. Each had a single large handle that allowed us to easily maneuver the basket and shake it to redistribute food midway through cooking. This kept our hands away from the air fryers' heating elements and gave us a place to hold the basket without using oven mitts. The baskets sat inside plastic or metal trays, which caught crumbs and debris for easy cleanup.

Wide Cooking Spaces: Just because an air fryer claims to have a larger capacity doesn't mean that it has more usable cooking space. Since air-fried food cooks best in one layer, the width of an air fryer's cooking surface mattered more than the height of its cooking space. We preferred one wide cooking surface to multiple racks for this reason. Our favorite models had cooking surfaces that measured more than 10 inches by 10 inches, offering enough room to accommodate recipes that serve up to four people.

Simple, Responsive Controls: Our top-performing models required only pushing a couple of buttons or turning a single knob to operate. While we did like a few of the analog models, our favorites had digital controls, since we were less likely to accidentally knock digital controls when adding or removing food. Digital models were also more precise.

Nonstick Interiors: Frying baskets and crumb-catching trays with nonstick coatings were easy to clean, even when they were covered in cooked-on cheese or sticky sauces. Because air fryers generally can't heat to more than 400 degrees, there's no risk of the nonstick coatings getting hot enough to release fumes.

Auto-Pause Timers: For the best results when cooking in an air fryer, you need to remove the basket or racks and shake, flip, or turn food as it cooks. We preferred models whose timers automatically paused when we opened the doors or lids and resumed when we closed them. This saved us from having to push another button to continue cooking, which was easy to forget.

Automatic Shutoff: The best models in our lineup also shut off automatically at the end of the programmed cooking cycle, ensuring that food didn't overcook if it lingered in the machine for a few extra minutes. Another perk: We didn't have to remember to turn off the models.

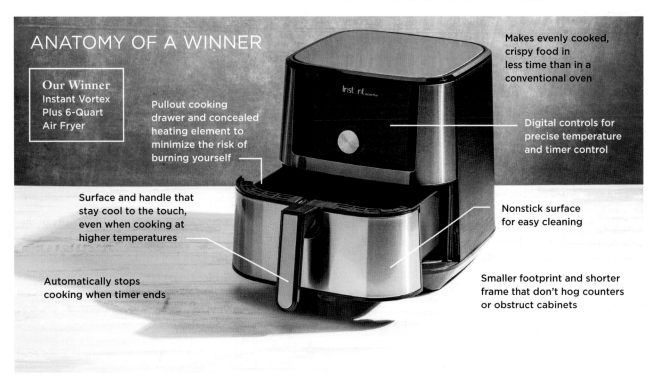

ANATOMY OF A WINNER

Our Winner
Instant Vortex
Plus 6-Quart
Air Fryer

Pullout cooking drawer and concealed heating element to minimize the risk of burning yourself

Makes evenly cooked, crispy food in less time than in a conventional oven

Digital controls for precise temperature and timer control

Surface and handle that stay cool to the touch, even when cooking at higher temperatures

Automatically stops cooking when timer ends

Nonstick surface for easy cleaning

Smaller footprint and shorter frame that don't hog counters or obstruct cabinets

highly recommended	performance	comments

Instant
Vortex Plus 6-Quart Air Fryer

MODEL N/A
PRICE $119.95
CONTROLS Digital
STYLE Drawer
HEIGHT 12.5 in

COOKING ★★★
CAPACITY ★★★
SAFETY ★★★
EASE OF USE ★★½

Our winner delivers on its promise to offer an extra-large capacity. Though it's only a foot tall, this drawer-style model was large enough to fit four chicken cutlets or two 15-ounce bags of frozen french fries, cooking everything to crispy, golden perfection. We were even able to cook a whole 4-pound chicken in it. A quick 2-minute preheat ensured that the interior was hot when we added food. The wide drawer-style basket was easy to remove and insert—and our hands were safeguarded from the heating element—and its sturdy handle allowed us to shake its contents for easy redistribution. Intuitive digital controls were brightly lit and easy to operate. This fryer is a great option for a family of four or anyone who is looking for more cooking space without adding much bulk. Our one gripe is that the basket liner occasionally fell out when we inverted the basket. We solved this by using tongs to remove food or being more careful when pouring.

Instant
Vortex Plus ClearCook
+ OdorErase 6-Quart

MODEL 140-3089-01
PRICE $149.99
CONTROLS Digital
STYLE Drawer
HEIGHT 12.5 in

COOKING ★★★
CAPACITY ★★★
SAFETY ★★★
EASE OF USE ★★½

This updated model of our previous winner has the same spacious interior, convenient preheating cycle, and stellar cooking ability as its predecessor. But for a bit more money, it includes a few bells and whistles that we appreciated. It's quieter than most of the other models in the lineup, and its viewing window allowed us to monitor cooking progress without losing heat. The only smells we detected were from the food we were cooking (no sign of the unpleasant odors of the predecessor), and we found the control panel even easier to use than that of our winner. Also, the basket liner rarely came loose when we inverted it. In sum, it performs well and is well worth paying a bit extra for it.

Cosori
Dual Blaze 6.8-Quart
Smart Air Fryer

MODEL CAF-P583S-KUS
PRICE $179.99
CONTROLS Digital
STYLE Drawer
HEIGHT 14.5 in

COOKING ★★★
CAPACITY ★★½
SAFETY ★★★
EASE OF USE ★★½

This powerful model included an additional heating element under the basket. As a result, it cooked chicken Parmesan and crisped up frozen french fries about 2 to 3 minutes faster than our favorite air fryers, though fries from scratch took about the same amount of time. Its basket was a touch smaller than those of our favorites, so chicken cutlets were cramped, though they still cooked evenly. We liked its simple digital controls and thought its smart-home compatibility was usually helpful. We only disliked its bulk; it took up too much space under our cabinets.

highly recommended (cont.)	performance	comments

Philips
Premium Airfryer with Fat Removal Technology

MODEL HD9741/99
PRICE $219.95
CONTROLS Digital
STYLE Drawer
HEIGHT 11 in

COOKING ★★★
CAPACITY ★★
SAFETY ★★★
EASE OF USE ★★★

We love this machine's slim, compact footprint, and we liked that its nonstick cooking basket was simple to clean and had a removable bottom for deeper cleaning. Its digital controls and dial-operated menu made setting the time and temperature easy and intuitive. It automatically stopped cooking as soon as the set time was up, and its drawer allowed us to remove its cooking basket without exposing our hands to the heating element. While it can't hold as much food as our winner can, it can handle small batches of frozen foods or recipes intended to serve two people.

recommended	performance	comments

GoWISE
USA 3.7-Quart 7-in-1 Air Fryer

MODEL GW22621
PRICE $75.15
CONTROLS Digital
STYLE Drawer
HEIGHT 13 in

COOKING ★★★
CAPACITY ★★
SAFETY ★★★
EASE OF USE ★★½

While this air fryer's digital controls aren't quite as intuitive as those of our favorite models, it was still easy to set the time and temperature once we got the hang of the multiple buttons. It cooked foods quickly, and its display was large and easy to read. Its drawer and automatic shutoff were a boon to safety, and its nonstick interior was easy to clean. Its small capacity wouldn't work for a crowd, but it cooked our recipes for two and small batches of frozen fries without issue.

Philips
Premium Analog Airfryer

MODEL HD9721/99
PRICE $169.95
CONTROLS Analog
STYLE Drawer
HEIGHT 11.2 in

COOKING ★★★
CAPACITY ★★
SAFETY ★★★
EASE OF USE ★★

This small model's stature and footprint make it easy to store, but it's large enough to cook small batches of frozen foods and our recipes evenly and quickly. Its nonstick interior was easy to clean, but its analog temperature and timer dials weren't as precise as digital controls.

recommended with reservations	performance	comments

Ninja
Air Fryer Max XL

MODEL AF161
PRICE $149.95
CONTROLS Digital
STYLE Drawer
HEIGHT 15 in

COOKING ★★½
CAPACITY ★★
SAFETY ★★★
EASE OF USE ★★

This model sported a powerful "Max Crisp" function that allowed it to reach 450 degrees and cook food quickly, if unevenly. We liked that its digital controls were simple to use. But while its cooking basket was deep, holding a full 2 pounds of frozen fries, it was too narrow to fit four chicken cutlets in a single layer, limiting its usefulness for larger recipes. The unit was tall and heavy with a cooking tray with silicone bumpers that clung tightly to the walls of its cooking basket and was hard to extract. We were also frustrated that it didn't automatically pause its timer when we removed the basket to shake or turn food.

recommended with reservations (cont.)	performance	comments

GoWISE USA
USA 8-in-1 XL 5.8QT Air Fryer

MODEL GW22731
PRICE $99.95
CONTROLS Digital
STYLE Drawer
HEIGHT 11.5 in

COOKING ★★
CAPACITY ★★
SAFETY ★★★
EASE OF USE ★★

This model took up more counter space than its smaller, 3.7-quart counterpart, and its cooking basket was a bit deeper, but its cooking surface was only about ½ inch wider. There wasn't enough room to cook double batches of our recipes, and when we tried making two bags of frozen french fries, they were undercooked, with the fries toward the center being flabby and raw—even though we frequently tossed them throughout cooking. Still, this model cooked single batches as well as the smaller version.

Instant Pot
Duo Crisp 6.5-Quart with
Ultimate Lid Multi-Cooker and
Air Fryer

MODEL 140-0068-01
PRICE $229.99
CONTROLS Digital
STYLE Flip-top
HEIGHT 13 in

COOKING ★★★
CAPACITY ★★½
SAFETY ★★★
EASE OF USE ★★½

This flip-top model had an interface with buttons that were intuitive to use. It had an exposed heating element on the inside of the lid, making us a little nervous we'd bump it and get burned. It had a small capacity, only fitting one 15-ounce bag of french fries or two chicken cutlets at a time. It cooked those cutlets well, producing juicy interiors and golden, crisp exteriors, but the fries cooked a bit unevenly, with fries toward the outside crisping more quickly than those on the inside. Because this machine has a flip-top design, we had to toss food using tongs, which mangled some fries in the process. As a multi-cooker, it was straightforward to use but delivered mushy pressure-cooked beans and slow-cooked beef stew with undercooked vegetables.

GoWISE USA
Vibe 11.6 qt. Air Fryer

MODEL GW77722
PRICE $119.99
CONTROLS Digital
STYLE Oven
HEIGHT 15 in

COOKING ★★
CAPACITY ★★
SAFETY ★★
EASE OF USE ★½

Despite touting an 11.6-quart capacity, this model couldn't really handle much more food than smaller drawer-style air fryers. Single layers of food cooked evenly and quickly, crisping up nicely. But food placed on the upper rack blocked heat from reaching the lower rack, resulting in unevenly cooked food. Its metal racks (called "fry baskets") trapped baked-on cheese and molasses and were tedious to clean.

recommended with reservations (cont.)	performance	comments

Ninja
Foodi XL 14-in-1 8-Qt. Pressure
Cooker Steam Fryer with
SmartLid

MODEL OL601
PRICE $279.99
CONTROLS Digital
STYLE Flip-top
HEIGHT 14 in

COOKING ★★
CAPACITY ★★
SAFETY ★★
EASE OF USE ★½

This flip-top model had a completely exposed heating element in its heavy lid, which made us worry that we'd burn ourselves or smash a finger when shutting it. The machine was capable of holding two 15-ounce bags of french fries in its tall basket insert, but it cooked them unevenly, with undercooked, limp fries in the center of the basket and burnt fries around the exterior. When we used just one bag of fries, they were evenly cooked and crispy throughout. The machine had wire racks that enabled us to cook in layers, holding up to four chicken cutlets, but this delivered uneven results too, with pale, undercooked chicken on the bottom and burned chicken on the top that was nearly touching the heating element. There's a slider on the lid that you have to shift to reveal all the settings under "Pressure," "Steamcrisp," or "Air Fry/Stovetop"; this takes a bit of time. We enjoyed using this machine as a multicooker, achieving great pressure-cooked and slow-cooked beef stew and baked beans.

Instant
Vortex Plus 10-Quart Air Fryer
Oven

MODEL N/A
PRICE $119.00
CONTROLS Digital
STYLE Oven
HEIGHT 14 in

COOKING ★★
CAPACITY ★★
SAFETY ★★
EASE OF USE ★½

Our hopes for an easy-to-use oven-style model were dashed with this air fryer. The instructions say to use an included rotisserie basket—a rotating mesh barrel designed to cook food more evenly—when cooking fries and other small foods. We found this accessory frustrating to open, fill, close, insert, and remove—especially when the metal was hot—and its cramped interior did little to ensure even cooking. We had better results when we prepared small batches of fries using the perforated oven-style racks. But the racks didn't help us prepare larger batches: When we doubled our Chicken Parmesan recipe and used two racks, the cutlets cooked unevenly. In short, this oven-style air fryer offers little advantage over smaller drawer-style fryers when it comes to capacity.

not recommended	performance	comments

Chefman
Turbofry Air Oven with
Auto-Stir Function

MODEL N/A
PRICE $127.99
CONTROLS Digital
STYLE Oven
HEIGHT 15 in

COOKING ★★
CAPACITY ★★
SAFETY ★★
EASE OF USE ★

We found that this model heated up quickly and efficiently. Unfortunately, cooking on multiple racks resulted in unevenly cooked food. This model also came with a frying basket that sported a propeller-like auto-stir attachment. When we tried to cook a double batch of frozen fries, the attachment mangled the fries, and the fries took almost an hour to fully cook. The racks were difficult to clean and hard to grip with an oven mitt.

THE 4 STYLES OF AIR FRYER WE USED

WINNER

DRAWER

A drawer-style air fryer has an easy-to-use basket that slides into the appliance in a drawer. The basket has one wide cooking surface and sits on a plastic or metal tray that catches crumbs and excess oil and drippings. A single large, stay-cool handle allows you to maneuver the basket easily and to shake it to redistribute the food in it partway through cooking. Our winning air fryer, the **Instant Vortex Plus 6-Quart Air Fryer**, is a drawer-style model.

PROS:

- We can't say enough good things about the drawer-style model of air fryer; it's the gold standard and by far our favorite to use. The basket acts like a vessel, and the enclosed space allows for the best layering of ingredients.

- No matter the size, drawer-style air fryers have the most real estate for cooking. We prefer one cooking surface to multiple racks.

CONS:

- None

INSTANT POT LID

Instant Pot makes a lid with a heating element that locks into place on certain Instant Pot multicookers, turning the multicooker into an air fryer. Inserts include two baskets with perforated bottoms that sit one on top of the other, but we don't recommend cooking with both baskets at the same time (we used only the upper basket).

PROS:

- The lid did well with all our recipes. You can roast a whole chicken with it if you remove the insert.

- A lid is a convenient option if you are trying to avoid having another whole appliance.

CONS:

- Its cooking space is limited, so it is harder to make doubled versions of recipes.

- There are no heatproof handles, so you need oven mitts or tongs to take out the baskets.

OVEN

The oven-style air fryer is designed like an oven, with two racks and a door that opens outward. The multiple cooking racks and baskets don't have handles, and their perforations allow crumbs and drips to fall through onto the oven base, or worse, the floor. The upper rack blocks heat from reaching the lower one, resulting in unevenly cooked food, even if you move and rotate the racks partway through cooking.

PRO:

- Even though this style has less space for cooking, it is able to handle large roasts well.

CONS:

- Don't be fooled by the 10-quart capacity: It has less space for cooking than a 6-quart drawer-style air fryer.

- The racks make stacking ingredients more challenging.

TOASTER OVEN

Some toaster ovens have an air-frying function. Good for kitchens with limited counter space, air-fryer toaster ovens are larger than drawer-style air fryers and can accommodate more food. But these ovens often cook food slower than other air fryers, and many need preheating. Our test kitchen favorite is the **Breville Smart Oven Air Fryer Pro**.

PRO:

- If you are trying to maximize the potential of your appliances, then this model is a smart choice. This model is also good if you want to cook traditional sheet-pan meals and other foods such as cookies that require a sheet pan.

CONS:

- Air-fryer toaster ovens are generally more expensive than other styles of air fryer.

- Some models have a fan located on the side, making rotating the hot handleless tray essential for even browning.

MAKING THE MOST OF YOUR AIR FRYER

We love the hands-off ease of cooking in an air fryer, but we found that getting the best results involved slightly more than simply turning it on and walking away. The following tricks had big effects on the overall flavor and texture of our food.

More Even Cooking

Avoid overfilling: Air fryers work by circulating hot air around food, but if the food is packed too tightly it will steam instead of crisp and will cook unevenly. (That said, proteins shrink as they cook, so a snug fit with meat is OK.) We took a "jigsaw puzzle" approach to fitting foods, cutting larger proteins in half and skewering smaller pieces to make it easier to arrange more food in the basket without overcrowding.

Rotate and flip meats: It may seem fussy given that the meat is surrounded by hot air, but we found that turning it partway through cooking helped it to cook more evenly.

Toss vegetables: We got more even browning when we tossed vegetables halfway through cooking them. For smaller cuts, such as fries, tossing them in a separate bowl proved to be more efficient; it also allowed us to add seasonings such as grated cheese partway through cooking.

Tuck in the tails: When cooking proteins of uneven thickness, such as pork tenderloins or fish fillets, we folded the thinner "tails" underneath to create a more uniform size.

Better Browning

Pat food dry: A dry surface browns more quickly than a wet one, since moisture on the surface will steam, so we patted meats and some vegetables with paper towels before cooking.

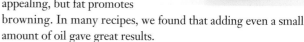

A little fat helps: Cooking without any oil whatsoever may sound appealing, but fat promotes browning. In many recipes, we found that adding even a small amount of oil gave great results.

Try a little honey: Fat isn't the only way to boost browning. The sugar in honey also browns well in the intense heat of the air fryer and flavors the food as it cooks. (Fruit preserves and hoisin sauce work too.)

Brush dough with egg wash: When cooking pastry dough in the air fryer, as for our Southwestern Beef Hand Pies (page 126), we found that brushing the tops with egg wash gave us even, glossy browning.

FROM FREEZER TO FRYER IN A FLASH
Because air fryers excel at crisping up frozen foods, we decided to create our own from-scratch recipes. They can be made ahead and frozen, then dropped into the air fryer at a moment's notice for an easy breakfast, weeknight dinner, or anytime snack. They include:

- **Make-Ahead Breakfast Burritos** (page 30)
- **Chicken Nuggets** (page 41)
- **Better-Than-Boxed Fish Sticks** (page 158)
- **Make-Ahead Lentil and Mushroom Burgers** (page 244)
- **Make-Ahead Chocolate Chip Cookies** (page 266)

TIPS AND TECHNIQUES FOR SUCCESS

An air fryer is a fairly easy appliance to use, but we want to make sure it's easy on you and that you're getting all you can out of it. Here are some tips and techniques from the test kitchen to help you do that.

Crisp Up Food

While cooking in the air fryer is low fat, it isn't no fat. Along with browning, a little fat can help food crisp up. We spray or brush meat and fish with vegetable oil (spraying makes it easy to focus the oil on top of the protein).

Skewer It

Threading pieces of chicken or vegetables onto wooden skewers provides an easy way to space food out in the basket and maximize air exposure. It also helps generate some flavorful charring.

"LINCOLN LOG" SKEWERS AND VEGETABLES

For easy multilayered cooking, arrange half the skewers or vegetable pieces in the basket, spaced evenly apart. Arrange the remaining skewers or vegetables on top, perpendicular to the first layer, log cabin-style.

Use a Container to Cook In

We figured out how to incorporate wet ingredients into our recipes. Using ovensafe vessels that fit into the basket—such as a bowl, ramekin, soufflé dish, or nonstick cake pan—meant we could cook liquid-y dishes in the air fryer. We baked eggs and porridge in bowls (that we could then eat out of), cooked saucy pasta and meatballs in a cake pan, and also baked a cheesecake and olive oil cake in a 6-inch cake pan.

MAKING AN ALUMINUM FOIL SLING

1 Fold one long sheet of foil so that it is 4 inches wide. Lay the sheet of foil widthwise across the basket or rack. Press the foil up and into the sides and fold any excess foil as needed so that the edges of the foil are flush with the lip of the basket.

2 After cooking, use the sling to carefully remove the fish from the air-fryer basket.

A Word About Preheating

A few newer models—including our winner—recommend preheating to ensure that the frying basket is hot when the food touches it. Some air fryers have automatic preheating times and presets indicating when to add or turn food. We found preheating unnecessary. To allow for differences across models, the cooking times in our recipes are meant to be counted as soon as you press "start."

Forget About Attachments

Some air fryers come with rotisserie baskets (barrel-shaped mesh cages) or frying baskets with auto-stir attachments. These accessories are designed to agitate the food, thus eliminating the need for manually shaking the baskets midcook, a common air fryer requirement. But they are fussy to use and don't make better food.

SCALING OUR RECIPES

To accommodate the widest variety of air fryers, we developed most of the recipes in this book to serve two. That said, many of the recipes can be easily scaled up to serve more people.

Doubling a Recipe

If a recipe can be doubled, we indicate this in the headnote of the recipe. If you are doubling a recipe, double all the ingredients.

If your air fryer has a capacity of 6 quarts or more, you can double a recipe and still cook it in a single batch. However, it is critical to leave enough room for air circulation around the ingredients to ensure even cooking. If you have a smaller air fryer (less than 6 quarts) and are doubling a recipe, you will need to cook in batches.

Scaling Proteins

For some stand-alone proteins such as salmon fillets and bone-in chicken breasts, the recipes offer the flexibility to cook one to four pieces, as indicated in the yield line. Here, again, be sure to leave space for the air to circulate around each piece. The number you'll be able to fit depends on the size of your air fryer; a smaller air fryer holds two pieces of fish or chicken. If a recipe calls for doubling steaks, use two steaks of the same size instead of one bigger steak.

Cooking Times

For a few recipes, such as Hearty Vegetable Hash with Golden Yogurt (page 249), a longer cooking time may be needed when doubling it. If that is the case, the increased time is listed in the recipe headnote.

Vessel Inserts

Ovensafe vessels work well in the air fryer to cook liquid-y ingredients (see page 15 for more information). Before you fill any vessel with ingredients, make sure that it fits in your air fryer.

DOUBLE IT

3-cup ovensafe bowl
Serves 1

1½-quart soufflé dish
Serves 2

HANDY EQUIPMENT TO USE WITH YOUR AIR FRYER

Ovensafe Bowl, Soufflé Dish, and Ramekin

We use a 3-cup (24-ounce) ovensafe bowl (which then can be conveniently eaten out of) or 1½-quart soufflé dish in many recipes to hold and cook wet or liquid-y ingredients in the air fryer. For individual portions of dessert, a 6-ounce ramekin works great.

6-Inch Round Nonstick or Silicone Cake Pan

Experimenting with a 6-inch nonstick cake pan opened up exciting new recipe possibilities since it allowed us to use liquid-y ingredients such as eggs for a frittata, tomato sauce for meatballs, and kimchi. We also used this pan to bake our snack bars. It's easy to put in and take out of the air fryer when hot; we recommend using tongs in one hand and an oven mitt on the other to help with that.

Aluminum Foil or Silicone Muffin-Tin Liners

Our test cooks found that both aluminum foil and silicone liners worked equally well when making muffins in the air fryer.

6-Inch Wooden Skewers

We use 6-inch wooden skewers to make chicken and vegetable kebabs. This length fits into any size air fryer.

Nonstick-Safe Spatula

Since many air-fryer baskets and inserts have a nonstick coating, we use a nonstick-safe spatula to retrieve cooked fish and more out of the air fryer. We especially like the long, narrow head of the **Matfer Bourgeat Exoglass Pelton Spatula**.

Kitchen Tongs

A good pair of tongs serves many a purpose in the kitchen. They are great for placing, moving, and tossing ingredients in the air fryer and are particularly helpful for lifting hot ramekins and cake pans out of the air fryer. Our favorite kitchen tongs are the **OXO Good Grips 12-Inch Tongs**.

Oven Mitts

Oven mitts are essential for keeping your hands protected when handling hot parts of the air fryer or pans or bowls inside. Our grip was secure even on the small handles or knobs on an air fryer when using our winning oven mitt, the heavily textured **OXO Silicone Oven Mitt**.

OIL MISTER

For a sustainable alternative to canned oil spray, you can use a refillable oil mister. We frequently spray the air-fryer basket to prevent sticking and spray ingredients such as chicken and pork to keep them moist and help with browning. We like to keep one mister filled with canola oil and another with olive oil, using the **Norpro Hard Plastic and Stainless Steel Sprayer Mister**.

Aluminum Foil

We use aluminum foil to tent meat while it rests and to wrap foods before freezing. We also use it sometimes to line the air-fryer basket and to make a foil sling (see page 13) to help lift delicate fish out of the air fryer so that it doesn't break apart.

EASY SNACKS AND TOPPINGS

You can use your air fryer to produce some great snacks, roast a fresh vegetable condiment or fruit topping, and toast nuts and sandwich buns. Here are some of our favorite ways to do all that.

Whole-Wheat Pita Chips with Salt and Pepper

Cook time: 6 minutes | Total time: 10 minutes, plus 30 minutes cooling

Traditional pita also works well here. This recipe can be easily doubled (see page 14).

Using kitchen shears, cut around perimeter of 1 (8-inch) 100% whole wheat pita and separate into 2 thin rounds. Lightly spray both sides of each cut round with olive oil spray and sprinkle with ⅛ teaspoon table salt and ⅛ teaspoon pepper. Cut each round into 8 wedges. Arrange wedges into two even layers in air-fryer basket. Place basket into air fryer and

set temperature to 300 degrees. Cook until wedges are light golden brown on edges, 3 to 5 minutes. Using tongs, toss wedges gently to redistribute and continue to cook until golden brown and crisp, 3 to 5 minutes. Let cool completely, about 30 minutes. Makes 16 chips. (Chips can be stored in airtight container for up to 3 days.)

Variation
Buttermilk-Ranch Whole-Wheat Pita Chips
Omit salt and pepper. Sprinkle each oiled pita round with ½ teaspoon buttermilk-ranch seasoning powder before cutting into wedges.

Crispy Barbecue Chickpeas

Cook time: 25 minutes
Total time: 30 minutes, plus 10 minutes cooling

This recipe can be easily doubled (see page 14).

Drain 1 (15-ounce) chickpeas thoroughly (do not rinse), then pat dry with paper towels. Toss chickpeas with 4 teaspoons extra-virgin olive oil until evenly coated, then transfer to air-fryer basket and spread into single layer. Place basket into air fryer and set temperature to 300 degrees. Cook until chickpeas appear dry, slightly shriveled, and deep golden brown, 25 to 35 minutes, tossing occasionally. (To test for doneness, remove a few paler chickpeas and let cool briefly before tasting; if interiors are soft, return to air fryer for 2 minutes before testing again.) Combine 1½ teaspoons chili powder, ¾ teaspoon sugar, ½ teaspoon garlic powder, pinch table salt, and pinch cayenne in large bowl. Add chickpeas and toss to coat. Let cool completely before serving, about 10 minutes. Makes about 1 cup. (Chickpeas can be stored in airtight container for up to 1 week.)

Variations
Crispy Coriander-Cumin Chickpeas
Reduce sugar to ¼ teaspoon. Substitute ½ teaspoon ground coriander, ¼ teaspoon ground turmeric, and ¼ teaspoon ground cumin for chili powder and garlic powder.

Crispy Smoked Paprika Chickpeas
Reduce sugar to ¼ teaspoon. Substitute 1½ teaspoons smoked paprika and ¼ teaspoon onion powder for chili powder and garlic powder.

Jalapeño Poppers

Cook time: 10 minutes | Total time: 20 minutes

Look for large jalapeños that are about 4 inches long and 1¼ inches thick at the stem end. If your jalapeños are smaller, do not overfill them; the filling should be level with the cut sides. This recipe can be easily doubled (see page 14). If doubling, cook the poppers in two batches.

Cut 6 jalapeños in half lengthwise, leaving stems intact but removing seeds and ribs. Arrange jalapeño halves cut side up on cutting board and sprinkle evenly with ¼ teaspoon table salt. Stir 4 ounces shredded cheddar, 4 ounces softened cream cheese, 1 thinly sliced scallion, 1 tablespoon chopped pickled jalapeños, 1 tablespoon minced fresh cilantro, 2 teaspoons cornstarch, and 1 teaspoon grated lime zest in bowl until well combined. Divide cheese mixture evenly among jalapeño halves (about 1 tablespoon per half), gently pressing filling into cavities so it is flush with cut edges. Slice 6 pieces bacon in half crosswise. Wrap each popper with bacon, overlapping ends of bacon pieces underneath jalapeño halves. (Bacon-wrapped poppers can be refrigerated for up to 24 hours; arrange on large plate and cover with plastic wrap until ready to cook.) Arrange poppers in even layer in air-fryer basket. Place basket into air fryer and set temperature to 400 degrees. Cook until jalapeños are tender and bacon is golden and crisp, 10 to 14 minutes. Makes 12 poppers.

Pigs in Blankets

Cook time: 7 minutes | Total time: 20 minutes

One 10- to 13-ounce package of cocktail franks usually contains 24 cocktail franks. Depending on the size of your air fryer, you may need to cook the cocktail franks in more than 2 batches.

Line air-fryer basket with aluminum foil, crimping edges to prevent foil from flapping. Cut 1 thawed (9½ by 9-inch) sheet puff pastry lengthwise into 8 even strips, then cut strips crosswise into 3-inch lengths. Lightly brush pastry with egg wash.

Roll 1 cocktail frank in each dough strip. Transfer half of bundles to prepared basket, seam side down, spaced ½ inch apart; keep remaining bundles refrigerated until ready to bake. Brush tops with egg wash and sprinkle with 1½ teaspoons bagel seasoning. Place basket into air fryer and set temperature to 400 degrees. Bake until pastry is golden brown, 7 to 10 minutes; let cool slightly before serving. Repeat with remaining bundles.

Roasted Garlic

Cook time: 20 minutes | Total time: 30 minutes

Use this garlic in spreads, compound butter, and dips such as hummus. This recipe can be easily doubled (see page 14). If doubling, wrap garlic heads separately.

Remove outer papery skins from 1 large head of garlic. Cut off top third of head to expose cloves and discard. Place garlic head, cut side up, in center of large piece of aluminum foil; drizzle with ½ teaspoon extra-virgin olive oil; and sprinkle with pinch table salt. Gather foil tightly around garlic to form packet and place packet in air-fryer basket. Place basket into air fryer; set temperature to 400 degrees; and cook until garlic is soft and golden, about 20 minutes. Carefully open packet to let garlic cool slightly. When cool enough to handle, squeeze cloves from skins; discard skins. Makes about 2 tablespoons. (Refrigerate whole head of garlic for up to 1 week. Let garlic come to room temperature before squeezing out of skins.)

Roasted Plum Tomatoes

Cook time: 20 minutes | Total time: 25 minutes

Use these tomatoes on a charcuterie board or as a sandwich topping, or serve them alongside roasted chicken, beef, pork, or fish. This recipe can be easily doubled (see page 14).

Toss 1 pound plum tomatoes, cored and halved lengthwise, with 1 tablespoon extra-virgin olive oil, 2 thinly sliced garlic cloves, 1 teaspoon sugar, ¼ teaspoon dried oregano, ¼ teaspoon dried thyme, ¼ teaspoon table salt, and pinch red pepper flakes in bowl. Arrange tomatoes in even layer in air-fryer basket. Place basket into air fryer and set temperature to 350 degrees. Cook until tomatoes are shriveled, dry, and dark around edges, 20 to 30 minutes. Serve warm or at room temperature. Makes about 1 cup. (Tomatoes can be refrigerated for up to 3 days.)

Roasted Peppers

Cook time: 25 minutes
Total time: 45 minutes

Cut ½ inch from top and bottom of up to 3 bell peppers; discard or save for another use. Using paring knife, remove ribs from peppers and discard along with core and seeds. Arrange peppers in air-fryer basket on their sides. (Peppers will fit snugly, but shouldn't come in contact with heating element.) Place basket into air fryer and set temperature to 400 degrees. Cook until peppers have collapsed and skins are browned and wrinkled, about 25 minutes, flipping and rotating peppers halfway through cooking. Transfer peppers to bowl, cover tightly with plastic wrap, and let steam for 10 minutes. Uncover bowl and let peppers cool slightly. When cool enough to handle, peel skin from flesh and discard. (Peppers can be refrigerated for up to 5 days.)

Croutons

Cook time: 6 minutes | Total time: 10 minutes

Cut 3 ounces baguette into ¾-inch pieces (you should have 3 cups). Toss bread with 2 tablespoons extra-virgin olive oil, ¼ teaspoon pepper, and ⅛ teaspoon table salt in bowl until evenly coated; transfer to air-fryer basket. Place basket into air fryer and set temperature to 350 degrees. Cook, returning croutons to now-empty bowl and tossing to redistribute every 2 minutes until golden and crisp, 6 to 10 minutes. Let croutons cool completely. Makes 3 cups. (Croutons can be stored in airtight container for up to 3 days.)

Crispy Shallots

Cook time: 10 minutes | Total time: 15 minutes

Toss 4 thinly sliced shallots with ½ teaspoon vegetable oil in bowl; transfer to air-fryer basket. Place basket into air fryer and set temperature to 300 degrees. Cook, tossing occasionally, until shallots are golden and crisp, 10 to 12 minutes. Season with table salt to taste. Makes about ¾ cup. (Shallots can be stored in airtight container for up to 1 month.)

Roasted Fruit Topping

Cook time: 15 minutes | Total time: 20 minutes

We had good success roasting apples, pears, peaches, plums, and pineapple. Add a pinch of cinnamon and/or 1 to 2 teaspoons of brown sugar, maple syrup, or honey (depending on the fruit's sweetness) before roasting. Spoon topping over porridge or layer it with yogurt and granola. You will need a 6-inch round nonstick or silicone cake pan for this recipe; before starting this recipe, confirm your air fryer allows enough space for the pan. This recipe can be easily doubled in a 1½-quart soufflé dish (see page 14).

Toss 3 cups 1-inch fruit pieces with 2 teaspoons vegetable oil and pinch table salt in 6-inch round nonstick or silicone cake pan. Place pan in air-fryer basket and place basket into air fryer. Set temperature to 400 degrees. Cook until fruit is tender and lightly browned, 15 to 20 minutes, stirring halfway through. Serve warm or at room temperature. Makes about 1 cup. (Roasted fruit can be refrigerated for up to 3 days.)

Toasted Nuts or Seeds (Walnuts, Almonds, Cashews, Pine Nuts, Pepitas)

Cook time: 6 minutes | Total time: 10 minutes

While we were able to toast most nuts and seeds in the basket of our winning air fryer, you may find that some smaller nuts and seeds (like sesame seeds and pine nuts) fall through the holes in your basket, as different air-fryer baskets are designed a little differently.

Place up to 1 cup nuts or seeds in air-fryer basket, place basket into air fryer, and set temperature to 350 degrees. Cook, shaking basket occasionally, until nuts or seeds are fragrant, 6 to 10 minutes. Makes 1 cup. (Nuts can be stored in airtight container for up to 5 days.)

Variations

Smoked Paprika Spiced Almonds

Toss 1 cup skin-on raw almonds with 1 tablespoon extra-virgin olive oil, 1 teaspoon table salt, and ¾ teaspoon smoked paprika. Place almonds in air-fryer basket, place basket into air fryer, and set temperature to 350 degrees. Cook, shaking basket occasionally, until almonds are fragrant, 6 to 10 minutes. Makes 1 cup.

Orange-Fennel Toasted Walnuts

Toss 1 cup walnuts with 1 tablespoon extra-virgin olive oil, 1 teaspoon table salt, 1 teaspoon grated orange zest, and ½ teaspoon ground fennel. Place walnuts in air-fryer basket, place basket into air fryer, and set temperature to 350 degrees. Cook, shaking basket occasionally, until walnuts are fragrant, 6 to 10 minutes. Makes 1 cup.

Warm-Spiced Pecans

Toss 1 cup pecans with 1 tablespoon extra-virgin olive oil, 1 tablespoon granulated sugar, ½ teaspoon ground cinnamon, and ⅛ teaspoon ground cloves. Place pecans in air-fryer basket, place basket into air fryer, and set temperature to 350 degrees. Cook, shaking basket occasionally, until pecans are fragrant, 6 to 10 minutes. Makes 1 cup.

Almond, Cherry, and Chocolate Trail Mix

Cook time: 14 minutes | Total time: 20 minutes, plus 1 hour cooling

You can substitute pistachios, cashews, walnuts, or peanuts for the almonds and dried cranberries for the cherries. Do not substitute quick oats, instant oats, or steel-cut oats in this recipe. Cool the oat-nut mixture completely before adding the cherries and chocolate. This recipe can be easily doubled (see page 14).

Lightly spray air-fryer basket with vegetable oil spray. Whisk 3 tablespoons pure maple syrup, 1 tablespoon extra-virgin olive oil, 1 teaspoon vanilla extract, ¼ teaspoon ground allspice, and ¼ teaspoon table salt together in large bowl. Stir in 1½ cups old-fashioned rolled oats, ½ cup whole almonds, ½ cup unsweetened flaked coconut, and ¼ cup raw pepitas until all ingredients are evenly moistened. Scrape oat mixture into prepared basket and spread into even layer. Place basket into air fryer; set temperature to 300 degrees; and cook, without stirring, until oat mixture is golden brown, 14 to 20 minutes. Remove basket from air fryer and let oat-almond mixture cool completely, about 1 hour. Transfer mixture to clean large bowl, breaking up larger clusters, and stir in ½ cup unsweetened dried cherries and 4 ounces coarsely chopped bittersweet chocolate. Makes 4 cups. (Trail mix can be stored in airtight container for up to 2 weeks.)

Toasted Burger or Sandwich Buns

Cook time: 2 minutes | Total time: 5 minutes

Wipe out air-fryer basket with paper towels after cooking burgers or other food and arrange 2 split buns cut side down in basket. Place basket in air fryer and set temperature to 400 degrees. Cook until lightly golden, 2 to 3 minutes.

BREAKFAST

EGG IN A HOLE WITH TOMATO, AVOCADO, AND HERB SALAD

Serves 1

| COOK TIME 8 minutes | TOTAL TIME 45 minutes |

why this recipe works For this skillet classic, you won't need a skillet nor have to stand at the stove to toast your bread and cook the egg. The air fryer's convection heat does both, leaving your hands free to make a lemony avocado, tomato, and herb salad. A flavorful olive oil–Dijon mustard mixture creates a barrier under the toasting bread, which prevents the egg white from leaking out. When the egg is nearly done, we turn off the air fryer and let the egg sit in the warm machine to finish setting the white without overcooking the yolk. If you don't have a round cutter, cut the toast hole with a sturdy drinking glass. Depending on the size of your air fryer, you may need to trim the bread slice to lay flat in the basket. This recipe can be easily doubled (see page 14).

Olive oil spray

1 teaspoon extra-virgin olive oil, plus extra for drizzling

1 teaspoon Dijon mustard

1 (½-inch-thick) slice rustic whole-grain bread

1 large egg

Pinch table salt

Pinch pepper

2 ounces cherry tomatoes, halved

½ avocado, cut into ½-inch pieces

⅓ cup torn fresh parsley leaves

1 scallion, sliced thin

2 teaspoons lemon juice

1 Line bottom of air-fryer basket with aluminum foil and lightly spray foil with oil spray.

2 Whisk oil and mustard together in medium bowl. Using 2-inch round cutter, cut and remove circle from center of bread. Brush both sides of bread slice and cut-out with oil mixture; do not clean bowl. Arrange bread slice and cutout in prepared basket. Place basket into air fryer; set temperature to 400 degrees; and cook until bread is heated through but still soft, about 4 minutes, flipping bread halfway through cooking.

3 Working quickly, crack egg into bread hole, lightly spray with oil spray, and sprinkle with salt and pepper. Return basket to air fryer and cook until egg white is opaque but still slightly jiggly, 4 to 6 minutes. Turn off air fryer and let bread sit, without moving, until egg white is set, 2 to 4 minutes.

4 Meanwhile, toss tomatoes, avocado, parsley, scallion, and lemon juice together in now-empty bowl. Season with salt and pepper to taste. Using spatula, transfer bread slice and cutout to plate. Top with salad and drizzle with extra oil. Serve.

BAKED EGGS WITH SMOKY ZUCCHINI, RED PEPPER, AND BREAD HASH

Serves 1

COOK TIME **14 minutes**
(30 minutes from refrigerated)

TOTAL TIME **45 minutes**

why this recipe works We know that the air fryer is hands-off and turns out perfectly cooked eggs with creamy, slightly runny yolks and tender whites. But we wanted something more to sink our teeth into. Instead of making potato hash, we added zucchini; roasted red peppers; and whole-grain bread, flavored with red wine vinegar and smoked paprika, to our eggs. The hash created insulation between the eggs and the very hot sides of the ovensafe bowl, preventing the eggs from cooking too quickly. Turning off the air fryer when the egg whites had just turned opaque but still jiggled and letting the eggs sit for 6 minutes in the warm machine completed the cooking. The residual heat set the whites without overcooking the yolks. You will need a 3-cup ovensafe bowl for this recipe; before starting this recipe, confirm your air fryer allows enough space for the dish. This recipe can be easily doubled in a 1½-quart soufflé dish (see page 14); make four indentations in step 3.

½ zucchini (4 ounces), cut into ½-inch pieces

¼ cup jarred roasted red peppers, rinsed, patted dry, and chopped

1 slice rustic whole-grain bread, cut into ½-inch pieces (1 cup)

1 tablespoon tomato paste

2 teaspoons extra-virgin olive oil, plus extra for drizzling

1 teaspoon red wine vinegar

1 teaspoon smoked paprika

2 large eggs

Olive oil spray

Pinch table salt

1 tablespoon chopped fresh parsley

1 Combine zucchini, peppers, bread, tomato paste, oil, vinegar, and paprika in 3-cup ovensafe bowl. (Vegetable-bread mixture can be covered and refrigerated for up to 24 hours.)

2 Place bowl in air-fryer basket. Place basket into air fryer; set temperature to 400 degrees; and cook until zucchini is tender and edges of bread begin to brown, 8 to 10 minutes, stirring halfway through cooking.

3 Remove basket from air fryer and reduce temperature to 250 degrees. Make two shallow 2-inch-wide indentations in vegetable-bread mixture using back of spoon. Crack 1 egg into each indentation, lightly spray with oil spray, and sprinkle with salt.

4 Return basket to air fryer and cook until egg whites are opaque but still slightly jiggly, 6 to 8 minutes. Turn off air fryer and let eggs sit, without moving, until whites are set, 6 to 8 minutes. Sprinkle eggs with parsley and drizzle with extra oil. Serve.

BAKED EGGS WITH SPINACH, ARTICHOKES, AND FETA

Serves 1

COOK TIME **14 minutes**
(30 minutes from refrigerated)

TOTAL TIME **45 minutes**

why this recipe works This easy air-fryer baked egg dish is packed with meaty artichokes, spinach, and tangy feta, which give you tons of flavor. It's also fuss-free. The vegetables can be prepped the night before, so this dish is perfect for a weekday breakfast. And you eat them out of the bowl you use to air-fry them. The air fryer's dry heat cooks refrigerated or frozen vegetables quickly, reducing prep, cook, and cleanup time. Creating two indentations in the spinach mixture separates the eggs slightly, helping them cook through, warmed by the vegetables, better than if they were nestled together, with whites touching. Lemon juice and dill cut the eggs' richness. We prefer the flavor and texture of jarred whole baby artichokes but you can substitute 3 ounces frozen artichokes, thawed, patted dry, and chopped coarse. You will need a 3-cup ovensafe bowl for this recipe; before starting this recipe, confirm your air fryer allows enough space for the dish. This recipe can be easily doubled in a 1½-quart soufflé dish (see page 14); make four indentations in step 2.

5 ounces frozen chopped spinach, thawed and squeezed dry

½ cup jarred whole baby artichokes, patted dry and chopped coarse

1 scallion, sliced thin

1 tablespoon minced fresh dill, divided

2 teaspoons extra-virgin olive oil, plus extra for drizzling

1 teaspoon lemon juice

Pinch ground nutmeg

2 large eggs

Olive oil spray

Pinch table salt

2 tablespoons crumbled feta cheese

1 Combine spinach, artichokes, scallion, 2 teaspoons dill, oil, lemon juice, and nutmeg in 3-cup ovensafe bowl, then spread into even layer. (Spinach mixture can be covered and refrigerated for up to 24 hours.)

2 Make two shallow 2-inch-wide indentations in spinach mixture using back of spoon, then place bowl in air-fryer basket. Place basket into air fryer; set temperature to 400 degrees; and cook until edges of spinach mixture begin to brown, about 8 minutes.

3 Remove basket from air fryer and reduce temperature to 250 degrees. Crack 1 egg into each indentation, lightly spray with oil spray, and sprinkle with salt. Return basket to air fryer and cook until egg whites are opaque but still slightly jiggly, 6 to 8 minutes.

4 Turn off air fryer and let eggs sit, without moving, until whites are set, 6 to 8 minutes. Sprinkle eggs and spinach mixture with feta and remaining 1 teaspoon dill and drizzle with extra oil. Serve.

KALE, ROASTED RED PEPPER, AND GOAT CHEESE FRITTATA

Serves 2

COOK TIME **15 minutes**　　　　　TOTAL TIME **30 minutes**

why this recipe works This frittata highlights the incredible convenience and even cooking offered by the air fryer. In about fifteen minutes (plus the time it takes to combine a few ingredients in a bowl), it transformed a simple egg-and-cheese custard packed with kale, roasted red peppers, and scallions into a delightful meal for two—fluffy and tender on the inside, golden and delicately sealed on the outside. The compact size and even heat of a non-stick cake pan made the occasional stirring of the egg mixture during cooking unnecessary. Using frozen vegetables (which are blanched before freezing) meant we didn't have to precook them. Any worries we had that frozen vegetables might taste soggy were put to rest by the air fryer's rapidly circulating hot air, which gently roasted the vegetables at the surface and edges of the frittata. You will need a 6-inch round nonstick or silicone cake pan for this recipe; before starting this recipe, confirm your air fryer allows enough space for the pan.

4　large eggs

1　tablespoon milk

⅛　teaspoon table salt

4　ounces frozen chopped kale or spinach, thawed and squeezed dry

¼　cup jarred roasted red peppers, rinsed, patted dry, and chopped

1　ounce goat cheese, crumbled (¼ cup)

2　scallions, sliced thin

1 Generously spray 6-inch round nonstick cake pan with vegetable oil spray. Whisk eggs, milk, and salt in medium bowl until well combined, then stir in kale, peppers, goat cheese, and scallions.

2 Transfer egg mixture to prepared pan and place pan in air-fryer basket. Place basket into air fryer; set temperature to 350 degrees; and cook until frittata is deep golden brown and registers 180 to 190 degrees, 15 to 25 minutes.

3 Transfer pan to wire rack and let rest for 5 minutes. Using rubber spatula, loosen frittata from pan and transfer to cutting board. Cut into wedges and serve.

HAM, PEA, AND SWISS CHEESE FRITTATA
Substitute 2 ounces chopped deli ham and ½ cup thawed frozen peas for kale and red peppers, and Swiss cheese for goat cheese.

BROCCOLI, SUN-DRIED TOMATO, AND CHEDDAR FRITTATA
Substitute 4 ounces frozen chopped broccoli florets, thawed and patted dry, and 2 tablespoons chopped oil-packed sun-dried tomatoes, rinsed and patted dry, for kale and red peppers, and cheddar cheese for goat cheese.

MAKE-AHEAD BREAKFAST BURRITOS

Makes 6 burritos

COOK TIME **5 minutes**
(30 minutes from frozen)

TOTAL TIME **45 minutes**

why this recipe works If you love a good breakfast burrito and want one quickly, this recipe is for you. Though the filling is made in a skillet, shaped burritos can be warmed in the air fryer from refrigerated or frozen. Unlike the microwave, the air fryer heats evenly, so there are no soggy or cold bits. While store-bought breakfast burritos often rely on greasy meat for bulk and flavor, we fill our burrito with healthier refried black beans and added frozen chopped kale to our fluffy scrambled eggs. To build a flavorful base for the beans, we sautéed aromatic scallions, cumin, and chili powder. We added the beans, mashing them while they cooked, to create a cohesive mixture. To freeze the burritos, wrap each one in foil. The number of burritos you can cook at one time will depend on the size of your air fryer. Serve with salsa, Greek yogurt, lime wedges, and hot sauce.

8	large eggs	6	scallions, sliced thin	¼	cup chopped fresh cilantro
¼	cup milk	1½	teaspoons ground cumin	2	tablespoons lime juice
⅛	teaspoon table salt	½	teaspoon chili powder	6	(10-inch) 100 percent whole-wheat tortillas
2	tablespoons extra-virgin olive oil, divided	1	(15-ounce) can black beans, undrained		
8	ounces frozen chopped kale or spinach, thawed and squeezed dry				

1 Whisk eggs, milk, and salt in large bowl until well combined. Heat 1 tablespoon oil in 12-inch nonstick skillet over medium heat until shimmering. Add egg mixture and, using rubber spatula, constantly and firmly scrape along bottom and sides of skillet until eggs are just set, 2 to 4 minutes. Off heat, fold in kale. Transfer egg mixture to plate and wipe skillet clean with paper towels.

2 Heat remaining 1 tablespoon oil in now-empty skillet over medium heat until shimmering. Add scallions, cumin, and chili powder and cook until fragrant, about 1 minute.

Stir in beans and their liquid and cook, mashing beans with back of spoon, until mixture is heated through and thickened, 3 to 5 minutes. Off heat, stir in cilantro and lime juice. Season with salt and pepper to taste.

3 Wrap tortillas in damp dish towel and microwave until warm and pliable, about 1 minute. Lay tortillas on counter and spread bean mixture evenly across each tortilla, close to bottom edge. Top with egg-kale mixture. Working with 1 tortilla at a time, fold sides, then bottom of tortilla over filling, then continue to roll tightly into wrap.

4 Arrange up to 4 burritos, seam side down, in air-fryer basket, spaced evenly apart. Place basket into air fryer; set temperature to 400 degrees; and cook until crisp, 5 to 8 minutes.

5 Individually wrap remaining burritos in greased aluminum foil. Transfer to zipper-lock bags and freeze for up to 2 months. To bake from frozen, place foil-wrapped burritos into air-fryer basket. Place basket into air fryer; set temperature to 325 degrees; and cook until heated through, about 30 minutes, flipping burritos halfway through cooking. Let rest, wrapped in foil, for 5 minutes before serving. (Alternatively, frozen wrapped burritos can be thawed in refrigerator overnight and baked for about 15 minutes.)

ROASTED FRUIT AND ALMOND BUTTER TOAST

Serves 1

COOK TIME **6 minutes** TOTAL TIME **15 minutes**

why this recipe works Why make toast in an air fryer? Because turning on that one appliance quickly gives you not only toasty bread but also melted almond or peanut butter and roasted fruit all in a single step. While developing this recipe, we weren't sure if we would have to pretoast the bread, take it out, top it with fruit, and put it back in the air fryer. But we found that the air fryer's rapidly circulating heat perfectly toasted the bread and caramelized the fruit all at once in less than 10 minutes. To save even more time, rather than tossing the uncooked fruit in sugar before laying it on the bread, we sweetened it afterward, drizzling the toast with a little honey or maple syrup. We preferred bananas, grapes, and berries here; citrus tends to dry up and turn bitter in the air fryer. Depending on the size of your air fryer, you may need to trim the bread slice to lay flat in the basket. Let your creativity run wild with the fruit you use; use a single variety or a combination. Customize your toast with additional toppings such as toasted nuts, seeds, or shredded coconut. This recipe can be easily doubled (see page 14).

2 ounces ripe banana, seedless grapes, blueberries, raspberries, and/or hulled strawberries

2 tablespoons natural, unsweetened almond or peanut butter

1 (½-inch-thick) slice rustic whole-grain bread

½ teaspoon honey or maple syrup

Slice banana ¼ inch thick, halve grapes, and/or quarter strawberries. Spread almond butter onto bread and top evenly with fruit. Place bread into air-fryer basket. Place basket into air fryer and set temperature to 400 degrees. Cook until fruit begins to caramelize and toast is golden brown around edges, 6 to 10 minutes. Transfer bread to plate and drizzle with honey. Serve.

OVERNIGHT BREAKFAST GRAIN BOWL

Serves 1

COOK TIME **45 minutes**	TOTAL TIME **1 hour, plus 8 hours soaking**

why this recipe works We love whole grains for a healthy breakfast, but they take a lot of attention to prepare. Could we use the air fryer's even temperature for hands-off cooking? We chose quinoa for this porridge and found that presoaking and cooking the grains in plenty of liquid encouraged them to swell, burst, and release their starches, creating creaminess. We air-fried the soaked grains and, in 45 minutes, our porridge was ready without boiling over or needing constant stirring. Maple syrup and berries are an appetizing topping, and a splash of fruity olive oil is a flavorful, healthy change from butter. For savory porridge, skip the syrup and fruit and mix in your favorite cheese and fresh herbs. For an accurate measurement of boiling water, bring a kettle of water to a boil and then measure out the desired amount. This recipe can be easily doubled using a 1½-quart soufflé dish (see page 14). You will need a 3-cup ovensafe bowl for this recipe; before starting this recipe, confirm your air fryer allows enough space for the dish. We like the convenience of prewashed quinoa; rinsing removes the quinoa's bitter protective coating (called saponin). If you buy unwashed quinoa, rinse it and then spread it out on a clean dish towel to dry for 15 minutes. Customize your porridge with additional toppings such as yogurt, toasted nuts and seeds, and/or our Roasted Fruit Topping (page 18).

5 tablespoons prewashed white quinoa

1¼ cups boiling water

⅛ teaspoon ground cinnamon

⅛ teaspoon table salt

2-4 tablespoons milk

1 tablespoon extra-virgin olive oil

1½ teaspoons maple syrup, plus extra for drizzling

¼ cup blackberries, blueberries, and/or raspberries

1 Add quinoa to 3-cup ovensafe bowl. Cover with cold water and soak at room temperature for at least 8 hours or up to 24 hours. Drain and rinse well.

2 Combine quinoa, boiling water, cinnamon, and salt in now-empty bowl and cover tightly with aluminum foil. Place bowl in air-fryer basket. Place basket into air fryer; set temperature to 400 degrees; and cook until quinoa is tender and beginning to burst, about 45 minutes.

3 Remove basket from air fryer. Stir 2 tablespoons milk, oil, and maple syrup into porridge and let sit, uncovered, for 5 minutes; porridge will thicken as it sits. Adjust consistency with remaining 2 tablespoons milk as needed. Top with berries and drizzle with extra maple syrup before serving.

OVERNIGHT BREAKFAST THREE-GRAIN BOWL

Reduce quinoa to 2 tablespoons. Soak 2 tablespoons millet and 1 tablespoon amaranth with quinoa in step 1.

CHICKEN AND TURKEY

CHICKEN PARMESAN

Serves 2

COOK TIME 13 minutes **TOTAL TIME** 45 minutes

why this recipe works Crisp and gooey when done right, chicken Parmesan seemed an ideal candidate for the air fryer. But, without a pan of hot oil, the coating of crunchy panko bread crumbs refused to brown. This was easily fixed: Pretoasting the panko in the microwave with a bit of oil turned it richly golden. To streamline the breading process, we whisked the flour and egg together, adding garlic powder and dried oregano for flavor. We dipped our chicken in this mixture, then pressed it in the toasted panko that we'd combined with grated Parmesan for an extra hit of cheesiness and an even crunchier texture. A short stint in the air fryer gave us chicken that was juicy inside and crunchy outside. We sprinkled on shredded mozzarella and cooked the cutlets just long enough to melt the cheese. A little warmed pasta sauce poured over the top kept our recipe simple and avoided soggy cutlets. Chopped basil added a fresh finish. Serve with pasta if desired. This recipe can be easily doubled (see page 14).

¾ cup panko bread crumbs

2 tablespoons extra-virgin olive oil

¼ cup grated Parmesan cheese

1 large egg

1 tablespoon all-purpose flour

¾ teaspoon garlic powder

½ teaspoon dried oregano

⅜ teaspoon table salt, divided

¼ teaspoon pepper, divided

2 (8-ounce) boneless, skinless chicken breasts, trimmed

2 ounces whole-milk mozzarella cheese, shredded (½ cup)

¼ cup jarred marinara sauce, warmed

2 tablespoons chopped fresh basil

1 Toss panko with oil in bowl until evenly coated. Microwave, stirring frequently, until light golden brown, 1 to 3 minutes. Transfer to shallow dish, let cool slightly, then stir in Parmesan. Whisk egg, flour, garlic powder, oregano, ⅛ teaspoon salt, and ⅛ teaspoon pepper together in second shallow dish.

2 Pound chicken to uniform thickness as needed. Pat dry with paper towels and sprinkle with remaining ¼ teaspoon salt and remaining ⅛ teaspoon pepper. Working with 1 breast at a time, dredge in egg mixture, letting excess drip off, then coat with panko mixture, pressing gently to adhere.

3 Lightly spray bottom of air-fryer basket with vegetable oil spray. Arrange breasts in prepared basket, spaced evenly apart, alternating ends. Place basket into air fryer and set temperature to 400 degrees. Cook until chicken is crisp and registers 160 degrees, 12 to 16 minutes, flipping and rotating breasts halfway through cooking.

4 Sprinkle chicken with mozzarella. Return basket to air fryer and cook until cheese is melted, about 1 minute. Transfer chicken to individual serving plates. Top each breast with 2 tablespoons warm marinara sauce and sprinkle with basil. Serve.

CHICKEN NUGGETS

Makes 36 nuggets; serves 4

COOK TIME 12 minutes   **TOTAL TIME** 1 hour, plus freezing time

why this recipe works These homemade nuggets are tender and juicy. And they're very convenient if made ahead and frozen. A 15-minute brine seasoned the white meat and guarded against dryness even after freezing. Two dipping sauces completed the picture. The air fryer cooks up to 18 nuggets at once; this recipe makes double that, so you'll have plenty on hand. The nuggets can be cooked from fresh; reduce the cooking time to 10 to 12 minutes, tossing halfway through cooking. Respray the basket before cooking additional batches.

4 (8-ounce) boneless, skinless chicken breasts, trimmed	3 cups panko bread crumbs	1 tablespoon onion powder
3 tablespoons table salt, for brining	¼ cup extra-virgin olive oil	¾ teaspoon garlic powder
3 tablespoons sugar, for brining	3 large eggs	1 teaspoon table salt
	3 tablespoons all-purpose flour	¼ teaspoon pepper

1 Pound chicken to uniform thickness as needed. Cut each breast diagonally into thirds, then cut each piece into thirds. Dissolve 3 tablespoons salt and sugar in 2 quarts cold water in large container. Add chicken, cover, and let sit for 15 minutes.

2 Meanwhile, toss panko with oil in bowl until evenly coated. Microwave, stirring frequently, until light golden brown, about 5 minutes. Transfer to shallow dish and let cool slightly. Whisk eggs, flour, onion powder, garlic powder, salt, and pepper together in second shallow dish.

3 Set wire rack in rimmed baking sheet. Remove chicken from brine and pat dry with paper towels. Working with several chicken pieces at a time, dredge in egg mixture, letting excess drip off, then coat with panko mixture, pressing gently to adhere; transfer to prepared rack. Freeze until firm, about 4 hours. (Frozen nuggets can be transferred to zipper-lock bag and stored in freezer for up to 1 month.)

4 to cook nuggets Lightly spray bottom of air-fryer basket with vegetable oil spray. Place up to 18 nuggets in prepared basket. Place basket into air fryer, set temperature to 400 degrees, and cook for 6 minutes. Transfer nuggets to clean bowl and toss gently to redistribute. Return nuggets to air fryer and cook until chicken is crisp and registers 160 degrees, 6 to 10 minutes. Serve.

SWEET-AND-SOUR DIPPING SAUCE
Whisk ¾ cup apple jelly, 1 tablespoon distilled white vinegar, ½ teaspoon soy sauce, ⅛ teaspoon garlic powder, pinch ground ginger, and pinch cayenne pepper together in bowl; season with salt and pepper to taste. (Sauce can be refrigerated for up to 4 days; bring to room temperature before serving.)

HONEY-DIJON DIPPING SAUCE
Whisk ½ cup Dijon mustard and ¼ cup honey together in bowl; season with salt and pepper to taste. (Sauce can be refrigerated for up to 4 days; bring to room temperature before serving.)

CRISPY BREADED CHICKEN BREASTS WITH CREAMY APPLE-FENNEL SALAD

Serves 2

COOK TIME 12 minutes   **TOTAL TIME** 45 minutes

why this recipe works The convection heat of the air fryer quickly produced delectable golden-brown, breaded chicken breasts that crisped up with very little oil and tasted rich. We also made a creamy salad to accompany the dish, dressed with yogurt instead of mayonnaise. For the chicken, we found that panko worked better than ordinary bread crumbs for a crisp coating. The challenge was that the panko browned unevenly in the air fryer. As we'd already discovered, pretoasting the panko bread crumbs in the microwave with a little olive oil helped, guaranteeing evenly golden crusts. We also pounded the chicken breasts to facilitate even cooking and browning. To streamline the breading process, we whisked flour into an egg, added a generous dollop of Dijon mustard for brightness and tang, and quickly dipped the chicken into this mixture before dredging it with the toasted panko. For our salad, we whisked together a creamy rémoulade-style dressing of yogurt, Dijon mustard, caper brine, and lemon juice, tossing it with a thinly sliced fennel bulb, chopped apple, and capers. If your fennel does not have fronds, substitute 1 tablespoon fresh chopped dill or parsley. This recipe can be easily doubled (see page 14).

- 1 cup panko bread crumbs
- 2 tablespoons extra-virgin olive oil
- 1 large egg
- 4 teaspoons Dijon mustard, divided
- 1 tablespoon all-purpose flour
- ¼ teaspoon table salt
- 2 (6-ounce) boneless, skinless chicken breasts, trimmed
- 1 tablespoon plain yogurt
- 1 teaspoon lemon juice
- 1 teaspoon capers, rinsed, plus 1 teaspoon brine
- 1 fennel bulb, 1 tablespoon fronds minced, stalks discarded, bulb halved, cored, and sliced thin
- 1 apple, cored and cut into 2-inch-long matchsticks

1 Toss panko with oil in shallow dish until evenly coated. Microwave, stirring frequently, until light golden brown, 1 to 3 minutes; let cool slightly. Whisk egg, 1 tablespoon mustard, flour, and salt together in second shallow dish.

2 Pound chicken to uniform thickness as needed. Pat dry with paper towels. Working with 1 breast at a time, dredge in egg mixture, letting excess drip off, then coat with panko, pressing gently to adhere.

3 Lightly spray bottom of air-fryer basket with vegetable oil spray. Arrange breasts in prepared basket, spaced evenly apart, alternating ends. Place basket into air fryer and set temperature to 400 degrees. Cook until chicken is crisp and registers 160 degrees, 12 to 18 minutes, flipping and rotating breasts halfway through cooking.

4 Whisk yogurt, lemon juice, caper brine, fennel fronds, and remaining 1 teaspoon mustard together in large bowl. Add apple, fennel bulb, and capers and toss to combine. Season with salt and pepper to taste. Serve chicken with salad.

SPICY FRIED-CHICKEN SANDWICH

Serves 4

COOK TIME 12 minutes   **TOTAL TIME** 40 minutes

why this recipe works Crunchy, juicy, and slicked with mayo, a spicy fried-chicken sandwich is a lunchtime favorite, but we aren't about to heat up a skillet of frying oil whenever the craving strikes. The air fryer gave us a less greasy route that was nearly as convenient as hitting up our favorite lunch spot. For our spicy chicken sandwich to live up to its name, we added heat in three stages. First, we whisked hot sauce into the egg-flour dredging mixture to ensure the heat was directly coating the chicken rather than getting lost in the breading, as it does in many recipes. Combining more hot sauce with mayonnaise for a creamy spread upped the heat level further. An unwritten rule of fried sandwiches states that a pickled element is a must; this was our opportunity to add even more heat with fiery, sweet pickled jalapeños in lieu of pickle chips. Shredded lettuce provided a crisp, fresh component that tempered the heat a bit. You can use your air fryer to toast the buns; see page 19 for more information.

1 cup panko bread crumbs

2 tablespoons extra-virgin olive oil

1 large egg

3 tablespoons hot sauce, divided

1 tablespoon all-purpose flour

½ teaspoon garlic powder

⅜ teaspoon table salt, divided

¼ teaspoon pepper, divided

2 (8-ounce) boneless, skinless chicken breasts, trimmed

¼ cup mayonnaise

4 hamburger buns, toasted, if desired

2 cups shredded iceberg lettuce

¼ cup jarred sliced jalapeño chiles

1 Toss panko with oil in bowl until evenly coated. Microwave, stirring frequently, until light golden brown, 1 to 3 minutes. Transfer to shallow dish and set aside to cool slightly. Whisk egg, 2 tablespoons hot sauce, flour, garlic powder, ⅛ teaspoon salt, and ⅛ teaspoon pepper together in second shallow dish.

2 Pound chicken to uniform thickness as needed. Halve each breast crosswise, pat dry with paper towels, and sprinkle with remaining ¼ teaspoon salt and remaining ⅛ teaspoon pepper. Working with 1 piece of chicken at a time, dredge in egg mixture, letting excess drip off, then coat with panko mixture, pressing gently to adhere.

3 Lightly spray bottom of air-fryer basket with vegetable oil spray. Arrange chicken pieces in prepared basket, spaced evenly apart. Place basket into air fryer and set temperature to 400 degrees. Cook until chicken is crisp and registers 160 degrees, 12 to 16 minutes, flipping and rotating chicken pieces halfway through cooking.

4 Combine mayonnaise and remaining 1 tablespoon hot sauce in small bowl. Spread mayonnaise mixture evenly over bun bottoms, then top with 1 piece chicken, lettuce, jalapeños, and bun tops. Serve.

APRICOT-THYME GLAZED BONELESS CHICKEN BREASTS

Serves 2

COOK TIME 12 minutes   **TOTAL TIME** 40 minutes

why this recipe works Glazed boneless chicken breasts are a fast and flavorful addition to anyone's weeknight meal rotation. To make them especially hands-off, we simply placed two breasts, rubbed with oil, in the air fryer and let the hot air work its magic, brushing on the glaze after flipping the chicken to prevent it from sticking to the basket. When it comes to glaze, many recipes invest too much time creating a mixture that just slides off and ends up in the bottom of the pan. For a slightly sweet, no-fuss glaze that stayed put, we reached for one of our favorite fruit condiments: apricot preserves. The chunkier preserves offered a more pleasant texture than jam or jelly, their thick, sticky consistency helped them adhere, and the chunky bits browned up nicely. Just a few seconds in the microwave made the preserves much easier to spread, and a little fresh thyme added a slight woodsy flavor that balanced the apricot's sweet tartness. For a simple variation, we combined the sweetness of pineapple preserves and the warm, spicy bite of fresh ginger. This recipe can be easily doubled (see page 14).

2 tablespoons apricot preserves

½ teaspoon minced fresh thyme or ⅛ teaspoon dried

2 (8-ounce) boneless, skinless chicken breasts, trimmed

1 teaspoon vegetable oil

¼ teaspoon table salt

⅛ teaspoon pepper

1 Microwave apricot preserves and thyme in bowl until fluid, about 30 seconds; set aside. Pound chicken to uniform thickness as needed. Pat dry with paper towels, rub with oil, and sprinkle with salt and pepper.

2 Arrange breasts skinned side down in air-fryer basket, spaced evenly apart, alternating ends. Place basket into air fryer, set temperature to 400 degrees, and cook chicken for 4 minutes. Flip and rotate chicken, then brush skinned side with apricot-thyme mixture. Return basket to air fryer and cook until chicken registers 160 degrees, 8 to 12 minutes.

3 Transfer chicken to serving platter, tent loosely with aluminum foil, and let rest for 5 minutes. Serve.

PINEAPPLE-GINGER BONELESS GLAZED CHICKEN BREASTS
Substitute pineapple preserves for apricot preserves and grated fresh ginger for thyme.

UNSTUFFED CHICKEN BREASTS
WITH DIJON MAYONNAISE

Serves 2

COOK TIME 13 minutes   **TOTAL TIME** 40 minutes

why this recipe works For all of the fun of rolled and stuffed chicken—the oozing cheese and savory filling—with none of the fuss, we left our chicken breasts unrolled and layered the "fillings" on the outside. First we wrapped chicken breasts (pounded to even thickness) in slices of ham, overlapping the pieces slightly and securing them with toothpicks. We cooked these savory packages in the air fryer until the ham was crisp and the chicken cooked through, then layered on sliced Swiss cheese, which became a gooey topping after just another minute in the air fryer. Delicious as the result was, tasters felt the dish lacked some of the dinner party flair of the original version, so we combined mayonnaise, Dijon mustard, and a little water to create a quick, velvety smooth sauce to drizzle over the chicken and finished it with a sprinkle of peppery chives. Thinly sliced ham is liable to tear, so for best results use slices that are about ⅛ inch thick. You will need four toothpicks for this recipe. This recipe can be easily doubled (see page 14).

2 (8-ounce) boneless, skinless chicken breasts, trimmed	4 thick slices ham (4 ounces)	1 tablespoon Dijon mustard
¼ teaspoon table salt	2 slices Swiss cheese (2 ounces)	1 teaspoon water
⅛ teaspoon pepper	2 tablespoons mayonnaise	1 tablespoon minced fresh chives

1 Pound chicken to uniform thickness as needed. Pat dry with paper towels and sprinkle with salt and pepper. For each chicken breast, shingle 2 slices of ham on counter, overlapping edges slightly, and lay chicken, skinned side down, in center. Fold ham around chicken and secure overlapping ends by threading toothpick through ham and chicken. Flip chicken and thread toothpick through ham and chicken on second side.

2 Lightly spray bottom of air-fryer basket with vegetable oil spray. Arrange breasts skinned side down in prepared basket, spaced evenly apart, alternating ends. Place basket into air fryer and set temperature to 400 degrees. Cook until edges of ham begin to brown and chicken registers 160 degrees, 12 to 16 minutes, flipping and rotating breasts halfway through cooking. Top each breast with 1 slice Swiss, folding cheese as needed. Return basket to air fryer and cook until cheese is melted, about 1 minute.

3 Transfer chicken to serving platter and discard toothpicks. Tent loosely with aluminum foil and let rest for 5 minutes. Meanwhile, combine mayonnaise, mustard, and water in small bowl. Drizzle chicken with 1 tablespoon sauce and sprinkle with chives. Serve, passing remaining sauce separately.

BROWN SUGAR–BALSAMIC GLAZED BONE-IN CHICKEN BREAST

Serves 1 to 4

COOK TIME 15 minutes   **TOTAL TIME** 30 minutes

why this recipe works When cooking for one, roasting a chicken breast in the oven can seem like too much effort. But what if you used your countertop air fryer, which doesn't need preheating? Bone-in chicken air-fries quickly and takes very little prep. We rubbed the breast with a little oil and sprinkled on salt and pepper. Starting the chicken skin side down helped the fat render. We roasted the chicken at 350 degrees, instead of 400, which we often use to quickly air-fry proteins. The lower temperature helped minimize moisture loss. For added flavor, we glazed one side of the breast with a mixture of brown sugar, balsamic vinegar, and garlic. If you plan to discard the chicken skin before serving, reserve the glaze and brush it on the chicken after removing the skin. This recipe is written to serve 1 but can be easily scaled to serve up to 4 people (see page 14).

1 (12-ounce) bone-in split chicken breast, trimmed

1 teaspoon extra-virgin olive oil

⅛ teaspoon table salt

⅛ teaspoon pepper

2 tablespoons packed brown sugar

2 teaspoons balsamic vinegar

1 small garlic clove, minced to paste

1 Pat chicken dry with paper towels, rub with oil, and sprinkle with salt and pepper. Arrange breast skin side down in air-fryer basket. (Space additional breasts evenly apart, alternating ends.) Place basket into air fryer, set temperature to 350 degrees, and cook for 10 minutes.

2 Microwave sugar, vinegar, and garlic in small bowl until mixture is fluid, about 30 seconds, stirring halfway through microwaving. Flip and rotate breast, then brush with glaze. Return basket to air fryer and cook until chicken is well browned and registers 160 degrees, 15 to 20 minutes. Discard skin, if desired. Let chicken rest for 5 minutes before serving.

PEACH-JALAPEÑO GLAZED BONE-IN CHICKEN BREAST
Substitute 1 tablespoon peach preserves for sugar, 1 teaspoon lime juice for vinegar, and 2 teaspoons minced jalapeño for garlic.

HONEY-MISO GLAZED BONE-IN CHICKEN BREAST
Substitute 1 tablespoon honey for sugar, 1 teaspoon unseasoned rice vinegar for balsamic, and 2 teaspoons white or red miso for garlic.

SPICED CHICKEN BREASTS WITH ASPARAGUS, ARUGULA, AND CANNELLINI BEAN SALAD

Serves 2

COOK TIME 20 minutes

TOTAL TIME 45 minutes

why this recipe works Boneless chicken breasts cook so quickly in the air fryer that we wondered, Why stop there? Here, we produce a complete meal by cooking chicken and vegetables in stages. We first softened red onion in the basket, then added asparagus. When the vegetables became tender, we stirred them into warmed cannellini beans tossed with a simple dressing. We let that marinate briefly while we air-fried chicken breasts jazzed up with coriander (for its citrus notes) and paprika (for depth). Baby arugula turned our vegetables and beans into a salad. Rinsing the cannellini beans eliminates any slimy texture. Look for asparagus spears no thicker than ½ inch. This recipe can be easily doubled (see page 14).

1 cup canned cannellini beans, rinsed

2 tablespoons extra-virgin olive oil, divided

1½ tablespoons red wine vinegar

1 garlic clove, minced

⅜ teaspoon table salt, divided

¼ teaspoon pepper, divided

½ red onion, sliced thin

8 ounces asparagus, trimmed and cut into 1-inch lengths

½ teaspoon ground coriander

¼ teaspoon paprika

2 (8-ounce) boneless, skinless chicken breasts, trimmed

2 ounces (2 cups) baby arugula

1 Microwave beans in large bowl until just warm, about 30 seconds. Stir in 1 tablespoon oil, vinegar, garlic, ¼ teaspoon salt, and pinch pepper; set aside.

2 Toss onion with 2 teaspoons oil, ⅛ teaspoon salt, and pinch pepper in clean bowl to coat. Place onion in air-fryer basket, set temperature to 400 degrees, and cook for 2 minutes. Stir in asparagus, return basket to air fryer, and cook until asparagus is tender and bright green, 6 to 8 minutes, tossing halfway through cooking. Transfer to bowl with beans and set aside.

3 Combine coriander, paprika, remaining ¼ teaspoon salt, and remaining ⅛ teaspoon pepper in small bowl.

Pound chicken to uniform thickness as needed. Pat dry with paper towels, rub with remaining 1 teaspoon oil, and sprinkle evenly with spice mixture. Arrange breasts skinned side down in now-empty air-fryer basket, spaced evenly apart, alternating ends. Place basket into air fryer and set temperature to 400 degrees. Cook until chicken registers 160 degrees, 12 to 16 minutes, flipping and rotating breasts halfway through cooking.

4 Transfer chicken to serving platter, tent loosely with aluminum foil, and let rest for 5 minutes. Add arugula to asparagus mixture in bowl and toss to combine. Season with salt and pepper to taste. Serve chicken with salad.

ROASTED BONE-IN CHICKEN BREASTS

Serves 2

COOK TIME 20 minutes   **TOTAL TIME** 30 minutes

why this recipe works When it's just two of you, roasting a whole chicken can feel like far too much trouble for a busy night. But roasting a pair of bone-in chicken breasts in the air fryer is a snap, and there are no leftovers to deal with. Bone-in chicken cooks beautifully in the air fryer, and the circulated hot air does nearly all the work. We rubbed the breasts with just a teaspoon of oil, starting them skin side down to help the fat in the skin to render. To ensure crispy skin, we flipped and rotated them halfway through cooking so that the skin could brown. A moderate 350 degrees minimized moisture loss and resulted in perfectly juicy meat. For a sauce to drizzle over our roasted breasts, we created two bright, fresh options, either of which can be prepared while the chicken cooks (one enlists the microwave, but neither requires a pan or even a blender, keeping the prep minimal and cutting down on dishes to wash). With our chicken roasted, all that remained was to toss a simple salad, perhaps open a bottle of wine, and voilà—a fancy dinner for two ready in 30 minutes. For an elegant presentation, cut the chicken breasts off the bone before serving. This recipe can be easily doubled (see page 14).

2 (12-ounce) bone-in split chicken breasts, trimmed

1 teaspoon extra-virgin olive oil

¼ teaspoon table salt

⅛ teaspoon pepper

Pat chicken dry with paper towels, rub with oil, and sprinkle with salt and pepper. Arrange breasts skin side down in air-fryer basket, spaced evenly apart, alternating ends. Place basket into air fryer and set temperature to 350 degrees. Cook until chicken registers 160 degrees, 20 to 25 minutes, flipping and rotating breasts halfway through cooking. Transfer chicken to serving platter, tent loosely with aluminum foil, and let rest for 5 minutes. Serve.

PEACH-GINGER CHUTNEY
Microwave 1 teaspoon extra-virgin olive oil, 1 small minced shallot, 1 minced garlic clove, 1 teaspoon grated fresh ginger, ⅛ teaspoon table salt, and pinch red pepper flakes in medium bowl until shallot has softened, about 1 minute.

Stir in 1½ cups frozen peaches, thawed and cut into ½-inch pieces; 2 tablespoons packed light brown sugar; and 1½ tablespoons cider vinegar. Microwave until peaches have softened and liquid is thick and syrupy, 6 to 8 minutes, stirring occasionally. Stir in 1 tablespoon chopped crystallized ginger.

LEMON-BASIL SALSA VERDE
Whisk ¼ cup minced fresh parsley, ¼ cup chopped fresh basil, 3 tablespoons extra-virgin olive oil, 1 tablespoon rinsed and minced capers, 1 tablespoon water, 2 minced garlic cloves, 1 rinsed and minced anchovy fillet, ½ teaspoon grated lemon zest and 2 teaspoons juice, and ⅛ teaspoon table salt together in bowl.

ROASTED BONE-IN CHICKEN BREASTS AND FINGERLING POTATOES WITH SUN-DRIED TOMATO RELISH

Serves 2

COOK TIME 20 minutes   **TOTAL TIME** 40 minutes

why this recipe works Roasting chicken on a pile of potatoes in the air fryer produces crispy results, as the hot air cooks the potatoes from all sides and the wire basket allows excess fat to drip below. We filled the basket with quick-cooking fingerling potatoes. Above them, we placed two bone-in chicken breasts. We started the chicken skin side down to render drippings, which seasoned the potatoes, then flipped it to allow the skin to crisp. Afterward, we collected a spoonful of drippings and used it to flavor a sun-dried tomato relish, which added savory depth to our meal. Look for fingerling potatoes about 3 inches in length.

- 1 pound fingerling potatoes, unpeeled
- 2 teaspoons extra-virgin olive oil, divided, plus extra as needed
- 2 teaspoons minced fresh thyme or ¾ teaspoon dried, divided

- 2 teaspoons minced fresh oregano or ¾ teaspoon dried, divided
- 1 garlic clove, minced
- ¾ teaspoon plus ⅛ teaspoon table salt, divided
- ½ teaspoon plus ⅛ teaspoon pepper, divided

- 2 (12-ounce) bone-in split chicken breasts, trimmed
- ¼ cup oil-packed sun-dried tomatoes, patted dry and chopped fine
- 1 small shallot, minced
- 1½ tablespoons red wine vinegar
- 1 tablespoon capers, rinsed and minced

1 Toss potatoes with 1 teaspoon oil, 1 teaspoon thyme, 1 teaspoon oregano, garlic, ¼ teaspoon salt, and ¼ teaspoon pepper in bowl to coat; transfer to air-fryer basket.

2 Pat chicken dry with paper towels. Rub with remaining 1 teaspoon oil, sprinkle with ½ teaspoon salt and ¼ teaspoon pepper, and sprinkle with remaining 1 teaspoon thyme and remaining 1 teaspoon oregano. Arrange breasts skin side down on top of potatoes, spaced evenly apart, alternating ends. Place basket into air fryer and set temperature to

350 degrees. Cook until potatoes are tender and chicken registers 160 degrees, 20 to 25 minutes, flipping and rotating breasts halfway through cooking.

3 Transfer chicken and potatoes to serving platter, tent loosely with aluminum foil, and let rest for 5 minutes. Pour off and reserve 1½ tablespoons juices from air-fryer drawer (add extra oil as needed to equal 1½ tablespoons). Combine tomatoes, shallot, vinegar, capers, remaining ⅛ teaspoon salt, remaining ⅛ teaspoon pepper, and reserved chicken juices in bowl. Serve chicken and potatoes with tomato relish.

BARBECUED BONE-IN CHICKEN BREASTS WITH CREAMY COLESLAW

Serves 2

COOK TIME 20 minutes   **TOTAL TIME** 45 minutes

why this recipe works Barbecued bone-in chicken on the grill can be tricky, what with flare-ups and unevenly cooked meat. For an easier indoor take, the air fryer stood in admirably, allowing us to cook the chicken nearly unattended. We used two bone-in chicken breasts and started cooking them skin side down to avoid drying them out. For plenty of barbecue flavor, we flipped the chicken and brushed the skin with a generous amount of barbecue sauce, finishing the cooking skin side up so that the sauce could caramelize a bit in the air fryer's circulated heat. For a convenient slaw that held its own, we started with bagged coleslaw mix. Salting the cabbage mixture for 30 minutes drew out excess moisture, avoiding a watery slaw, and softened the vegetables. For a dressing, we cut the standard mayonnaise with an equal amount of sour cream, which improved the texture and added richness and tang. White vinegar and a small amount of sugar gave the dressing balance. This recipe can be easily doubled (see page 14).

- 3 cups (8 ounces) shredded coleslaw mix
- ½ teaspoon table salt, plus salt for salting coleslaw
- 2 (12-ounce) bone-in split chicken breasts, trimmed
- ¼ teaspoon plus pinch pepper, divided
- 1 teaspoon vegetable oil
- 2 tablespoons barbecue sauce, plus extra for serving
- 2 tablespoons mayonnaise
- 2 tablespoons sour cream
- 1 teaspoon distilled white vinegar, plus extra for seasoning
- ¼ teaspoon sugar

1 Toss coleslaw mix and ¼ teaspoon salt in colander set over bowl. Let sit until wilted slightly, about 30 minutes. Rinse, drain, and dry well with dish towel.

2 Meanwhile, pat chicken dry with paper towels, rub with oil, and sprinkle with salt and ¼ teaspoon pepper. Arrange breasts skin side down in air-fryer basket, spaced evenly apart, alternating ends. Place basket into air fryer, set temperature to 350 degrees, and cook for 10 minutes. Flip and rotate breasts, then brush skin side with barbecue sauce. Return basket to air fryer and cook until well browned and chicken registers 160 degrees, 10 to 15 minutes.

3 Transfer chicken to serving platter, tent loosely with aluminum foil, and let rest for 5 minutes. While chicken rests, whisk mayonnaise, sour cream, vinegar, sugar, and remaining pinch pepper together in large bowl. Stir in coleslaw mix and season with salt, pepper, and additional vinegar to taste. Serve chicken with coleslaw, passing extra barbecue sauce separately.

SPICY PEANUT CHICKEN WITH CHARRED GREEN BEANS AND TOMATOES

Serves 2

COOK TIME 39 minutes	TOTAL TIME 1 hour

why this recipe works To give weeknight chicken and vegetables some pizzazz, we developed a peanut-hoisin sauce that was a glaze for the chicken, dressing for the green bean and cherry tomato salad, and sauce for passing at the table. We tossed the green beans with a little oil and air-fried them until they were tender and developed great char. Then we tossed them with tomatoes, scallions, and some peanut sauce. We brushed one side of the chicken with peanut sauce before air frying and glazed the other halfway through cooking, so the meat was well browned and flavorful. For an accurate measurement of boiling water, bring a kettle of water to a boil and then measure out the desired amount. If you plan to discard the chicken skin, do not set aside sauce for brushing in step 1. This recipe can be easily doubled (see page 14).

¼ cup boiling water

2 tablespoons creamy peanut butter

2 tablespoons hoisin sauce

1 tablespoon tomato paste

1 tablespoon chili-garlic sauce

1 pound green beans, trimmed

2 teaspoons toasted sesame oil, divided

2 (12-ounce) bone-in split chicken breasts, trimmed

¼ teaspoon table salt

6 ounces cherry tomatoes, halved

3 scallions, sliced thin

1 tablespoon chopped dry-roasted unsalted peanuts

¼ cup shredded fresh basil

Lime wedges

1 Whisk boiling water, peanut butter, hoisin, tomato paste, and chili-garlic sauce in bowl until combined; set aside 2 tablespoons sauce for brushing on chicken.

2 Toss green beans with 1 teaspoon oil in large bowl. Arrange in even layer in air-fryer basket. Place basket into air fryer and set temperature to 400 degrees. Cook until green beans are tender and spotty brown, 14 to 19 minutes, tossing halfway through cooking. Return green beans to now-empty bowl; set aside.

3 Pat chicken dry with paper towels, rub with remaining 1 teaspoon oil, and sprinkle with salt. Arrange chicken skin side down in now-empty basket, spaced evenly apart, alternating ends. Place basket into air fryer, set temperature to 350 degrees, and cook for 10 minutes. Flip and rotate chicken, then brush with reserved sauce. Return basket to air fryer and cook until chicken is well browned and registers 160 degrees, 15 to 20 minutes. Transfer chicken to plate and discard skin, if desired. Tent with aluminum foil and let rest while finishing green beans.

4 Add half of remaining sauce, tomatoes, scallions, peanuts, and basil to bowl with green beans and toss to combine. Season with salt and pepper to taste. Serve chicken with salad and lime wedges, passing remaining sauce separately.

RED CURRY CHICKEN KEBABS WITH PEANUT DIPPING SAUCE

Serves 2

COOK TIME 6 minutes   **TOTAL TIME** 30 minutes

why this recipe works "Air-grilled" chicken kebabs are just the ticket since they can double as a light meal or an appetizer. We took a cue from the herbal, savory flavors of Southeast Asian satay dishes (which vary widely in sweetness, aroma, spiciness, and richness) and used store-bought red curry paste as a starting point. We combined the paste with sugar, fish sauce, and lime zest and juice to achieve a balance of salty, sweet, sour, bitter, and umami. We used 2 tablespoons of the mixture to coat thin slices of chicken breast that were easy to thread onto skewers. The remaining mixture served as the base of a creamy peanut dipping sauce. We arranged the kebabs in the air fryer in two layers like Lincoln Logs (see page 13) to facilitate even cooking. After just 6 to 8 minutes (the time it took to make the sauce), the chicken was lightly browned and tender. This recipe can be easily doubled (see page 14).

- 2 tablespoons Thai red curry paste
- 1 tablespoon packed brown sugar
- 2 teaspoons fish sauce
- 1 teaspoon grated lime zest plus 1 tablespoon juice, plus lime wedges for serving
- 12 ounces boneless, skinless chicken breasts
- 2 teaspoons vegetable oil
- 12 (6-inch) wooden skewers
- 3 tablespoons smooth peanut butter
- 2 tablespoons chopped fresh basil or cilantro

1 Whisk curry paste, sugar, fish sauce, and lime zest and juice together in large bowl. Transfer 2 tablespoons curry paste mixture to medium bowl; set aside.

2 Slice each chicken breast lengthwise ¼ inch thick (you should have at least 12 slices) and pat dry with paper towels. Whisk oil into remaining curry paste mixture in large bowl. Add chicken and toss to coat. Weave chicken slices evenly onto each skewer, leaving 1 inch at bottom of skewer exposed. (Kebabs and reserved curry paste mixture can be refrigerated separately for up to 24 hours.)

3 Arrange half of kebabs in air-fryer basket, parallel to each other and spaced evenly apart. Arrange remaining skewers on top, perpendicular to bottom layer. Place basket into air fryer and set temperature to 400 degrees. Cook until chicken is spotty browned, 6 to 8 minutes.

4 Whisk peanut butter into reserved curry paste mixture until smooth and sauce has consistency of heavy cream. Adjust consistency with hot water as needed. Transfer kebabs to serving platter and sprinkle with basil. Serve with sauce and lime wedges.

SPICED CHICKEN KEBABS WITH VEGETABLE AND BULGUR SALAD

Serves 2

COOK TIME 20 minutes   **TOTAL TIME** 1 hour

why this recipe works For this recipe, we used skewers to raise the vegetables and chicken in the air fryer, allowing heat to circulate around them to generate better browning and charring for both. Partway through cooking, we stacked the chicken kebabs on the vegetable kebabs, placed crosswise for maximum air circulation, bringing the chicken closer to the heat source. A garlicky yogurt mixture spiced with baharat, an East Mediterranean spice blend, acted as a marinade for the chicken and sauce for the finished dish. Using bigger pieces of chicken and packing them tightly onto skewers kept the meat juicy. Skewering the vegetables separately allowed us to tailor cooking times so that the chicken and vegetables were ready at the same time. The vegetables retained their great charred flavor even after being chopped further for the bulgur salad. Look for medium-grind bulgur (labeled "#2"), which is roughly the size of mustard seeds. Avoid coarsely ground bulgur; it will not cook through in time. If you can't find baharat, you can substitute ½ teaspoon paprika, ¼ teaspoon pepper, ⅛ teaspoon ground cumin, and pinch ground cloves. We arranged the skewers in the air fryer in two layers like Lincoln Logs (see page 13) to facilitate even cooking. Serve with warmed pitas or naans, if desired. This recipe can be easily doubled (see page 14).

½ cup medium-grind bulgur, rinsed

⅓ cup boiling water

1 teaspoon baharat, divided

½ teaspoon table salt, divided

⅔ cup plain Greek yogurt

2 teaspoons grated lemon zest plus ¼ cup lemon juice, divided (2 lemons)

2 tablespoons extra-virgin olive oil, divided

1 small garlic clove, minced to paste

12 ounces boneless, skinless chicken breasts, trimmed and cut into 1½-inch pieces

½ cup coarsely chopped fresh mint, divided

½ cup coarsely chopped fresh parsley, divided

1 small red bell pepper, stemmed, seeded, and cut into 1½-inch pieces

1 small red onion, halved and cut through root end into 6 equal wedges

Olive oil spray

5 (6-inch) wooden skewers

2 tablespoons toasted chopped pistachios, almonds, or walnuts

1 Combine bulgur, boiling water, ¾ teaspoon baharat, and ¼ teaspoon salt in large bowl. Cover tightly with plastic wrap and let sit while preparing kebabs.

2 Combine yogurt, lemon zest, 2 tablespoons lemon juice, 1 tablespoon oil, garlic, remaining ¼ teaspoon baharat, and remaining ¼ teaspoon salt in bowl. Transfer ¼ cup yogurt mixture to medium bowl, add chicken, and toss to coat; let marinate for at least 15 minutes or up to 1 hour. Stir ¼ cup mint and ¼ cup parsley into remaining yogurt mixture and season with salt and pepper to taste; set aside for serving.

3 Thread bell pepper and onion evenly onto 3 skewers; lightly spray with oil spray. Arrange kebabs in air-fryer basket, parallel to each other and spaced evenly apart. Place basket into air fryer, set temperature to 375 degrees, and cook for 5 minutes.

4 Meanwhile, thread chicken evenly onto remaining 2 skewers. Arrange chicken kebabs on top of vegetable kebabs, perpendicular to bottom layer. Return basket to air fryer and cook until chicken is lightly browned and registers 160 degrees, 15 to 20 minutes, flipping and rotating chicken kebabs halfway through cooking. Transfer chicken kebabs to plate, tent with aluminum foil, and let rest while finishing salad.

5 Transfer vegetable kebabs to cutting board. When cool enough to handle, slide vegetables off skewers and chop coarse. Add vegetables, pistachios, remaining 2 tablespoons lemon juice, remaining 1 tablespoon oil, remaining ¼ cup mint, and remaining ¼ cup parsley to bulgur and toss to combine. Season with salt and pepper to taste. Serve chicken kebabs and salad with yogurt sauce.

AIR-FRIED CHICKEN

Serves 2

COOK TIME 16 minutes   **TOTAL TIME** 50 minutes

why this recipe works This basic air-fried chicken recipe turns out chicken that is golden and crispy on the outside and moist and juicy on the inside, and needs only a light spray of vegetable oil to become crisp. The secret was removing the fatty skin and finding a coating that would become crunchy without needing to be fried in a pan of hot oil. In a side-by-side taste test, crushed cornflakes won out over bread crumbs and Melba toast, offering the best color and crispness, but the results tasted a bit like breakfast cereal. Spicing up the cornflakes with poultry seasoning, paprika, and cayenne pepper gave the coating the savory element it needed. Dredging the floured chicken pieces in buttermilk added tang and ensured the crumbs stuck to the chicken. To crush the cornflakes, place them inside a zipper-lock bag and use a rolling pin or the bottom of a large skillet to break them into fine crumbs. To help remove the skin from the chicken, use a paper towel to grasp the skin. If you prefer, you can use a combination of two 5-ounce thighs and two 5-ounce drumsticks instead of the chicken breasts; if using drumsticks and thighs, be sure to cook them until they register 175 degrees, 20 to 25 minutes. This recipe can be easily doubled (see page 14).

Vegetable oil spray

2 (12-ounce) bone-in split chicken breasts, skin removed, halved crosswise, trimmed

1¼ teaspoons table salt, divided

½ teaspoon pepper, divided

⅓ cup buttermilk

½ teaspoon dry mustard

½ teaspoon garlic powder

¼ cup all-purpose flour

2 cups (2 ounces) cornflakes, finely crushed

1½ teaspoons poultry seasoning

½ teaspoon paprika

⅛ teaspoon cayenne pepper

1 Lightly spray bottom of air-fryer basket with vegetable oil spray. Pat chicken dry with paper towels and sprinkle with ½ teaspoon salt and ¼ teaspoon pepper. Whisk buttermilk, mustard, garlic powder, ½ teaspoon salt, and remaining ¼ teaspoon pepper together in medium bowl. Spread flour in shallow dish. Combine cornflakes, poultry seasoning, paprika, remaining ¼ teaspoon salt, and cayenne in second shallow dish.

2 Working with 1 piece of chicken at a time, dredge in flour, dip in buttermilk mixture, letting excess drip off, then coat with cornflake mixture, pressing gently to adhere; transfer to large plate. Lightly spray chicken with oil spray.

3 Arrange chicken pieces in prepared basket, spaced evenly apart. Place basket into air fryer and set temperature to 400 degrees. Cook until chicken is crisp and registers 160 degrees, 16 to 24 minutes, flipping and rotating pieces halfway through cooking. Serve.

CHIPOTLE-HONEY FRIED CHICKEN WITH BRUSSELS SPROUT AND CITRUS SALAD

Serves 2

COOK TIME 15 minutes   **TOTAL TIME** 1 hour

why this recipe works Our air-fried chicken is golden and crunchy on the outside and moist and juicy on the inside, just as fried chicken should be. It needs just a light spray of vegetable oil to cook. The secret was finding a coating that would get crunchy without needing to be deep-fried and, again, crushed cornflakes crushed the competition. To add a punch of smoky, spicy flavor, we incorporated chipotle chile in adobo in two ways: in the buttermilk mixture and in an aromatic, warm honey glaze to drizzle on the chicken before serving. For a fresh accompaniment, we made a salad of shaved brussels sprouts with tangy citrus and a mustard-cider vinaigrette. To crush the cornflakes, place them inside a zipper-lock bag and use a rolling pin or the bottom of a large skillet to break them into fine crumbs.

- 1 orange
- 1 tablespoon extra-virgin olive oil
- 1 tablespoon cider vinegar
- 1 tablespoon whole-grain mustard
- 1 tablespoon honey, divided
- ¼ teaspoon table salt, divided

- ¼ teaspoon pepper, divided
- 8 ounces brussels sprouts, trimmed, halved, and sliced very thin
- Vegetable oil spray
- ⅓ cup buttermilk
- 2 tablespoons minced canned chipotle chile in adobo sauce, divided

- 1 tablespoon all-purpose flour
- 2 cups (2 ounces) cornflakes, finely crushed
- 1¼ pounds bone-in chicken pieces (split breasts cut in half, drumsticks, and/or thighs), skin removed, trimmed

1 Cut away peel and pith from orange. Quarter orange, then slice crosswise ½ inch thick. Whisk oil, vinegar, mustard, 1 teaspoon honey, ⅛ teaspoon salt, and ⅛ teaspoon pepper together in large bowl. Add brussels sprouts and orange pieces and toss gently to combine; set aside for serving.

2 Lightly spray bottom of air-fryer basket with vegetable oil spray. Whisk buttermilk, 1 tablespoon chipotle, flour, remaining ⅛ teaspoon salt, and remaining ⅛ teaspoon pepper in medium bowl until smooth. Spread cornflakes in shallow dish.

3 Pat chicken dry with paper towels. Working with 1 piece of chicken at a time, dredge in buttermilk mixture, letting excess drip off, then coat with cornflakes, pressing gently to adhere. Lightly spray chicken pieces with oil spray and arrange in prepared basket, spaced evenly apart. Place basket into air fryer and set temperature to 400 degrees. Cook until chicken is crisp and registers 160 degrees, 15 to 25 minutes, flipping and rotating pieces halfway through cooking.

4 Meanwhile, microwave remaining 1 tablespoon chipotle and remaining 2 teaspoons honey in small bowl until mixture is fluid, about 20 seconds, stirring halfway through microwaving. Drizzle chicken with chipotle mixture and serve with salad.

CORIANDER CHICKEN THIGHS WITH ROASTED CAULIFLOWER AND SHALLOTS

Serves 2

COOK TIME 25 minutes	TOTAL TIME 1 hour

why this recipe works The fragrance of lemony-coconutty coriander seed is so potent, we wanted to use it in several ways for this dish, which contains more vegetables—cauliflower, shallots, and tomatoes—than chicken. We seasoned the vegetables and the chicken with ground coriander, creating a flavorful spice crust, and also added the spice to the citrusy dressing. Toasting and grinding coriander seeds right before using ensured the freshest flavor. Cutting the cauliflower into 2-inch florets meant the cauliflower cooked in the same amount of time as the chicken. Poking holes in the chicken thighs with a skewer helped render the fat as they cooked; cooking them skin side up made the skin golden and crisp. Toast coriander seeds in a dry skillet over medium heat until fragrant (about 2 minutes), and then remove the skillet from the heat so that the coriander won't scorch. If you plan to discard the chicken skin, skip poking with skewer. Instead, loosen skin covering thighs and rub coriander mixture under skin. This recipe can be easily doubled (see page 14).

2 teaspoons coriander seeds, toasted

½ teaspoon paprika

½ teaspoon table salt

½ teaspoon pepper

1 pound cauliflower florets, cut into 2-inch pieces

2 shallots, peeled and quartered

2 tablespoons extra-virgin olive oil, divided

1½ tablespoons lime juice

1 small garlic clove, finely grated

2 (5- to 7-ounce) bone-in, skin-on chicken thighs, trimmed

8 ounces cherry tomatoes, halved

⅓ cup chopped fresh cilantro

1 Crush coriander in mortar and pestle or spice grinder until coarsely ground; transfer to small bowl. Stir in paprika, salt, and pepper.

2 Toss cauliflower and shallots with 1 tablespoon oil and 1 teaspoon coriander mixture in large bowl. Transfer to air-fryer basket and spread into even layer. Combine lime juice, garlic, 1 teaspoon coriander mixture, and remaining 1 tablespoon oil in now-empty bowl; set aside.

3 Using metal skewer, poke skin side of chicken 10 to 15 times. Pat chicken dry with paper towels and rub evenly with remaining coriander mixture. Arrange chicken skin side up on top of vegetables, spaced evenly apart. Place basket into air fryer and set temperature to 400 degrees. Cook until vegetables are tender and chicken is well browned and crisp and registers 195 degrees, 25 to 35 minutes, stirring vegetables and rotating chicken halfway through cooking (do not flip chicken).

4 Transfer chicken to plate and let rest for 5 minutes. Transfer vegetables to bowl with lime juice–garlic mixture. Add tomatoes and cilantro and toss to coat. Season with salt and pepper to taste. Serve chicken with vegetables.

CHICKEN-TOMATILLO TACOS WITH ROASTED PINEAPPLE SALSA

Serves 2

COOK TIME 30 minutes   **TOTAL TIME** 1 hour

why this recipe works The chicken filling for tacos is often simmered. But if overcooked, the meat dries out, so to ensure that our chicken stayed juicy and flavorful, we used chicken thighs instead of breasts. We were excited to use the air fryer for the other elements of the dish: roasting tomatillos and the ingredients for a deeply flavorful fruit salsa. We kept the seasoning on the chicken and tomatillos simple because this salsa has it all: poblanos for heat, red onion for zip, and pineapple for sweetness. We found that the air fryer heightened the pineapple's yellow color and enhanced its sweetness. Roasting the chicken on a bed of tomatillos allowed the chicken juices to saturate the tomatillos while their skins charred and started to break down. The tartness of the tomatillos complemented the sweet pineapple salsa, and a garnish of thinly sliced radishes and queso fresco brought crunch and richness to the tacos. If fresh tomatillos are unavailable, substitute one (11-ounce) can of tomatillos, drained, rinsed, and patted dry. You can lightly char the tortillas one at a time over a gas burner or stack tortillas, wrap tightly in aluminum foil, and warm in the air fryer set to 350 degrees for 5 minutes, flipping halfway through cooking. This recipe can be easily doubled (see page 14).

- 2 poblano chiles, stemmed, quartered, and seeded
- 2 jalapeño chiles, stemmed, halved, and seeded (optional)
- 1 small red onion, quartered
- 1 cup 1-inch fresh or thawed frozen pineapple pieces
- 1 tablespoon extra-virgin olive oil, divided

- ¼ teaspoon table salt, divided
- ¼ teaspoon pepper, divided
- ½ cup coarsely chopped fresh cilantro
- 1 tablespoon lime juice, plus lime wedges for serving
- 12 ounces tomatillos, husks and stems removed, rinsed well, patted dry, and halved

- 12 ounces boneless, skinless chicken thighs, trimmed
- 6 (6-inch) corn tortillas, warmed
- 1 ounce queso fresco, crumbled (¼ cup)
- 2 radishes, trimmed and sliced thin

1 Toss poblanos; jalapeños, if using; onion; and pineapple with 2 teaspoons oil, ⅛ teaspoon salt, and ⅛ teaspoon pepper in bowl. Transfer to air-fryer basket and spread into even layer; do not clean bowl.

2 Place basket into air fryer and set temperature to 400 degrees. Cook until chile-pineapple mixture is tender and spotty brown, 15 to 20 minutes, stirring halfway through cooking. Transfer mixture to cutting board, let cool slightly, then chop coarse. Combine chile-pineapple mixture, cilantro, and lime juice in bowl and season with salt and pepper to taste; set aside for serving.

3 Toss tomatillos with remaining 1 teaspoon oil and arrange in even layer in now-empty basket. Pat chicken dry with paper towels and sprinkle with remaining ⅛ teaspoon salt and remaining ⅛ teaspoon pepper. Arrange chicken on top of tomatillos, spaced evenly apart. Return basket to air fryer and cook until tomatillos are blistered and chicken registers 175 degrees, 15 to 20 minutes, flipping and rotating chicken halfway through cooking.

4 Transfer chicken to cutting board, let cool slightly, then shred into bite-size pieces using 2 forks. Serve chicken and tomatillos with warmed tortillas, passing salsa, queso fresco, radishes, and extra lime wedges separately.

HOISIN-GINGER CHICKEN SALAD WITH NAPA CABBAGE, SHIITAKES, AND BELL PEPPER

Serves 2

COOK TIME 15 minutes	TOTAL TIME 45 minutes

why this recipe works The air fryer's intense circulating heat creates the perfect condition for sealing in the juices and flavors of chicken thighs (and other meats). These same conditions help generate even, deeply burnished glazes. The trick is to use a glaze that isn't too thick (which can become gloppy) or too thin (which can slide off), and to add it at the right time so that it doesn't burn before the meat reaches the proper temperature—that time is when the meat is parcooked. We thinned store-bought hoisin sauce with fresh ginger and a splash of vinegar, which also added welcome brightness and acidity to the sweet and savory hoisin. We first cooked the chicken on a layer of shiitake mushrooms, which steamed while absorbing flavorful chicken juices. Then we brushed on some glaze and continued to cook the chicken. By the time the chicken reached the correct temperature, the glaze had reduced and adhered to the thighs. We glazed the second side, and after a few more minutes in the air fryer, our chicken and shiitakes were ready to be sliced into a hearty topping for a colorful salad with napa cabbage, bell pepper, scallions, cilantro, and peanuts. You can substitute sliced romaine lettuce for the napa cabbage. This recipe can be easily doubled (see page 14).

4 teaspoons toasted sesame oil, divided

2 tablespoons unseasoned rice vinegar, divided

1 tablespoon grated fresh ginger, divided

2 teaspoons soy sauce

4 cups thinly sliced napa cabbage

1 small red bell pepper, stemmed, seeded, and cut into ¼-inch-wide strips

2 scallions, sliced thin on bias

4 ounces shiitake mushrooms, stemmed

12 ounces boneless, skinless chicken thighs, trimmed

3 tablespoons hoisin sauce

¼ cup fresh cilantro leaves

¼ cup unsalted dry-roasted peanuts

1 Whisk 1 tablespoon oil, 1 tablespoon vinegar, 1 teaspoon ginger, and soy sauce together in large bowl. Add cabbage, bell pepper, and scallions and toss to combine; set aside.

2 Toss mushrooms with remaining 1 teaspoon oil and arrange gill side up in even layer in air-fryer basket. Pat chicken dry with paper towels and arrange in even layer on top of mushrooms. Place basket into air fryer, set temperature to 400 degrees, and cook for 5 minutes.

3 Whisk hoisin, remaining 1 tablespoon vinegar, and remaining 2 teaspoons ginger together in small bowl. Brush tops of chicken thighs with half of hoisin mixture. Return basket to air fryer and cook until chicken is well browned and registers 175 degrees, 10 to 15 minutes. Flip chicken; brush with remaining hoisin mixture; and cook until glaze is bubbly, about 2 minutes.

4 Transfer chicken and mushrooms to cutting board, let cool slightly, then slice thin. Toss cabbage mixture to recombine and season with salt and pepper to taste. Divide salad among individual serving bowls and top with chicken, mushrooms, cilantro, and peanuts. Serve.

THAI-STYLE CHICKEN LETTUCE WRAPS

Serves 2 to 4

COOK TIME 12 minutes

TOTAL TIME 40 minutes

why this recipe works Based on a light yet bold Thai salad known as larb, these chicken lettuce wraps embody the cuisine's signature balance of sweet, sour, salty, and hot flavors. But even the most flavorful salad can't compensate for dry chicken. Choosing boneless chicken thighs ensured the meat would be moist. The air fryer made quick work of cooking the chicken while we mixed a pungent dressing from lime juice, fish sauce, brown sugar, shallot, garlic, and pepper flakes. We let the chicken cool slightly and then shredded it; this subtle but significant step created loads of surface area that allowed the dressing to soak into the meat, ensuring every bite would be saturated with flavor. Fresh herbs (mint, cilantro, and Thai basil), mango, and Thai chiles brought more freshness to our salad, which we spooned into Bibb lettuce cups and sprinkled with chopped peanuts for crunch. If you can't find Thai basil, you can substitute regular basil. If you can't find Thai chiles, you can substitute two Fresno or red jalapeño chiles.

1 pound boneless, skinless chicken thighs, trimmed

1 teaspoon vegetable oil

2 tablespoons lime juice

1 shallot, minced

1 tablespoon fish sauce, plus extra for serving

2 teaspoons packed brown sugar

1 garlic clove, minced

⅛ teaspoon red pepper flakes

1 mango, peeled, pitted, and cut into ¼-inch pieces

⅓ cup chopped fresh mint

⅓ cup chopped fresh cilantro

⅓ cup chopped fresh Thai basil

1 head Bibb lettuce (8 ounces), leaves separated

¼ cup dry-roasted peanuts, chopped

2 Thai chiles, stemmed and sliced thin

1 Pat chicken dry with paper towels and rub with oil. Place chicken in air-fryer basket. Place basket into air fryer and set temperature to 400 degrees. Cook until chicken registers 175 degrees, 12 to 16 minutes, flipping and rotating chicken halfway through cooking.

2 Meanwhile, whisk lime juice, shallot, fish sauce, sugar, garlic, and pepper flakes together in large bowl; set aside.

3 Transfer chicken to cutting board, let cool slightly, then shred into bite-size pieces using 2 forks. Add shredded chicken, mango, mint, cilantro, and basil to bowl with dressing and toss to coat. Serve chicken in lettuce leaves, passing peanuts, Thai chiles, and extra fish sauce separately.

JERK CHICKEN LEG QUARTERS

Serves 2

COOK TIME 27 minutes
TOTAL TIME 50 minutes

why this recipe works Spicy, sweet, and herbal, this simple take on Jamaican jerk chicken delivers authentic flavors from a spice rub composed of easily available pantry ingredients. We substituted black pepper, dry mustard, and cayenne pepper for the heat of the usual Scotch bonnet peppers, which can be hard to come by. Ground allspice was key, and dried thyme rounded out the traditional seasonings while brown sugar sweetened things up and helped to create a deep brown, crackly, and crusted skin on our chicken. We chose skin-on chicken leg quarters, a cut that's forgiving to cook and tender down to the last nibble on the bone. It also offered lots of surface area for our jerk rub. To get both tender meat and crispy skin using our air fryer, we pierced the skin in several places to allow the fat underneath to render more quickly, and kept the leg quarters skin side up throughout, ensuring they had time to become deeply colored. Served with lime wedges and a sprinkling of scallion, our jerk chicken legs were mouthwatering; all that was missing was a warm Caribbean breeze. Some leg quarters are sold with the backbone attached. Be sure to remove it (we like to use a heavy chef's knife for this task) before cooking so that the chicken fits in the air-fryer basket and to make serving easier. This recipe can be easily doubled (see page 14; alternate thicker and thinner ends of legs quarters in basket).

1 tablespoon packed brown sugar	¾ teaspoon dry mustard	2 (10-ounce) chicken leg quarters, trimmed
1 teaspoon ground allspice	¾ teaspoon dried thyme	1 teaspoon vegetable oil
1 teaspoon pepper	½ teaspoon table salt	1 scallion, green part only, sliced thin
1 teaspoon garlic powder	¼ teaspoon cayenne pepper	Lime wedges

1 Combine sugar, allspice, pepper, garlic powder, mustard, thyme, salt, and cayenne in bowl. Pat chicken dry with paper towels. Using metal skewer, poke 10 to 15 holes in skin of each chicken leg. Rub with oil and sprinkle evenly with spice mixture.

2 Arrange chicken skin side up in air-fryer basket, spaced evenly apart. Place basket into air fryer and set temperature to 400 degrees. Cook until chicken is well browned and crisp and registers 195 degrees, 27 to 30 minutes, rotating chicken halfway through cooking (do not flip).

3 Transfer chicken to plate, tent loosely with aluminum foil, and let rest for 5 minutes. Sprinkle with scallion. Serve with lime wedges.

BUFFALO CHICKEN DRUMSTICKS

Serves 2

COOK TIME 22 minutes   **TOTAL TIME** 45 minutes

why this recipe works An air fryer produces great Buffalo chicken with the crunch that typically comes from deep frying. The catch is that, for well-crisped pieces, you must cook wings in batches—even for two servings—which didn't thrill us. To avoid this, we opted for more substantial drumsticks, turning the snack into a main dish, and found we liked the meatier pieces (still with plenty of crispy skin) prepared Buffalo style. We poked holes in the skin to render the fat efficiently and rubbed them with a touch of oil to ensure that they crisped up. To build flavor, we coated the drumsticks with a blend of paprika, cayenne, salt, and pepper before cooking. For the namesake sauce, we microwaved equal parts melted butter and hot sauce but found the coating to be greasy. Using less butter fixed that problem but did not keep the sauce from sliding off the chicken. Adding just ¼ teaspoon of cornstarch yielded a thicker, glazy sauce that coated the drumsticks perfectly, and a bit of molasses deepened its flavor and brought a hint of sweetness. Instead of preparing a blue cheese sauce, we simply crumbled blue cheese over the drumsticks, which balanced the Buffalo sauce's seductive heat. Classic Buffalo sauce is made with Frank's RedHot Original Cayenne Pepper Sauce. This recipe can be easily doubled (see page 14).

1½ teaspoons paprika	4 (5-ounce) chicken drumsticks, trimmed	2 tablespoons unsalted butter
½ teaspoon cayenne pepper	1 teaspoon vegetable oil	2 teaspoons molasses
¼ teaspoon table salt	3 tablespoons hot sauce	¼ teaspoon cornstarch
¼ teaspoon pepper		2 tablespoons crumbled blue cheese

1 Combine paprika, cayenne, salt, and pepper in bowl. Pat drumsticks dry with paper towels. Using metal skewer, poke 10 to 15 holes in skin of each drumstick. Rub with oil and sprinkle evenly with spice mixture.

2 Arrange drumsticks in air-fryer basket, spaced evenly apart, alternating ends. Place basket into air fryer and set temperature to 400 degrees. Cook until chicken is crisp and registers 195 degrees, 22 to 25 minutes, flipping and rotating chicken halfway through cooking. Transfer chicken to large plate, tent loosely with aluminum foil, and let rest for 5 minutes.

3 Meanwhile, microwave hot sauce, butter, molasses, and cornstarch in large bowl, stirring occasionally, until hot, about 1 minute. Add chicken and toss to coat. Transfer to serving platter and sprinkle with blue cheese. Serve.

LEMON-PEPPER CHICKEN WINGS

Serves 2

COOK TIME 18 minutes   **TOTAL TIME** 30 minutes

why this recipe works Once you make chicken wings in your air fryer, you may never go back to conventional frying or oven roasting again. With their delicate skin and paper-thin layer of fat, chicken wings are a perfect candidate for air frying. In the intense, evenly circulating heat, the fat renders as the skin crisps and then conveniently accumulates at the bottom of the air fryer without smoking up your kitchen. Rather than toss our wings in gloppy, sugar- or fat-heavy sauces, we tossed them with our choice of superflavorful combinations: simple lemon and pepper with herbs, slightly more complex Parmesan and garlic (to round out the lemon, pepper, and herbs), and feisty cilantro and lime with jalapeño. These added a lot of zing to the wings without compromising their perfectly crisped exteriors. If you buy chicken wings that are already split, with the tips removed, you will need only 1 pound. This recipe can be easily doubled (see page 14).

- 1¼ pounds chicken wings, halved at joints, wingtips discarded
- ⅛ teaspoon table salt
- ¼ teaspoon pepper
- 1 tablespoon grated lemon zest, plus lemon wedges for serving
- 1 tablespoon minced fresh parsley, dill, and/or tarragon

1 Pat wings dry with paper towels and sprinkle with salt and pepper. Arrange wings in even layer in air-fryer basket. Place basket into air fryer and set temperature to 400 degrees. Cook until wings are golden brown and crisp, 18 to 24 minutes, flipping wings halfway through cooking.

2 Combine lemon zest and parsley in large bowl. Add wings and toss until evenly coated. Serve with lemon wedges.

PARMESAN-GARLIC CHICKEN WINGS
Add 1 tablespoon grated Parmesan cheese and 1 minced garlic clove to lemon zest–parsley mixture.

CILANTRO-LIME CHICKEN WINGS
Substitute lime zest and wedges for lemon and cilantro for parsley. Add 1 tablespoon minced jalapeño chile to lime zest–cilantro mixture.

ROASTED CHICKEN SAUSAGES WITH BUTTERNUT SQUASH AND RADICCHIO

Serves 2

COOK TIME 18 minutes   **TOTAL TIME** 45 minutes

why this recipe works For a quick, easy dinner, sausages can't be beat. Pairing them with hearty, sweet butternut squash gave us a satisfying meal. The squash got a 10-minute head start in the air fryer so that it was fully tender by the time the sausages were cooked through. A swipe of honey helped speed up the browning of the sausage, which stayed juicy on the inside. Bitter radicchio added bulk and balanced out the sweet roasted squash, a cider vinegar–honey dressing tied everything together, and toasted walnuts added crunch. Chicken sausage is available in a variety of flavors; feel free to use any flavor that you think will work well in this dish. Turkey sausage can be substituted for the chicken sausage. For more information on toasting nuts in the air fryer, see page 19. This recipe can be easily doubled (see page 14).

1½ pounds butternut squash, peeled, seeded, and cut into 1-inch pieces (4 cups)

4 teaspoons extra-virgin olive oil, divided, plus extra for drizzling

½ teaspoon minced fresh thyme or ⅛ teaspoon dried

⅛ teaspoon table salt

Pinch cayenne pepper (optional)

6 ounces raw chicken sausage (2 sausages)

2 teaspoons honey, warmed, divided

2 teaspoons cider vinegar

1 teaspoon Dijon mustard

¼ teaspoon pepper

½ small head radicchio (3 ounces), cored and sliced ½ inch thick

2 tablespoons chopped toasted walnuts

2 tablespoons chopped fresh basil or parsley

1 Toss squash with 2 teaspoons oil; thyme; salt; and cayenne, if using. Transfer to air-fryer basket and spread into even layer. Place basket into air fryer; set temperature to 400 degrees; and cook until beginning to brown, 10 to 15 minutes, stirring halfway through cooking.

2 Brush sausages with 1 teaspoon honey. Stir squash, then arrange sausages on top, spaced evenly apart. Return basket to air fryer and cook until squash is tender and

sausages are lightly browned and register 165 degrees, 8 to 13 minutes, flipping and rotating sausages halfway through cooking.

3 Transfer sausages to plate and let rest while finishing squash. Whisk vinegar, mustard, pepper, remaining 2 teaspoons oil, and remaining 1 teaspoon honey together in large bowl. Add squash, radicchio, walnuts, and basil and toss to coat. Season with salt and pepper to taste. Serve sausages with vegetables.

WHOLE ROAST CHICKEN WITH LEMON, DILL, AND GARLIC

Serves 4

COOK TIME 45 minutes   **TOTAL TIME** 1½ hours

why this recipe works Cooking space is compact even in larger air fryers (one of the reasons foods cook so evenly) but with a few adjustments, we were able to roast a whole chicken successfully. The convection heat helped seal the exterior and lock in flavors and juices while creating a golden layer of crackly crisp skin. To ensure that our bird fit in the air fryer with room for good air circulation, we did two things: First, we forewent the usual step of tying the legs, as this tends to increase the chicken's height. Leaving them untied allowed for greater air circulation and faster cooking around the legs and thighs, which needed to cook to a higher temperature than the breast meat. Next, we pressed down gently on the breast so that it would sit flatter in the air fryer. We started the chicken breast side down, which gave the legs a jump start. Halfway through cooking, we flipped the chicken breast side up, so the breast meat and skin could finish to perfection. Finally, we created several aromatic blends to rub underneath the skin (we found that aromatics rubbed on the outside quickly burned). We had the best success with chickens weighing between 3½ and 4 pounds; larger chickens will require increased cooking time and may not fit in your air fryer. For a simpler roast, skip the aromatics and season the outside of the chicken with just salt and pepper. You will need an air fryer with at least a 6-quart capacity for this recipe. If using an air-fryer lid for a multi-cooker, do not use basket insert; place the chicken directly into the pot.

1 tablespoon extra-virgin olive oil	2 teaspoons dried dill weed	¼ teaspoon pepper
2 teaspoons grated lemon zest	½ teaspoon garlic powder	1 (3½- to 4-pound) whole chicken, giblets discarded
	½ teaspoon table salt	

1 Combine oil, lemon zest, dill, garlic powder, salt, and pepper in small bowl. Pat chicken dry with paper towels. Use your fingers to gently loosen skin covering breast and thighs. Carefully spoon spice mixture under skin, directly on meat on each side of breast and on thighs. Distribute spices over meat gently with fingertips. Arrange chicken breast side up in center of cutting board and, using heels of palms, firmly press on breast to flatten slightly.

2 Arrange chicken breast side down in air-fryer basket. Place basket into air fryer and set temperature to 400 degrees. Cook until chicken is light golden brown and skin is lightly crisped, about 30 minutes.

3 Using tongs, flip chicken breast side up. Return basket to air fryer and continue to cook chicken until breasts register 160 degrees and thighs register 175 degrees, 15 to 30 minutes.

4 Transfer chicken to carving board and let rest for 15 minutes. Carve chicken, discarding skin, if desired. Serve.

WHOLE ROAST CHICKEN WITH ORANGE, ALEPPO, AND CINNAMON
Substitute orange zest for lemon zest, ground dried Aleppo pepper for dill, and cinnamon for garlic.

WHOLE ROAST CHICKEN WITH GINGER, CUMIN, AND CARDAMOM
Substitute grated fresh ginger for lemon zest, ground cumin for dill, and ground cardamom for garlic.

CALIFORNIA TURKEY BURGERS

Serves 2

COOK TIME 10 minutes   **TOTAL TIME** 45 minutes

why this recipe works The air fryer seemed like a convenient way to make turkey burgers, but it wasn't as simple as forming two ground turkey patties and tossing them in the basket. On its own, ground turkey cooks up dry and dense—the extra-lean meat can't hold on to its own moisture during cooking. But we found that mixing in yogurt and panko gave the burgers structure and kept them moist. Making a slight indentation in the raw patties prevented them from puffing up too much as they cooked. And what's a California turkey burger without avocado? We decided to give the fruit a bit of a twist by pickling it, which added vibrancy and zip to the creamy avocado. Be sure to use ground turkey, not ground turkey breast (also labeled 99 percent fat-free), in this recipe. Ground chicken also works well here. You can use your air fryer to toast the buns; see page 19 for more information. This recipe can be easily doubled (see page 14).

½ avocado	3 tablespoons plain yogurt	2 slices Swiss, provolone, or pepper Jack cheese
1 small shallot, minced	2 tablespoons panko bread crumbs	2 hamburger buns, toasted, if desired
1 teaspoon distilled white vinegar	¼ teaspoon pepper	½ tomato, sliced thin
¼ teaspoon sugar	8 ounces ground turkey	1 ounce (½ cup) alfalfa sprouts
¼ teaspoon table salt, divided		

1 Using fork, mash avocado, shallot, vinegar, sugar, and ⅛ teaspoon salt to coarse paste in bowl; set aside for serving.

2 Lightly spray bottom of air-fryer basket with vegetable oil spray. Using fork, mash yogurt, panko, pepper, and remaining ⅛ teaspoon salt to paste in medium bowl. Add turkey and lightly knead with hands until mixture forms cohesive mass. Using lightly moistened hands, divide turkey mixture into 2 lightly packed balls, then flatten each gently into ½-inch-thick patty. Press center of each patty with your fingertips to create ¼-inch-deep depression.

3 Arrange patties in prepared basket, spaced evenly apart. Place basket into air fryer and set temperature to 350 degrees. Cook until burgers are lightly browned and register 160 degrees, 10 to 15 minutes, flipping halfway through cooking.

4 Turn off air fryer. Top burgers with cheese and let sit in warm air fryer until melted, about 1 minute. If desired, arrange bun tops and bottoms cut side up in now-empty basket. Return basket to air fryer, set temperature to 400, and cook until buns are lightly toasted, 4 to 6 minutes. Serve burgers on buns, topped with avocado mixture, tomato, and alfalfa sprouts.

MINI GLAZED TURKEY MEATLOAVES

Serves 2

COOK TIME 25 minutes   **TOTAL TIME** 1 hour

why this recipe works It might come as a surprise that you can cook meatloaf in an air fryer, but we found that the circulated hot air was the ideal cooking environment for this comfort food classic. For a lighter version of meatloaf, we started with ground turkey, perking up its mild flavor with garlic, shallot, and thyme. Worcestershire sauce provided some savory meatiness, while cayenne added subtle heat. To hold the loaf together, we mixed in an egg and a panade made from white sandwich bread and milk, which also helped the meatloaf to remain moist. Shaping two free-form mini loaves, rather than one big loaf, enabled the dish to cook in just 25 minutes and provided more surface area to be glazed. We made a flavor-packed glaze from ketchup, cider vinegar, brown sugar, and hot sauce. To ensure that it stuck, we applied a first coat to the meatloaves and let them cook until the glaze was tacky, then added a second coat of glaze, which stuck to this base coat in an even layer. Since the loaves were delicate, we placed them on an aluminum foil sling, which allowed us to rotate and also remove them easily. Be sure to use ground turkey, not ground turkey breast (also labeled 99 percent fat-free). For more information on making a foil sling, see page 13. Serve with Air-Fried Brussels Sprouts (page 203) and Crispy Smashed Potatoes (page 223), if desired.

- 1 shallot, minced
- 1 tablespoon vegetable oil
- 1 garlic clove, minced
- ½ teaspoon minced fresh thyme or ⅛ teaspoon dried
- Pinch cayenne pepper

- 1 slice hearty white sandwich bread, crust removed, torn into ½-inch pieces
- 1 large egg, lightly beaten
- 1 tablespoon whole milk
- 1 tablespoon Worcestershire sauce
- ¼ teaspoon table salt

- ¼ teaspoon pepper
- 1 pound ground turkey
- ¼ cup ketchup
- 1 tablespoon cider vinegar
- 1 tablespoon packed brown sugar
- ½ teaspoon hot sauce

1 Make foil sling for air-fryer basket by folding 1 long sheet of aluminum foil so it is 4 inches wide. Lay sheet of foil widthwise across basket, pressing foil into and up sides of basket. Fold excess foil as needed so that edges of foil are flush with top of basket. Lightly spray foil and basket with vegetable oil spray.

2 Microwave shallot, oil, garlic, thyme, and cayenne in large bowl until fragrant, about 1 minute. Add bread, egg, milk, Worcestershire, salt, and pepper and mash mixture to paste using fork. Break up ground turkey into small pieces over bread mixture and knead with hands until well combined. Shape turkey mixture into two 5 by 3-inch loaves. Arrange loaves on sling in prepared basket, spaced evenly apart.

3 Combine ketchup, vinegar, sugar, and hot sauce in small bowl, then brush loaves with half of ketchup mixture. Place basket into air fryer and set temperature to 350 degrees. Cook until meatloaves register 160 degrees, 25 to 30 minutes, brushing with remaining ketchup mixture and rotating meatloaves using sling halfway through cooking.

4 Using foil sling, carefully remove meatloaves from basket. Tent loosely with foil and let rest for 5 minutes. Serve.

TURKEY-ZUCCHINI MEATBALLS WITH ORZO, SPICED TOMATO SAUCE, AND FETA

Serves 2

COOK TIME 31 minutes   **TOTAL TIME** 1 hour

why this recipe works Cooking pasta or grains in the air fryer can be tricky since the environment encourages rapid evaporation, which can lead to uneven cooking. Enter orzo—a rice-shaped pasta with a rare talent for maintaining its shape and texture when cooked, especially when pretoasted. So we pretoasted the orzo in olive oil and garlic, using a 6-inch cake pan. Then we parcooked the pasta in a warmly spiced tomato sauce. Meanwhile, we shaped our turkey meatballs using shredded zucchini, a good way to add vegetables to the dish, replace the traditional panade, and give the meatballs moisture and tenderness. We nestled the meatballs into the parcooked orzo and sauce, then air-fried the meatballs until they had simmered on the bottom and were lightly roasted on the top. Finally, we added crumbled feta and air-fried everything together for the last few minutes. By the time the meatballs had reached their proper temperature, the cheese had melted and was just beginning to brown. You can substitute traditional orzo for the whole-wheat orzo; do not substitute other pasta shapes. Be sure to use ground turkey, not ground turkey breast (also labeled 99 percent fat-free), in this recipe. Ground chicken also works well here. You will need a 6-inch round nonstick or silicone cake pan for this recipe; before starting this recipe, confirm your air fryer allows enough space for the pan.

½ cup 100 percent whole-wheat orzo

1 tablespoon extra-virgin olive oil, plus extra for drizzling

2 garlic cloves, minced, divided

1 (8-ounce) can tomato sauce

¾ cup water

¼ teaspoon pepper, divided

⅛ teaspoon ground cinnamon

Pinch ground cloves

8 ounces ground turkey

4 ounces zucchini, grated (¾ cup)

1 tablespoon minced fresh oregano, plus extra for serving

⅛ teaspoon table salt

1 ounce crumbled feta cheese (¼ cup)

1 Combine orzo, oil, and half of garlic in 6-inch round nonstick cake pan, then spread into even layer. Place pan into air-fryer basket and place basket into air fryer. Set temperature to 400 degrees and cook until orzo is lightly browned and fragrant, 3 to 5 minutes, stirring halfway through cooking.

2 Stir tomato sauce, water, ⅛ teaspoon pepper, cinnamon, and cloves into orzo mixture until evenly combined. Return basket to air fryer and cook until orzo is al dente, 18 to 22 minutes.

3 Using hands, lightly knead turkey, zucchini, oregano, salt, remaining garlic, and remaining ⅛ teaspoon pepper in medium bowl until mixture forms cohesive mass. Using lightly moistened hands, pinch off and roll mixture into 8 meatballs. (Meatballs can be refrigerated for up to 24 hours.)

4 Stir orzo mixture gently to recombine. Nestle meatballs into orzo and cook until meatballs are lightly browned, 8 to 10 minutes. Sprinkle feta over meatballs and cook until meatballs register 160 degrees and feta is spotty brown, 2 to 4 minutes.

5 Transfer pan to wire rack and let meatballs and orzo rest for 5 minutes. Drizzle with extra oil and sprinkle with extra oregano before serving.

BEEF, PORK, AND LAMB

SPICE-RUBBED STEAK WITH SNAP PEA AND CUCUMBER SALAD

Serves 4

COOK TIME 15 minutes   **TOTAL TIME** 45 minutes

why this recipe works Looking to make juicy, perfectly cooked steak in the air fryer, we set our sights on 1½-inch-thick steak. These hefty cuts often command equally hefty prices, but we wanted a reasonably priced option ideal for an easy weeknight meal. Top sirloin, known for its lean texture and nice flavor, fit the bill. Cutting the steak into two pieces enabled it to fit snugly in the air fryer. Since the air fryer would essentially be roasting, rather than searing, the meat, we applied a fragrant spice rub to give it a bold crust. Rubbing the steak with a little oil first helped the spices adhere to the lean meat. We placed our steak in the air fryer and set it to 400 degrees to blast it with heat. Even with the circulated hot air, we found that flipping and rotating the pieces halfway through cooking produced more even results. After 15 minutes, our steaks emerged juicy and a perfect medium-rare. Since the beef could cook virtually unattended in the air fryer, we used the downtime to prepare a simple salad. Fresh snap peas, crisp radishes, and peppery baby arugula tossed in a creamy dill dressing offset the rich flavor of the spice-rubbed steak.

1½ teaspoons ground cumin	1 (1½-pound) boneless top sirloin steak, 1½ inches thick, trimmed and halved crosswise	½ English cucumber, halved lengthwise and sliced thin
1½ teaspoons chili powder		8 ounces sugar snap peas, strings removed, cut in half on bias
1⅜ teaspoons table salt, divided	1 teaspoon plus 1½ tablespoons extra-virgin olive oil, divided	
⅜ teaspoon pepper, divided		2 ounces (2 cups) baby arugula
¾ teaspoon ground coriander	3 tablespoons mayonnaise	2 radishes, trimmed, halved, and sliced thin
⅛ teaspoon ground cinnamon	1½ tablespoons white wine vinegar	
⅛ teaspoon cayenne pepper	1 tablespoon minced fresh dill	
	1 small garlic clove, minced	

1 Combine cumin, chili powder, 1¼ teaspoons salt, ½ teaspoon pepper, coriander, cinnamon, and cayenne in bowl. Pat steaks dry with paper towels, rub with 1 teaspoon oil, and sprinkle evenly with spice mixture.

2 Arrange steaks in air-fryer basket, spaced evenly apart. Place basket into air fryer and set temperature to 400 degrees. Cook until steaks register 120 to 125 degrees (for medium-rare) or 130 to 135 degrees (for medium),

15 to 20 minutes, flipping and rotating steaks halfway through cooking. Transfer steaks to cutting board, tent with aluminum foil, and let rest while preparing salad.

3 Whisk remaining 1½ tablespoons oil, mayonnaise, vinegar, dill, garlic, remaining ⅛ teaspoon salt, and remaining ⅛ teaspoon pepper together in large bowl. Add cucumber, snap peas, arugula, and radishes and toss gently to combine. Season with salt and pepper to taste. Slice steaks and serve with salad.

LEMON-SAGE TOP SIRLOIN STEAK WITH ROASTED CARROTS AND SHALLOTS

Serves 2

COOK TIME 25 minutes   **TOTAL TIME** 45 minutes

why this recipe works The key to this steak dinner was to combine some flavorful ingredients (earthy carrots, piquant shallots, and beefy sirloin) with aromatic complements (sage, lemon, and olive oil) and to nail the order of operations, using the air fryer's intense, even heat to bring out the best in the ingredients. First, we roasted carrots and halved shallots until they were just softened. Then we transferred them to a bowl and tossed them simply with lemon zest, separately coating the steak in sage and lemon zest. The time it took to cook the steak perfectly was just right for roasting the coating gently without burning it. While the steak rested, we finished air-frying the vegetables so that they would be spotty brown, tender, and warm when it was time to eat. This recipe can be easily doubled using two steaks (see page 14).

1 pound carrots, peeled and halved crosswise, thicker pieces halved lengthwise

6 shallots, halved through root end

1 tablespoon extra-virgin olive oil, divided

½ teaspoon table salt, divided

¼ teaspoon pepper, divided

1 tablespoon grated lemon zest, divided, plus lemon wedges for serving

1 tablespoon minced fresh sage

1 (8- to 12-ounce) boneless top sirloin steak, 1½ inches thick, trimmed

1 Toss carrots and shallots with 2 teaspoons oil, ¼ teaspoon salt, and ⅛ teaspoon pepper in large bowl. Arrange vegetables in even layer in air-fryer basket. Place basket into air fryer and set temperature to 400 degrees. Cook until vegetables are softened, 8 to 10 minutes. Return vegetables to bowl and toss gently with 1½ teaspoons lemon zest; cover to keep warm.

2 Combine sage, remaining 1 teaspoon oil, remaining ¼ teaspoon salt, remaining ⅛ teaspoon pepper, and remaining 1½ teaspoons lemon zest in bowl. Pat steak dry with paper towels and rub with sage mixture. Place steak in now-empty basket, return basket to air fryer, and set temperature to 400 degrees. Cook until steak is lightly browned and registers 120 to 125 degrees (for medium-rare) or 130 to 135 degrees (for medium), 14 to 20 minutes, flipping and rotating steak halfway through cooking.

3 Transfer steak to cutting board, tent with aluminum foil, and let rest while finishing vegetables. Return vegetables to basket. Place basket into air fryer; set temperature to 400 degrees; and cook until vegetables are tender and spotty brown, 3 to 5 minutes. Slice steak thin and serve with vegetables and lemon wedges.

TOP SIRLOIN STEAK WITH ROASTED MUSHROOMS AND BLUE CHEESE SAUCE

Serves 4

COOK TIME 25 minutes   **TOTAL TIME** 50 minutes

why this recipe works Steak with blue cheese sauce, golden-brown mushrooms, and tender onions is typically restaurant fare. For an unfussy version to make at home, we employed our air fryer to cook both steaks and vegetables in one go. We started with relatively inexpensive but well-marbled top sirloin and robust cremini mushrooms. Frozen pearl onions kept the prep light. Ensuring the steaks and vegetables finished cooking at the same time presented a challenge—they cooked at different rates and the mushrooms took up a lot of space in the basket. Our solution: Give the vegetables a head start. Since mushrooms shrink as they cook, we soon had room to rest our steaks on top; this arrangement also lifted the steaks closer to the heating element, enhancing browning. While the steaks rested, we microwaved a little blue cheese and cream to create a simple sauce, then stirred in more blue cheese chunks.

- 1½ pounds cremini mushrooms, trimmed and halved if large or left whole if small
- 1 cup frozen pearl onions, thawed
- 1 tablespoon extra-virgin olive oil, divided
- 4 garlic cloves, minced
- 2 teaspoons minced fresh thyme or ½ teaspoon dried
- 1 teaspoon table salt, divided
- 1 (1½-pound) boneless top sirloin steak, 1½ inches thick, trimmed and halved crosswise
- ¼ teaspoon pepper
- 2 ounces blue cheese, crumbled (½ cup), divided
- ¼ cup heavy cream
- 1 tablespoon chopped fresh parsley

1 Toss mushrooms and onions with 2 teaspoons oil, garlic, thyme, and ½ teaspoon salt in bowl; transfer to air-fryer basket. Place basket into air fryer and set temperature to 400 degrees. Cook until mushrooms and onions begin to brown, 12 to 15 minutes, stirring halfway through cooking.

2 Pat steaks dry with paper towels, rub with remaining 1 teaspoon oil, and sprinkle with remaining ½ teaspoon salt and pepper. Stir mushrooms and onions, then arrange steaks on top, spaced evenly apart. Return basket to air fryer and cook until steaks register 120 to 125 degrees (for medium-rare) or 130 to 135 degrees (for medium),

13 to 18 minutes, flipping and rotating steaks halfway through cooking. Transfer steaks to cutting board and mushroom-onion mixture to serving bowl. Tent each with aluminum foil and let rest while preparing sauce.

3 Microwave ¼ cup blue cheese and cream in bowl, whisking occasionally, until blue cheese is melted and smooth, about 30 seconds, stirring once halfway through. Let sauce cool slightly, then stir in remaining ¼ cup blue cheese. Stir parsley into mushroom-onion mixture and season with salt and pepper to taste. Slice steaks and serve with mushroom-onion mixture and sauce.

STEAK FRITES

Serves 2

| **COOK TIME** 23 minutes | **TOTAL TIME** 1 hour |

why this recipe works The classic bistro meal steak frites features perfectly cooked steak and really crisp french fries, each of which we'd made solo in the air fryer. After some delicious trial and error, our reward was being able to air-fry the meat and potatoes together. For the steak, using thicker sirloin meant that we got nice color on the meat while the middle stayed juicy. Making crunchy fries with fluffy interiors required a three-step process: a rinse and a 10-minute soak in hot water, a low-temperature fry to parcook the potatoes, and a high-temperature fry to finish cooking and crisping them. Coating the potato sticks with oil was another key to good browning. The fries often broke when we tossed them in the air-fryer basket, so we moved them to a bowl to toss, resulting in fewer broken pieces. To time the cooking of the potatoes and steak so that both would be ready at the same time, we added the steak to the air fryer partway through cooking the potatoes, placing the meat on the fries. While the cooked steak rested, we crisped the fries, then served our steak frites with parsley-shallot sauce. This recipe can be easily doubled using two steaks (see page 14).

Parsley-Shallot Sauce

- ¼ cup minced fresh parsley
- 1 tablespoon extra-virgin olive oil
- 1 tablespoon minced shallot
- 1 tablespoon red wine vinegar

- 1 garlic clove, minced
- ⅛ teaspoon table salt
- Pinch red pepper flakes

Steak and Fries

- 1 pound russet potatoes, peeled
- 5 teaspoons extra-virgin olive oil, divided

- 1 (8- to 12-ounce) boneless top sirloin steak, 1½ inches thick, trimmed
- ½ teaspoon table salt, divided
- ¼ teaspoon pepper

1 for the parsley-shallot sauce Combine parsley, oil, shallot, vinegar, 1 tablespoon water, garlic, salt, and pepper flakes in bowl; set aside for serving. (Sauce can be refrigerated for up to 2 days; let come to room temperature and whisk to recombine before serving.)

2 for the steak and fries Cut potatoes lengthwise into ½-inch-thick planks. Stack 3 or 4 planks and cut into ½-inch-thick sticks; repeat with remaining planks. Submerge potatoes in large bowl of water and rinse to remove excess

starch. Drain potatoes and repeat process as needed until water remains clear. Cover potatoes with hot water and let sit for 10 minutes. Drain potatoes, transfer to paper towel–lined rimmed baking sheet, and thoroughly pat dry.

3 Toss potatoes with 2 teaspoons oil in clean, dry large bowl. Arrange potatoes in even layer in air-fryer basket. Place basket into air fryer, set temperature to 350 degrees, and cook for 8 minutes. Transfer potatoes to now-empty bowl and toss gently to redistribute. Return potatoes to

basket; place basket into air fryer; and cook until softened and potatoes have turned from white to blond (potatoes may be spotty brown at tips), 5 to 10 minutes.

4 Pat steak dry with paper towels, rub with 1 teaspoon oil, and sprinkle with ¼ teaspoon salt and pepper. Transfer potatoes to now-empty bowl and toss with remaining 2 teaspoons oil and remaining ¼ teaspoon salt. Return potatoes to basket and place steak on top. Return basket to air fryer; increase temperature to 400 degrees; and cook until steak is lightly browned and registers 120 to 125 degrees (for medium-rare) or 130 to 135 degrees (for medium), 10 to 15 minutes, flipping and rotating steak halfway through cooking. Transfer steak to cutting board, tent with aluminum foil, and let rest while finishing potatoes.

5 Transfer potatoes to now-empty bowl and toss gently to redistribute. Return potatoes to basket; return basket to air fryer; and cook until golden brown and crisp, 5 to 10 minutes. Season with salt and pepper to taste. Slice steak thin and serve with fries and sauce.

FLANK STEAK WITH CORN AND BLACK BEAN SALAD

Serves 2

COOK TIME 8 minutes   TOTAL TIME 35 minutes

why this recipe works For your next taco night, try using the air fryer and these bright Southwestern flavors. For the black bean and corn salad that accompanies our flank steak, we roasted a poblano chile and scallion whites but liked the convenience of canned beans and frozen corn. Instead of cooking the meat separately, we placed it on top of our poblano and scallion whites to cook, which reduced the cooking time. Chipotle chile powder added smokiness to the steak, and a yogurt-lime dressing, scallion greens, and cilantro flavored the corn and black beans. The dressing also became an aromatic sauce for the meat. If fire-roasted corn is unavailable, substitute traditional frozen corn; avoid canned corn here. This recipe can be easily doubled using two steaks (see page 14). Serve with warm tortillas.

¼ cup plain Greek yogurt

1 teaspoon grated lime zest plus 2 tablespoons juice, plus lime wedges for serving

1½ cups frozen fire-roasted corn, thawed

1 (15-ounce) can black beans, rinsed

1 poblano chile, stemmed, halved, and seeded

4 scallions, white parts cut into 2-inch pieces, green parts sliced thin

1 tablespoon extra-virgin olive oil, divided

1 (8- to 12-ounce) flank steak, 1 inch thick, trimmed

½ teaspoon chipotle chile powder

¼ teaspoon table salt

3 tablespoons chopped fresh cilantro

1 Whisk yogurt and lime zest and juice together in large bowl; measure out and reserve 2 tablespoons dressing for serving. Add corn and beans to remaining dressing and toss to combine; set aside.

2 Toss poblano and scallion whites with 2 teaspoons oil in separate bowl. Transfer to air-fryer basket and spread into even layer. Pat steak dry with paper towels, rub with remaining 1 teaspoon oil, and sprinkle with chile powder and salt. Place steak on top of vegetables. Place basket into air fryer and set temperature to 400 degrees. Cook until steak is lightly browned and registers 120 to 125 degrees (for medium-rare) or 130 to 135 degrees (for medium), 8 to 14 minutes, flipping and rotating steak halfway through cooking.

3 Transfer steak to cutting board, tent with aluminum foil, and let rest while finishing salad. Chop poblano and scallion whites coarse and add to corn mixture along with cilantro and scallion greens. Season with salt and pepper to taste. Slice steak thin against grain and serve with salad, reserved dressing, and lime wedges.

BEEF SATAY WITH RED CURRY NOODLES

Serves 2

COOK TIME 6 minutes   **TOTAL TIME** 1 hour

why this recipe works Topped with "air-grilled" skewers of seasoned beef, this red curry noodle bowl is like two meals in one yet requires far less juggling than such dishes typically do. Air-frying the beef, rather than grilling it, vastly streamlined the process and let us focus on the noodles. We coated sliced flank steak with a brown sugar–coriander mixture that would complement the red curry sauce, then threaded the slices onto skewers, which we stacked in the air fryer in a crisscross pattern for optimal air circulation (see page 13). To build an easy noodle bowl, we used thin vermicelli noodles, which needed only a quick soak in boiling water. Strips of bell pepper and snow peas required no cooking and added color and crunch. To create an easy sauce with multidimensional flavor, we microwaved coconut milk and red curry paste to bloom the flavors. Adding lime juice, sugar, and fish sauce gave us a sauce that incorporated each taste: salty, sweet, sour, bitter, and umami. A final sprinkling of chopped basil added pleasant freshness to complete our noodle bowl.

1 tablespoon packed light brown sugar, divided

2 teaspoons vegetable oil

1 teaspoon ground coriander

¼ teaspoon table salt

⅛ teaspoon cayenne pepper

1 (12-ounce) flank steak, ½ to ¾ inch thick, trimmed

10 (6-inch) wooden skewers

4 ounces rice vermicelli

½ cup canned coconut milk

2 teaspoons Thai red curry paste

1 tablespoon lime juice, plus extra for seasoning

2 teaspoons fish sauce, plus extra for seasoning

1 small red bell pepper, stemmed, seeded, and cut into 2-inch-long matchsticks

4 ounces snow peas, strings removed and sliced lengthwise into matchsticks

½ cup chopped fresh basil

1 Combine 1 teaspoon sugar, oil, coriander, salt, and cayenne in bowl. Slice steak against grain into ½-inch-thick slices (you should have at least 10 slices) and pat dry with paper towels. Add beef to sugar mixture and toss to coat. Weave beef evenly onto skewers, leaving 1 inch at bottom of skewer exposed.

2 Arrange half of beef skewers in air-fryer basket, parallel to each other and spaced evenly apart. Arrange remaining skewers on top, perpendicular to bottom layer. Place basket into air fryer and set temperature to 400 degrees. Cook until beef is lightly browned, 6 to 8 minutes, flipping and rotating skewers twice during cooking. Transfer skewers to serving platter, tent with aluminum foil, and let rest while preparing noodles.

3 Place noodles in large bowl and pour 6 cups boiling water over top. Stir noodles briefly to ensure they are completely submerged, then let soak, stirring occasionally, until tender, about 2 minutes. Drain noodles and set aside.

4 Whisk coconut milk, red curry paste, and remaining 2 teaspoons sugar together in now-empty bowl and microwave until fragrant, about 1 minute. Whisk in lime juice and fish sauce. Add noodles, bell pepper, snow peas, and basil and toss gently to coat. Season with extra lime juice and fish sauce to taste. Adjust consistency with hot water as needed. Serve beef skewers with noodles.

STEAK TACOS

Serves 2 to 4

COOK TIME 13 minutes　　　　　　　　　　**TOTAL TIME** 40 minutes

why this recipe works When a taco craving strikes, the air fryer is a cook's best friend. With little oversight—thanks to its regulated heat and built-in timer—this automated sous chef turned out juicy, perfectly cooked steak (flank steak offered nice beefy flavor; cutting it in half sped up the cooking) while we warmed tortillas and prepared a few garnishes. For a hands-off, zingy topping, we quick-pickled sliced red onion, jalapeño, and radishes, letting the vegetables steep until crisp-tender in a hot mixture of red wine vinegar and sugar while the steak cooked. To finish, crumbled queso fresco and sliced avocado added pleasant richness, and cilantro leaves gave our tacos a pop of freshness.

1 cup red wine vinegar

⅓ cup sugar

½ red onion, sliced thin

2 radishes, trimmed, halved, and sliced thin

1 jalapeño chile, stemmed and sliced thin into rounds

1 (1-pound) flank steak, trimmed and halved with grain

1 teaspoon vegetable oil

¾ teaspoon ground cumin

¼ teaspoon table salt

⅛ teaspoon pepper

6–12 (6-inch) corn tortillas, warmed

2 ounces queso fresco, crumbled (½ cup)

1 avocado, halved, pitted, and sliced thin

Fresh cilantro leaves

Lime wedges

1 Microwave vinegar and sugar in medium bowl until steaming, about 5 minutes. Stir in onion, radishes, and jalapeño and set aside.

2 Pat steaks dry with paper towels. Rub steaks with oil, sprinkle with cumin, salt, and pepper. Arrange steaks in air-fryer basket, spaced evenly apart. Place basket into air fryer and set temperature to 400 degrees. Cook until steaks are browned and register 120 to 125 degrees (for medium-rare) or 130 to 135 degrees (for medium), 13 to 18 minutes, flipping and rotating steaks halfway through cooking. Transfer steaks to cutting board, tent with aluminum foil, and let rest for 5 minutes.

3 Drain pickled vegetables and return to now-empty bowl. Slice steaks thin against grain. Serve with warm tortillas, pickled vegetables, queso fresco, avocado, cilantro, and lime wedges.

GOCHUJANG-SESAME STEAK TIPS WITH NAPA SLAW

Serves 4

COOK TIME 13 minutes   **TOTAL TIME** 45 minutes

why this recipe works Inspired by Korean barbecue, these succulent morsels of beef offer a fantastic combination of spicy, sweet, sour, and salty flavors. We built a simple marinade by blooming ginger and garlic with sesame oil in the microwave, then whisking in honey, gochujang, and soy sauce. We used this to coat sirloin steak tips; the combo was so tender and flavorful, the meat needed no marinating period but could be cooked straightaway in the air fryer. For contrast, we made a crunchy napa cabbage and carrot slaw in a bright rice vinegar dressing. Sprinkling the beef with scallions and sesame seeds added a fresh and toasty finish. Sirloin steak tips, also called flap meat, are sold as whole steaks, cubes, and strips. To ensure uniform pieces, we prefer to purchase whole steak tips and cut them ourselves.

2 tablespoons toasted sesame oil, divided

2 teaspoons grated fresh ginger, divided

1 garlic clove, minced to paste

2 tablespoons honey, divided

2 tablespoons gochujang

1 teaspoon plus 1 tablespoon soy sauce, divided

1½ pounds sirloin steak tips, trimmed and cut into 2-inch pieces

3 tablespoons unseasoned rice vinegar

½ small head napa cabbage, cored and sliced thin (4 cups)

1 carrot, peeled and grated

2 tablespoons toasted sesame seeds, divided

3 scallions, sliced thin on bias

1 Microwave 1 tablespoon oil, 1 teaspoon ginger, and garlic in large bowl until fragrant, about 30 seconds, stirring once halfway through. Whisk in 4 teaspoons honey, gochujang, and 1 teaspoon soy sauce until smooth. Add steak tips and toss to coat.

2 Arrange steak tips in air-fryer basket, spaced evenly apart. Place basket into air fryer and set temperature to 400 degrees. Cook until steak tips are lightly browned and register 130 to 135 degrees (for medium), 13 to 18 minutes, flipping and rotating steak tips halfway through cooking. Transfer steak tips to serving platter, tent with aluminum foil, and let rest while preparing slaw.

3 Whisk vinegar, remaining 1 tablespoon oil, remaining 1 teaspoon ginger, remaining 2 teaspoons honey, and remaining 1 tablespoon soy sauce together in large bowl. Add cabbage and carrot and toss to coat. Let sit for 5 minutes, then stir in 1 tablespoon sesame seeds. Sprinkle steak tips with remaining 1 tablespoon sesame seeds and scallions and serve with slaw.

ROASTED STEAK TIPS WITH TOMATOES AND GORGONZOLA

Serves 2

COOK TIME 12 minutes

TOTAL TIME 30 minutes

why this recipe works Beefy steak tips and a summery tomato salad make for a quick and elegant dinner when you don't want to spend a lot of time in the kitchen. Steak tips deliver a lot of meatiness with very little cooking time, and roasting them in the air fryer effortlessly produces tender meat with rich flavor and great color. Seasoning the steak with just salt and pepper allowed its beefiness to shine. We coated the meat with a little oil to keep it from drying out in the high heat. As the steak rested (to allow its juices to distribute evenly), we created a light counterpoint to the beef by making a salad of ripe tomatoes, tangy dressing, and a sprinkle of Gorgonzola. Sirloin steak tips, also called flap meat, are sold as whole steaks, strips, and cubes. To ensure uniform pieces, we prefer to purchase whole steak tips and cut them ourselves. For the best results, use peak-of-the-season tomatoes. This recipe can be easily doubled (see page 14).

2 teaspoons red wine vinegar

½ teaspoon Dijon mustard

½ teaspoon table salt, divided

½ teaspoon pepper, divided

1 small shallot, sliced thin

8–12 ounces sirloin steak tips, trimmed and cut into 2-inch pieces

4 teaspoons extra-virgin olive oil, divided

1 tablespoon chopped fresh parsley

1 pound mixed tomatoes, cored

2 tablespoons crumbled Gorgonzola cheese

1 Whisk vinegar, mustard, ¼ teaspoon salt, and ¼ teaspoon pepper together in small bowl; stir in shallot and set aside.

2 Toss steak tips with 1 teaspoon oil, remaining ¼ teaspoon salt, and remaining ¼ teaspoon pepper. Arrange steak tips in air-fryer basket, spaced evenly apart. Place basket into air fryer and set temperature to 400 degrees. Cook until steak tips are lightly browned and register 130 to 135 degrees (for medium), 12 to 18 minutes, flipping and rotating steak tips halfway through cooking.

3 Transfer steak tips to plate, tent with aluminum foil, and let rest for 5 minutes. Meanwhile, whisk parsley and remaining 1 tablespoon oil into vinegar mixture. Halve or quarter small tomatoes, cut medium tomatoes into ½-inch wedges, and slice large tomatoes ¼ inch thick. Arrange tomatoes attractively on serving platter, spoon dressing over top, and sprinkle with Gorgonzola. Serve steak tips with tomato salad.

GINGER-SOY BEEF AND VEGETABLE KEBABS

Serves 2

COOK TIME 18 minutes   **TOTAL TIME** 1 hour

why this recipe works Whether you cook beef and vegetable kebabs on the grill or in the air fryer, the advice is the same: Resist the urge to thread both meat and veggies onto a single skewer. This arrangement may look pretty, but the meat will likely dry out long before the vegetables are done. For juicy chunks of beef and browned, tender-firm vegetables, we first chose well-marbled steak tips, cutting them into generous 1½-inch cubes. A quick ginger-soy marinade added deep flavor in 10 minutes, and we reserved some for a sauce. Meanwhile, we cooked our vegetable skewers—a mix of red onion, shiitake mushrooms, and zucchini. Partway through cooking, we stacked our beef kebabs on top, placed crosswise for maximum air circulation (see page 13); this also brought the meat closer to the heat source for better browning. Soon, our kebabs all emerged perfectly cooked. Sirloin steak tips, also called flap meat, are sold as whole steaks, cubes, and strips. To ensure uniform pieces, we prefer to purchase whole steak tips and cut them ourselves.

- 2 tablespoons vegetable oil, divided
- 1 teaspoon grated fresh ginger
- 1 garlic clove, minced
- ¼ teaspoon red pepper flakes
- 1 tablespoon toasted sesame oil
- 2 teaspoons soy sauce

- 1½ teaspoons honey
- ½ teaspoon grated orange zest plus 1 tablespoon juice
- 12 ounces sirloin steak tips, trimmed and cut into 1½-inch pieces
- 1 small red onion, halved and cut through root end into 6 equal wedges

- 4 ounces shiitake mushrooms, stemmed and halved if large
- 1 zucchini, sliced into ½-inch-thick rounds
- ¼ teaspoon table salt
- ¼ teaspoon pepper
- 5 (6-inch) wooden skewers

1 Microwave 4 teaspoons vegetable oil, ginger, garlic, and pepper flakes in large bowl until fragrant, about 30 seconds, stirring once halfway through. Whisk in sesame oil, soy sauce, honey, and orange zest and juice until combined. Measure out and reserve 3 tablespoons oil mixture. Add beef to remaining oil mixture and toss to coat; set aside.

2 Meanwhile, toss red onion, mushrooms, and zucchini with remaining 2 teaspoons vegetable oil, salt, and pepper in bowl. Thread 1 piece of onion onto wooden skewer. Thread one-third of zucchini and mushrooms onto skewer, followed by second piece of onion. Repeat skewering remaining vegetables with 2 more skewers. Arrange skewers in air-fryer basket, parallel to each other and spaced evenly apart. Place basket into air fryer and set temperature to 400 degrees. Cook until vegetables are beginning to brown, about 8 minutes.

3 While vegetable skewers cook, thread beef evenly onto remaining 2 skewers. Flip and rotate vegetable skewers, then arrange beef skewers on top, perpendicular to vegetable skewers. Return basket to air fryer and cook until beef registers 130 to 135 degrees (for medium) and vegetables are crisp-tender, 10 to 14 minutes, flipping and rotating beef skewers halfway through cooking.

4 Transfer skewers to serving platter, tent with aluminum foil, and let rest for 5 minutes. Whisk reserved oil mixture to recombine. Using fork, push beef and vegetables off skewers onto platter and drizzle with oil mixture. Serve.

COFFEE- AND FENNEL-RUBBED BONELESS SHORT RIBS WITH CELERY ROOT SALAD

Serves 2

COOK TIME 38 minutes   **TOTAL TIME** 1 hour

why this recipe works Boneless short ribs (which are cut from a less tough part of the cow than bone-in short ribs) can be roasted with excellent results. Two slabs fit neatly in the air fryer, offering a hands-off, luxurious meal for two. For a seasoning that stood up to the rich meat, we applied a fennel-coffee rub. Since there was room in the basket, we added subtly sweet celery root, a perfect pairing. We roasted the celery root until it just became tender, then added our short ribs and lowered the temperature to let the meat cook gently and evenly. A sprinkle of pomegranate seeds and parsley brightened the earthy celery root. The thickness and marbling of boneless short ribs can vary; look for lean ribs cut from the chuck. Do not substitute bone-in English-style short ribs. Because they are cooked gently and not seared, the short ribs will be rosy throughout. This recipe can be easily doubled (see page 14).

- 2 pounds celery root, peeled and cut into ¾-inch pieces
- 2 tablespoons extra-virgin olive oil, divided
- ⅜ teaspoon table salt, divided
- ⅜ teaspoon pepper, divided

- 1½ teaspoons ground fennel
- 1 teaspoon ground coffee
- 1 teaspoon packed brown sugar
- ½ teaspoon garlic powder

- 12 ounces boneless short ribs, 1½ to 2 inches thick and 4 to 5 inches long, trimmed
- ½ cup pomegranate seeds
- ½ cup fresh parsley leaves
- 1 teaspoon lemon juice

1 Toss celery root with 2 teaspoons oil, ⅛ teaspoon salt, and ⅛ teaspoon pepper in bowl; transfer to air-fryer basket. Place basket into air fryer and set temperature to 400 degrees. Cook celery root until just tender, about 20 minutes, tossing halfway through cooking.

2 Combine fennel, coffee, sugar, garlic powder, remaining ¼ teaspoon salt, and remaining ¼ teaspoon pepper in small bowl. Pat short ribs dry with paper towels, rub with 1 teaspoon oil, and sprinkle evenly with spice mixture.

3 Stir celery root, then arrange short ribs on top, spaced evenly apart. Return basket to air fryer and set temperature to 250 degrees. Cook until beef registers 130 to 135 degrees (for medium) and celery root is tender, 18 to 24 minutes, flipping and rotating short ribs halfway through cooking. Transfer short ribs to cutting board, tent with aluminum foil, and let rest while preparing salad.

4 Transfer celery root to large bowl; add pomegranate seeds, parsley, lemon juice, and remaining 1 tablespoon oil and toss to coat. Slice short ribs thin and serve with salad.

ROASTED BONELESS SHORT RIBS WITH RED PEPPER RELISH

Serves 4

COOK TIME 18 minutes   **TOTAL TIME** 35 minutes

why this recipe works In Argentina, short ribs are often cooked over hardwood coals until tender, smoky, and rosy within. To replicate this in our air fryer, we started with boneless short ribs, "slow-roasting" them at 250 degrees until evenly cooked (in reality, this took only 18 minutes). As they roasted, the wire basket allowed excess fat to drip away. A spice rub of smoked paprika, brown sugar, and cumin gave our ribs a smoky flavor reminiscent of grilling. To cut the richness, we prepared a piquant red pepper relish. To avoid using the stovetop, we microwaved red bell pepper with minced shallot, olive oil, garlic, and a pinch of cayenne until the bell pepper was softened. Cilantro and lemon juice brought freshness and balanced the acidity. The thickness and marbling of boneless short ribs can vary; look for lean ribs cut from the chuck. Do not substitute bone-in English-style short ribs. Because they are cooked gently and not seared, the short ribs will be rosy throughout.

- 2 teaspoons smoked paprika
- 2 teaspoons packed brown sugar
- 1½ teaspoons ground cumin
- ⅜ teaspoon table salt, divided
- ¼ teaspoon pepper

- 1½ pounds boneless short ribs, 1½ to 2 inches thick and 4 to 5 inches long, trimmed
- 2 teaspoons plus 2 tablespoons extra-virgin olive oil, divided
- ¼ cup finely chopped red bell pepper

- 1 small shallot, minced
- 2 garlic cloves, minced
- Pinch cayenne pepper
- 2 tablespoons minced fresh cilantro
- 2 teaspoons lemon juice

1 Combine paprika, sugar, cumin, ½ teaspoon salt, and pepper in bowl. Pat short ribs dry with paper towels, rub with 2 teaspoons oil, and sprinkle evenly with spice mixture. Arrange short ribs in air-fryer basket, spaced evenly apart. Place basket into air fryer and set temperature to 250 degrees. Cook until beef registers 130 to 135 degrees (for medium), 18 to 24 minutes, flipping and rotating short ribs halfway through cooking. Transfer short ribs to cutting board, tent with aluminum foil, and let rest while preparing relish.

2 Microwave bell pepper, shallot, garlic, cayenne, remaining ⅛ teaspoon salt, and remaining 2 tablespoons oil in bowl, stirring occasionally, until vegetables are softened, about 2 minutes. Let cool slightly, then stir in cilantro and lemon juice. Season with salt and pepper to taste. Slice short ribs thin and serve with relish.

BIG ITALIAN MEATBALLS WITH ZUCCHINI NOODLES

Serves 2

COOK TIME 35 minutes	TOTAL TIME 1 hour

why this recipe works This wonderful air-fryer take on spaghetti and meatballs offers a lighter and simpler way to enjoy the comfort classic. How do you air-fry spaghetti? Trade pasta for spiralized zucchini, which cooks in minutes in the air fryer, eliminating the need to boil a pot of water. To top our noodles, four giant meatballs seemed more fun than smaller ones. A milk and bread panade kept the meatballs tender and moist (it also held them together) while Parmesan, basil, shallot, garlic powder, and an egg gave them richness and flavor. We cooked the meatballs at a low temperature to prevent the exterior from drying out before the middle was done. Spiralized zucchini noodles can be found in the produce section of the supermarket. If you own a spiralizer, two 12-ounce zucchini will yield the necessary amount of zucchini noodles for this recipe. This recipe can be easily doubled (see page 14).

- 1 slice hearty white sandwich bread, crust removed, torn into ½-inch pieces
- 1 large egg
- 3 tablespoons milk
- 1 shallot, minced
- 1 ounce Parmesan cheese, grated (½ cup), plus extra for serving
- ¼ cup chopped fresh basil, divided
- 1 teaspoon garlic powder
- ¼ teaspoon table salt
- ¼ teaspoon pepper
- 1 pound 93 percent lean ground beef
- 1 pound zucchini noodles
- 2 teaspoons extra-virgin olive oil
- ¾ cup jarred marinara sauce, warmed

1 Mash bread, egg, and milk into paste in large bowl using fork. Stir in shallot, Parmesan, 2 tablespoons basil, garlic powder, salt, and pepper. Break up ground beef into small pieces over bread mixture in bowl and lightly knead with hands until well combined. Pinch off and roll mixture into four meatballs.

2 Arrange meatballs in air-fryer basket, spaced evenly apart. Place basket into air fryer, set temperature to 250 degrees, and cook for 20 minutes. Flip and rotate meatballs and continue to cook until well browned and register 160 degrees, 10 to 15 minutes. Transfer meatballs to serving platter, tent with aluminum foil, and let rest while preparing noodles.

3 Toss zucchini noodles in clean bowl with oil and season with salt and pepper. Arrange noodles in even layer in now-empty air-fryer basket. Return basket to air fryer and set temperature to 400 degrees. Cook until noodles are just tender, 5 to 7 minutes. Divide zucchini noodles and meatballs between individual serving bowls and top with warm marinara sauce. Sprinkle with remaining 2 table-spoons basil and serve, passing extra Parmesan separately.

BEEF-AND-BULGUR MEATBALLS WITH TAHINI-YOGURT DIPPING SAUCE

Serves 2

COOK TIME 7 minutes   **TOTAL TIME** 35 minutes

why this recipe works These meatballs are so flavorful that they're bound to make their way onto your dinner or cocktail party menu. We used bulgur instead of bread crumbs for the panade. Bulgur, a whole grain packed with vitamins and fiber, and used to make tabbouleh, inspired our Mediterranean flavor profile. We also incorporated yogurt, first combining it with herbs, garlic, and lots of lemon, reserving some for a sauce, and then using the rest in our 90 percent lean ground beef alongside warm spices. While the formed meatballs took a quick trip to the air fryer (which develops beautiful browning), we added some tahini and a little water to the reserved yogurt mixture, giving the dipping sauce an added nuttiness. Look for medium-grind bulgur (labeled "#2"), which is roughly the size of mustard seeds. Avoid coarsely ground bulgur; it will not cook through in time. For an accurate measurement of boiling water, bring a half kettle of water to a boil and then measure out the desired amount. This recipe can be easily doubled (see page 14).

¼ cup medium-grind bulgur

3 tablespoons boiling water, plus 1 tablespoon cold water

¾ cup plain yogurt

2 tablespoons minced fresh cilantro, mint, or parsley

1 garlic clove, minced

½ teaspoon grated lemon zest plus 2 teaspoons juice

½ teaspoon table salt, divided

¼ teaspoon pepper, divided

½ teaspoon ground cumin

¼ teaspoon ground coriander

8 ounces 90 percent lean ground beef

1 tablespoon tahini

1 Combine bulgur and boiling water in large bowl; cover and let sit until bulgur is tender and all water has been absorbed, about 15 minutes.

2 Whisk yogurt, cilantro, garlic, lemon zest and juice, ¼ teaspoon salt, and ⅛ teaspoon pepper in small bowl until well combined. Stir ¼ cup yogurt mixture, cumin, coriander, remaining ¼ teaspoon salt, and remaining ⅛ teaspoon pepper into bulgur; set remaining yogurt mixture aside. Break up ground beef into small pieces over bulgur mixture and lightly knead with hands until well combined. Pinch off and roll mixture into 12 meatballs. (Meatballs and reserved yogurt mixture can be refrigerated separately for up to 24 hours.)

3 Arrange meatballs in air-fryer basket, spaced evenly apart. Place basket into air fryer and set temperature to 400 degrees. Cook until meatballs are lightly browned and register 160 degrees, 7 to 9 minutes, turning halfway through cooking.

4 Whisk tahini and cold water into reserved yogurt mixture until smooth and sauce has consistency of heavy cream. Adjust consistency with extra water as needed. Serve meatballs with yogurt sauce.

JUICY WELL-DONE CHEESEBURGERS

Serves 2

COOK TIME 19 minutes	TOTAL TIME 30 minutes

why this recipe works Typical burger recipes require hovering over a hot pan or grill, waiting for the right moment to flip the patties to avoid turning out a dry hockey puck. But not this one—and not only because the air fryer's timer tells you when they need flipping. The real key was using a panade of mashed bread and milk, which kept the patties moist and juicy even when cooked to well-done. How? The bread's starches swell when mixed with liquid, forming a gel that holds juices in and prevents meat proteins from toughening when cooked. Giving the burgers a slight dimple in the middle before cooking also prevented them from puffing up in the hot air. With our burgers done, we wondered if we could use the air fryer to cook other burger components and found that it could toast hamburger buns (see page 19) and even caramelize onions for our onion and blue cheese variation. Serve with your favorite burger toppings. This recipe can be easily doubled (see page 14).

½ slice hearty white sandwich bread, crust removed, torn into ¼-inch pieces

1 tablespoon milk

½ teaspoon garlic powder

½ teaspoon onion powder

12 ounces 85 percent lean ground beef

¼ teaspoon table salt

⅛ teaspoon pepper

2 slices American cheese (2 ounces)

2 hamburger buns, toasted, if desired

1 Mash bread, milk, garlic powder, and onion powder into paste in medium bowl using fork. Break up ground beef into small pieces over bread mixture in bowl and lightly knead with hands until well combined. Divide mixture into 2 lightly packed balls, then gently flatten each into 1-inch-thick patty. Press center of each patty with fingertips to create ¼-inch-deep depression. Sprinkle with salt and pepper.

2 Arrange patties in air-fryer basket, spaced evenly apart. Place basket into air fryer and set temperature to 350 degrees. Cook until burgers are lightly browned and register 140 to 145 degrees (for medium-well) or 150 to 155 degrees (for well-done), 18 to 21 minutes, flipping and rotating burgers halfway through cooking.

3 Top each burger with 1 slice cheese. Return basket to air fryer and cook until cheese is melted, about 30 seconds. Serve burgers on buns.

JUICY WELL-DONE GREEN CHILE CHEESEBURGERS

Omit onion powder. Substitute pepper Jack cheese for American cheese. Add ¼ cup canned chopped green chiles, drained and patted dry, to beef mixture in step 1.

JUICY WELL-DONE BURGERS WITH CARAMELIZED ONIONS AND BLUE CHEESE

Omit onion powder. Substitute ¼ cup crumbled blue cheese for American cheese. Slice 1 small red onion into ¼-inch-thick rounds, then separate rounds into rings. Toss onion rings with 1 teaspoon vegetable oil, ¼ teaspoon sugar, and ⅛ teaspoon table salt in bowl. Arrange onion rings evenly in air-fryer basket, then place patties on top and cook as directed in step 2. Top burgers with caramelized onions before serving.

SOUTHWESTERN BEEF HAND PIES

Makes 8 pies

COOK TIME 12 minutes	TOTAL TIME 1 hour, plus 1 hour freezing

why this recipe works Easily prepared with store-bought pie dough, these spiced ground-beef hand pies can be made ahead and frozen, then quickly baked in the air fryer for a flaky, steaming-hot meal or snack anytime. Microwaving beef, aromatics, and spices bloomed flavors and let us drain away excess liquid that would sog out the dough. We then stirred in cheese, which added richness and created a cohesive filling; salsa for depth of flavor; and cilantro for freshness. We were able to cut eight 5-inch rounds from two 12-inch pastry rounds to make four hand pies. Hand pies can also be cooked immediately without freezing; reduce the cooking time in step 3 to 10 to 12 minutes.

- 8 ounces 93 percent lean ground beef
- 3 garlic cloves, minced
- 2 teaspoons chili powder
- 1 teaspoon ground cumin
- 1 teaspoon minced fresh oregano or ¼ teaspoon dried
- 4 ounces Monterey Jack cheese, shredded (1 cup)
- 1 cup mild tomato salsa, drained
- 2 tablespoons chopped fresh cilantro
- 1 package store-bought pie dough
- 1 large egg, lightly beaten

1 Microwave beef, garlic, chili powder, cumin, and oregano in bowl, stirring occasionally and breaking up meat with wooden spoon, until beef is no longer pink, about 3 minutes. Transfer beef mixture to fine-mesh strainer set over large bowl and let drain for 10 minutes; discard juices. Return drained beef mixture to now-empty bowl and stir in Monterey Jack, salsa, and cilantro.

2 Roll 1 dough round into 12-inch circle on lightly floured counter. Using 5-inch round biscuit cutter, stamp out 4 rounds; discard dough scraps. Repeat with remaining dough round. Mound beef mixture evenly in center of each stamped round. Fold dough over filling and crimp edges with fork to seal. Transfer hand pies to parchment paper–lined rimmed baking sheet, brush with egg, and freeze until firm, about 1 hour. (Hand pies can be transferred to zipper-lock bag and stored in freezer for up to 2 weeks; do not thaw before cooking.)

3 to cook hand pies Lightly spray bottom of air-fryer basket with vegetable oil spray. Arrange up to 2 hand pies in prepared basket, spaced evenly apart. Place basket into air fryer and set temperature to 350 degrees. Cook until hand pies are golden brown, 12 to 15 minutes. Transfer to wire rack and let cool slightly. Serve.

SOUTHWESTERN BEAN AND CORN HAND PIES

Omit ground beef. Substitute 1 cup drained tomatillo salsa (salsa verde) for tomato salsa. Add 1 tablespoon extra-virgin olive oil to spice mixture in step 1 and microwave until fragrant, about 30 seconds. Stir 1¼ cups canned black beans, rinsed, and ¾ cup frozen corn into spice mixture with Monterey Jack.

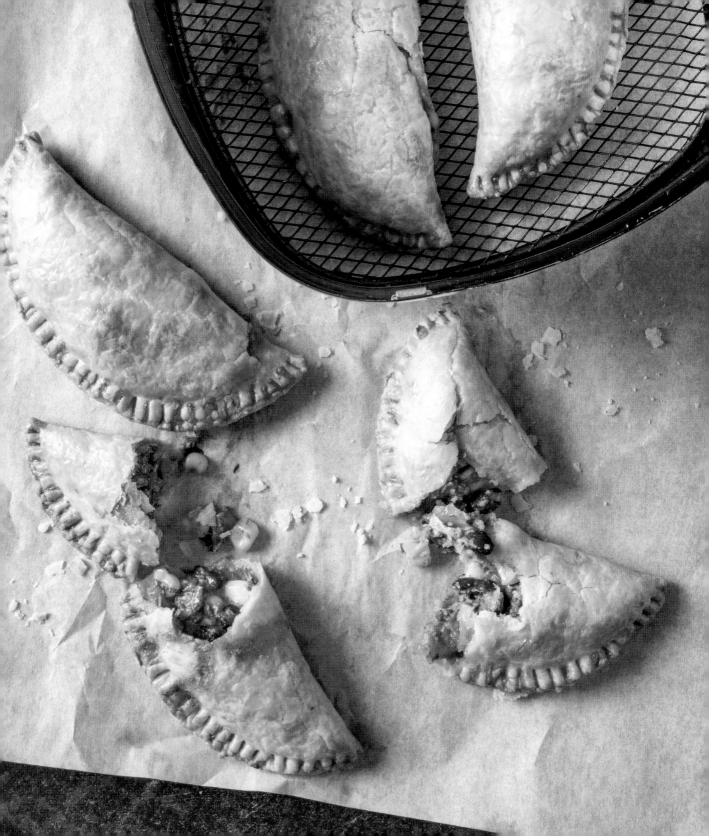

ROASTED BONE-IN PORK CHOP

Serves 2

COOK TIME 20 minutes   **TOTAL TIME** 40 minutes

why this recipe works A bone-in pork chop offers a simple but special meal, with meat that's juicy and full of flavor down to the last gnaw of the bone. Aiming to roast bone-in pork chops for two in our air fryer, we first tried using two 8-ounce chops, but rotating and flipping them proved too awkward; they didn't quite fit. Since bone-in chops are often found thick-cut, we switched to a single 1-pound chop, which was sufficient for two people and easier to fit in the basket, and it made for a dramatic presentation. With such a thick chop, however, we needed a way to cook the meat through without the exterior drying out. While 400 degrees promised better browning, the intense heat dried out the sizable cut too quickly. Roasting at a more moderate 350 degrees resulted in an evenly cooked, juicy chop, and—to our pleasant surprise— also gave the chop more color because of the longer roasting time. Cutting two slits in the sides of the chop prevented it from curling during cooking. To contrast with the rich, roasted meat, we created two bold sauces, a peach-mustard sauce (made with frozen peaches) and an herbaceous, smoky chermoula. If making the chermoula, prepare it before roasting the chops to allow its flavors to meld. This recipe can be easily doubled (see page 14).

1 (1-pound) bone-in pork rib or center-cut chop, 1½ to 1¾ inches thick, trimmed

1 teaspoon vegetable oil

¼ teaspoon table salt

⅛ teaspoon pepper

1 Pat chop dry with paper towels. Using sharp knife, cut 2 slits, about 2 inches apart, through fat on edge of chop. Rub with oil and sprinkle with salt and pepper.

2 Place chop into air-fryer basket, then place basket in air fryer. Set temperature to 350 degrees and cook until pork registers 140 degrees, 20 to 25 minutes, flipping and rotating chop halfway through cooking.

3 Transfer chop to cutting board, tent with aluminum foil, and let rest for 5 minutes. Carve pork from bone and slice ½ inch thick. Serve.

PEACH-MUSTARD SAUCE
Microwave 5 ounces frozen sliced peaches, cut into 1-inch pieces; 2 tablespoons water; 1 tablespoon sugar; and 2 teaspoons white wine vinegar in medium bowl, stirring occasionally, until peaches have softened and mixture is slightly thickened, about 8 minutes. Let cool slightly, then stir in ¾ teaspoon whole-grain mustard and ½ teaspoon minced fresh thyme or rosemary.

CHERMOULA
Whisk ⅓ cup extra-virgin olive oil, ⅓ cup minced fresh cilantro, 1 tablespoon lemon juice, 2 minced garlic cloves, ½ teaspoon ground cumin, ½ teaspoon paprika, and ⅛ teaspoon cayenne in bowl until combined. Season with salt and pepper to taste.

ROASTED BONE-IN PORK CHOP WITH SWEET POTATOES AND MAPLE-ROSEMARY SAUCE

Serves 2

COOK TIME 28 minutes	TOTAL TIME 45 minutes

why this recipe works For this savory pork chop and potato meal, we again chose a single thick-cut 16-ounce chop to serve two. We cooked the chop long enough for the meat to get tender without the exterior drying out. Roasting at 350 degrees gave us juicy meat and great color. Cutting two slits in the sides of the chop prevented it from curling during cooking. We roasted sweet potatoes under the pork and let the fat from the meat drip onto them, adding rich flavor to their sweetness. The potatoes finished cooking while the pork rested and we served the dish with an aromatic maple syrup sauce. This recipe can be easily doubled (see page 14).

1 pound sweet potatoes, unpeeled, halved lengthwise and sliced crosswise ¾ inch thick

1 tablespoon vegetable oil, divided

½ teaspoon table salt, divided

1 (1 pound) bone-in pork rib or center-cut chop, 1 to 1½ inches thick, trimmed

¼ teaspoon pepper

3 tablespoons maple syrup

2 teaspoons cider vinegar

½ teaspoon minced fresh rosemary

¼ teaspoon cornstarch

Pinch cayenne pepper

Pinch ground cloves

1 Toss potatoes with 2 teaspoons oil and ¼ teaspoon salt in bowl and arrange in even layer in air-fryer basket. Place basket into air fryer, set temperature to 350 degrees, and cook for 10 minutes.

2 Pat pork chop dry with paper towels. Using sharp knife, cut 2 slits, about 2 inches apart, through fat on edge of chop. Rub with remaining 1 teaspoon oil, then sprinkle with pepper and remaining ¼ teaspoon salt. Place chop on top of potatoes. Return basket to air fryer and cook until chop is lightly browned and registers 140 degrees, 15 to 20 minutes, flipping and rotating chop halfway through cooking.

3 Transfer chop to cutting board, tent with aluminum foil, and let rest while finishing potatoes and sauce. Return basket to air-fryer and cook until potatoes are browned and tender, 3 to 5 minutes.

4 Whisk maple syrup, vinegar, rosemary, cornstarch, cayenne, and cloves together in small bowl. Microwave until thickened, about 30 seconds, stirring halfway through microwaving. Season with salt and pepper to taste. Carve pork from bone and slice ½ inch thick. Serve pork with potatoes and sauce.

CRISPY PORK CHOPS WITH ROASTED PEACH, BLACKBERRY, AND ARUGULA SALAD

Serves 2

COOK TIME 22 minutes

TOTAL TIME 1 hour

why this recipe works This sensational recipe pairs ripe in-season peaches and blackberries with a delicious breaded pork chop. We coated boneless pork chops with bread crumbs before air-frying them. We also used the air fryer to roast peaches until they were tender and juicy. As we've found with coatings for other proteins, toasted panko gave us the most crunch out of any bread crumbs we tested. However, the crumb topping flaked off when we flipped the chops during cooking. To help it stick, we scored the surface of the chops in a crosshatch pattern, creating additional surface area for the coating to cling to. We also cut two slits on the edges of the chops to prevent them from buckling in the hot air. We tossed our roasted peaches with arugula, juicy blackberries, almonds, and basil for a mouthwatering salad that complemented the rich crunch of the chops. Instead of peaches, you can use nectarines or plums. For more information on toasting nuts in the air fryer, see page 19. This recipe can be easily doubled (see page 14).

- 2 tablespoons extra-virgin olive oil, divided
- 1 small shallot, minced
- 1 tablespoon white wine vinegar
- 1 tablespoon honey
- ½ teaspoon table salt, divided

- 2 ripe but firm peaches, halved and pitted
- 1 cup panko bread crumbs
- 1 large egg
- 1 tablespoon all-purpose flour
- 2 (4- to 6-ounce) boneless pork chops, ¾ to 1 inch thick, trimmed

- 3 ounces (3 cups) baby arugula
- 2½ ounces (½ cup) blackberries or raspberries
- ½ cup torn fresh basil, mint, and/or tarragon
- ¼ cup whole almonds, toasted and chopped coarse

1 Whisk 1 tablespoon oil, shallot, vinegar, honey, and ¼ teaspoon salt together in large bowl. Lightly spray bottom of air-fryer basket with vegetable oil spray. Arrange peaches cut side up in prepared basket and brush tops with portion of dressing; set aside remaining dressing.

Place basket into air fryer and set temperature to 400 degrees. Cook until peaches are tender and spotty brown, 10 to 15 minutes. Transfer peaches to cutting board and let cool while preparing pork chops.

2 Toss panko with remaining 1 tablespoon oil in shallow dish until evenly coated. Microwave, stirring frequently, until light golden brown, 1 to 3 minutes; let cool slightly. Whisk egg, flour, and remaining ¼ teaspoon salt together in second shallow dish.

3 Pat chops dry with paper towels. Using sharp knife, cut 2 slits, about 2 inches apart, through fat on edges of each chop. Cut 1/16-inch-deep slits, spaced ½ inch apart, in crosshatch pattern on both sides of chops. Working with 1 chop at a time, dredge in egg mixture, letting excess drip off, then coat with panko mixture, pressing gently to adhere.

4 Arrange chops in now-empty basket, spaced evenly apart. Return basket to air fryer and cook until chops are crispy and register 140 degrees, 12 to 18 minutes, flipping and rotating chops halfway through cooking. Transfer chops to plate and let rest while finishing salad.

5 Cut peaches into 1-inch wedges. Add peaches, arugula, blackberries, basil, and almonds to bowl with reserved dressing and toss gently to combine. Season with salt and pepper to taste. Serve chops with salad.

LEMON-OREGANO ROASTED PORK CHOPS WITH TOMATO-FETA SALAD

Serves 2

COOK TIME 16 minutes   **TOTAL TIME** 50 minutes

why this recipe works Boneless pork chops make an easy weeknight meal and are especially convenient when cooked in an air fryer. Because the boneless meat can dry out quickly, we set the maximum heat of 400 degrees, which ensured the chops stayed juicy, but they needed a boost of color, particularly at the center, which didn't get as brown as the fattier edges. Knowing that browning happens when sugars and proteins react with heat, we brushed the chops with honey; because of its high fructose content, the honey gave our chops more color. We added flavor to the honey with fresh oregano, garlic, and lemon zest. A salad of cherry tomatoes, arugula, and feta came together while the meat rested. We tossed it with a lemon-yogurt dressing, adding in more oregano. This recipe can be easily doubled (see page 14).

- 2 tablespoons minced fresh oregano, divided
- 2 teaspoons plus 2 tablespoons extra-virgin olive oil, divided
- 2 teaspoons honey
- 2 garlic cloves, minced, divided

- 1½ teaspoons grated lemon zest, divided plus 2 teaspoons juice
- 2 (8-ounce) boneless pork chops, about 1½ inches thick, trimmed
- ½ teaspoon table salt, divided
- ⅜ teaspoon pepper, divided

- 2 tablespoons plain yogurt
- 12 ounces cherry tomatoes, halved
- 1 cup baby arugula
- 2 ounces feta cheese, crumbled (½ cup)
- 1 small shallot, sliced thin

1 Microwave 1 tablespoon oregano, 2 teaspoons oil, honey, half of garlic, and ½ teaspoon lemon zest in bowl until fragrant, about 30 seconds, stirring once halfway through.

2 Pat chops dry with paper towels. Using sharp knife, cut 2 slits, about 2 inches apart, through fat on edges of each chop. Brush chops with oil mixture and sprinkle with ¼ teaspoon salt and ⅛ teaspoon pepper. Arrange chops in air-fryer basket, spaced evenly apart. Place basket into air fryer and set temperature to 400 degrees. Cook until pork registers 140 degrees, 16 to 20 minutes, flipping

and rotating chops halfway through cooking. Transfer chops to plate, tent with aluminum foil, and let rest while making salad.

3 Whisk yogurt, remaining 2 tablespoons oil, remaining 1 tablespoon oregano, remaining garlic, remaining 1 teaspoon lemon zest, lemon juice, remaining ¼ teaspoon salt, and remaining ¼ teaspoon pepper together in large bowl. Add tomatoes, arugula, feta, and shallot and toss to coat. Season with salt and pepper to taste. Serve chops with salad.

SWEET AND SPICY GLAZED PORK CHOPS WITH SESAME BOK CHOY

Serves 2

COOK TIME 21 minutes

TOTAL TIME 45 minutes

why this recipe works The sheen on a glazed pork chop tempts you to cut into it right away. But in the air fryer, glazes tend to slide off meat. Since a thick glaze adheres better, the natural pectin in fruit preserves helped us build such a glaze here. We combined pineapple preserves and rice vinegar as its sweet-and-sour components, with toasted sesame oil, ginger, and chili-garlic sauce lending umami and spice. We parcooked the meat and then brushed the glaze onto the pork in two batches to prevent too much from dripping off at one time. The sweet-and-sour pork paired well with baby bok choy, which fit easily in the air fryer. The bulbs turned tender and the leaves became slightly crispy in the air fryer while the pork rested. We tossed the tender vegetable with a dash of toasted sesame oil, giving it a sheen and echoing the flavor of the oil on the meat. If baby bok choy is unavailable, substitute 12 ounces of traditional bok choy, cut into 2-inch pieces. Bok choy can sometimes be sandy within the base of the head; make sure to remove any sand during washing. For a spicier dish, use the greater amount of chili sauce. This recipe can be easily doubled (see page 14).

- 2 (4- to 6-ounce) boneless pork chops, ¾ to 1 inch thick, trimmed
- 2 tablespoons toasted sesame oil, divided
- ¼ teaspoon table salt
- 2 tablespoons pineapple or apricot preserves
- 1 teaspoon unseasoned rice vinegar
- 1 teaspoon grated fresh ginger
- ¼–¾ teaspoon chili-garlic sauce
- 2 heads baby bok choy (4 to 5 ounces each)
- 2 teaspoons soy sauce
- 2 teaspoons sesame seeds, toasted

1 Pat pork chops dry with paper towels. Using sharp knife, cut 2 slits, about 2 inches apart, through fat on edges of each chop. Rub chops with 1 teaspoon oil, then sprinkle with salt. Arrange chops in air-fryer basket, spaced evenly apart. Place basket into air fryer; set temperature to 400 degrees; and cook until chops begin to brown at edges, 8 to 10 minutes.

2 Microwave preserves, vinegar, ginger, and chili-garlic sauce in small bowl until mixture is fluid, about 30 seconds, stirring halfway through microwaving. Flip and rotate chops, then brush with half of glaze. Return basket to air fryer and cook for 5 minutes. Brush chops with remaining glaze; return basket to air fryer; and continue to cook until chops are lightly browned and register 140 degrees, 3 to 5 minutes. Transfer chops to plate, tent with aluminum foil, and let rest while preparing bok choy.

3 Halve bok choy lengthwise, wash thoroughly, and spin dry. Toss bok choy with 2 teaspoons oil in large bowl and arrange in even layer in now-empty basket. Place basket into air fryer; set temperature to 350 degrees; and cook until bok choy is crisp-tender, about 5 minutes. Transfer bok choy to now-empty bowl and toss with soy sauce, sesame seeds, and remaining 1 tablespoon oil. Serve chops with bok choy.

FENNEL-RUBBED PORK TENDERLOIN WITH ZUCCHINI RIBBON SALAD

Serves 4

COOK TIME 16 minutes   **TOTAL TIME** 50 minutes

why this recipe works Pork tenderloin is a favorite choice for a weeknight meal, but its long shape wasn't an obvious fit for the air fryer. The solution? We cut it in half and found we could accommodate two tenderloins in the basket that way. Since the pork benefits from a crust, we brushed on a mixture of garlic, honey, lemon zest, and fennel seeds. Coarsely ground whole fennel seeds gave the meat a beautiful flavor and aroma. For an easy side dish, we shaved ribbons of zucchini, showcasing the squash's crunchier side. We tossed it with toasted pine nuts, basil, and shaved Parmesan, dressing the salad just before serving to avoid wilting. Use a spice grinder to coarsely grind the fennel (about six 1-second pulses); you can also pound the seeds with a skillet or meat mallet. Use a vegetable peeler or a mandoline to shave the zucchini. For more information on toasting nuts in the air fryer, see page 19.

- ¼ cup extra-virgin olive oil, divided
- 4 garlic cloves, minced
- 1 tablespoon honey
- 1 teaspoon grated lemon zest plus 2 tablespoons juice
- ¾ teaspoon table salt, divided
- ½ teaspoon pepper, divided
- 2 (1-pound) pork tenderloins, trimmed and halved crosswise
- 2 tablespoons fennel seeds, coarsely ground
- 4 small zucchini (6 ounces each), shaved lengthwise into ribbons
- 2 ounces Parmesan cheese, shaved
- 2 tablespoons shredded fresh basil
- 2 tablespoons pine nuts, toasted (optional)

1 Microwave 1 tablespoon oil, garlic, honey, lemon zest, ½ teaspoon salt, and ¼ teaspoon pepper in large bowl until fragrant, about 30 seconds, stirring once halfway through. Pat pork dry with paper towels, add to oil mixture, and toss to coat.

2 Sprinkle pork pieces with fennel seeds, pressing to adhere, then arrange in air fryer basket. (Tuck thinner tail ends of tenderloins under themselves as needed to create uniform pieces.) Place basket into air fryer and set temperature to 350 degrees. Cook until pork is lightly browned

and registers 140 degrees, 16 to 21 minutes, flipping and rotating tenderloin pieces halfway through cooking. Transfer pork to cutting board, tent with aluminum foil, and let rest while preparing salad.

3 Gently toss zucchini with remaining 3 tablespoons oil, lemon juice, remaining ¼ teaspoon salt, and remaining ¼ teaspoon pepper in clean bowl. Arrange attractively on serving platter and sprinkle with Parmesan, basil, and pine nuts, if using. Slice pork ½ inch thick and serve with salad.

PORK TENDERLOIN WITH PROSCIUTTO AND SAGE

Serves 4

COOK TIME 20 minutes   **TOTAL TIME** 45 minutes

why this recipe works Inspired by saltimbocca, the Roman dish of veal cutlets topped with prosciutto and sage, these savory bundles deliver a fancy meal with absurdly little effort. We started with pork tenderloin, which, like veal, is mild and tender but is easier to find and pairs beautifully with sage. While getting prosciutto to adhere to veal cutlets can be a fussy business involving toothpicks, here we simply halved two pork tenderloins to create four portions and wrapped each in prosciutto—layering fresh sage leaves in between—to create an attractive parcel, brushing melted butter both under and over the prosciutto; this step helped it to cling to the tenderloins and brought needed richness to the lean proteins as well as plenty of herbal flavor. In the circulated heat of the air fryer, the meat cooked evenly even without flipping and the prosciutto crisped up. A spritz of fresh lemon added pleasant brightness to our perfectly cooked tenderloins.

- 2 (1-pound) pork tenderloins, trimmed and halved crosswise
- 6 tablespoons unsalted butter, melted, divided
- ¼ teaspoon pepper
- 12 thin slices prosciutto (6 ounces)
- 8 large fresh sage leaves
-    Lemon wedges

1 Pat pork dry with paper towels, brush with 3 tablespoons melted butter, and sprinkle with pepper. For each piece of pork, shingle 3 slices of prosciutto on cutting board, overlapping edges slightly, and lay pork in center. (Tuck thinner tail ends of tenderloins under themselves as needed to create uniform bundles.) Top with 2 sage leaves, then fold prosciutto around pork, pressing on overlapping ends to secure. Brush pork bundles with remaining 3 tablespoons melted butter and arrange seam side down in air-fryer basket.

2 Place basket into air fryer and set temperature to 400 degrees. Cook until pork registers 140 degrees, 20 to 25 minutes. Transfer pork to cutting board, tent with aluminum foil, and let rest for 5 minutes. Slice pork ½ inch thick and serve with lemon wedges.

LEMON-THYME PORK TENDERLOIN WITH GREEN BEANS AND HAZELNUTS

Serves 2

COOK TIME 18 minutes   **TOTAL TIME** 45 minutes

why this recipe works Mild, buttery pork tenderloin is a great choice for a weeknight because it cooks quickly, easily takes on the flavor of an herb or spice rub, and makes a complete meal when accompanied by a vegetable side—here we use green beans and hazelnuts. We easily fit the tenderloin in the air fryer by cutting it in half crosswise. A concentrated paste of honey, mustard, thyme, and lemon zest flavored the pork and helped it brown, and a relatively low roasting temperature ensured that the meat cooked evenly and didn't dry out. Lemon and thyme made a second appearance, dressing the cooked green beans to punch up the flavor, while roasted red peppers, fresh parsley, and crunchy toasted hazelnuts rounded out the side dish for the pork. For more information on toasting nuts in the air fryer, see page 19. This recipe can be easily doubled (see page 14).

- 1 pound green beans, trimmed
- 2 tablespoons extra-virgin olive oil, divided
- ⅜ teaspoon table salt, divided
- ¼ teaspoon pepper, divided

- 2 teaspoons grated lemon zest, divided, plus 1 tablespoon juice
- 1½ teaspoons minced fresh thyme, divided
- 1 small garlic clove, minced to paste
- 1 teaspoon Dijon mustard
- 1 teaspoon honey

- 1 (12-ounce) pork tenderloin, trimmed and halved crosswise
- ½ cup jarred roasted red peppers, rinsed, patted dry, and sliced thin
- ¼ cup chopped fresh parsley
- ¼ cup hazelnuts or almonds, toasted, skinned, and chopped

1 Toss green beans with 1 tablespoon oil, ⅛ teaspoon salt, and ⅛ teaspoon pepper in large bowl. Arrange green beans in even layer in air-fryer basket. Combine 2 teaspoons oil, 1 teaspoon lemon zest, lemon juice, ½ teaspoon thyme, and garlic in now-empty bowl; set aside.

2 Combine mustard, honey, remaining 1 teaspoon oil, remaining ¼ teaspoon salt, remaining ⅛ teaspoon pepper, remaining 1 teaspoon lemon zest, and remaining 1 teaspoon thyme in separate bowl. Pat pork dry with paper towels, then rub with mustard mixture. Arrange pork on top of green beans, spaced evenly apart. (Tuck thinner

tail end of tenderloin under itself as needed to create uniform pieces.) Place basket into air fryer and set temperature to 350 degrees. Cook until green beans are tender and pork is lightly browned and registers 140 degrees, 18 to 24 minutes, flipping and rotating pork halfway through cooking.

3 Transfer pork to cutting board, tent with aluminum foil, and let rest for 5 minutes. Add green beans, red peppers, parsley, and hazelnuts to bowl with dressing and toss to combine. Season with salt and pepper to taste. Slice pork thin and serve with green bean mixture.

MARINATED PORK GYROS

Serves 2

COOK TIME 8 minutes	**TOTAL TIME** 45 minutes

why this recipe works Though the pork for these wraps is not made on the traditional spit used for gyros, the air fryer's high heat on the exterior of the meat helps it cook in a similar fashion to its inspiration. We opted to use country-style pork ribs, which are meatier than pork chops. They take a bit longer to cook than pork chops, allowing more time to develop color and crispy, tasty char. Before cooking, we coated the ribs in a flavorful marinade of garlic, oregano, coriander, and paprika, reserving half of it to use once the pork was cooked. While the pork roasted, we assembled a quick tzatziki (a Greek yogurt, cucumber, and garlic sauce). Persian, aka "mini," cucumbers were perfectly suited here. Rather than peel and seed half an English cucumber, all we had to do was shred one Persian cucumber, seeds and all, and slice a second one thin as a topping. Other toppings included a shallot and baby kale. Any baby green you have on hand would work fine too. Remember the remaining marinade? We turned it into a dressing by whisking in some lemon juice. After slicing the pork thin, we tossed the meat with the dressing before assembling the gyros, making sure that every inch of the meat was coated in spiced, garlicky goodness. Use half an English cucumber if you can't find Persian ones. This recipe can be easily doubled (see page 14).

- 1 tablespoon extra-virgin olive oil
- 3 garlic cloves, minced, divided
- 1 teaspoon dried oregano
- 1 teaspoon ground coriander
- 1 teaspoon paprika
- ½ teaspoon table salt, divided

- ½ teaspoon pepper, divided
- 8 ounces boneless country-style pork ribs, trimmed
- 2 Persian cucumbers, divided
- 6 tablespoons plain Greek yogurt

- 1 tablespoon lemon juice, divided, plus lemon wedges for serving
- 1 teaspoon minced fresh dill
- 2 (8-inch) pitas
- 1 cup baby kale or spinach
- 1 shallot, halved and sliced thin

1 Microwave oil, two-thirds garlic, oregano, coriander, paprika, ¼ teaspoon salt, and ¼ teaspoon pepper in medium bowl until fragrant, about 30 seconds.

2 Rub ribs with half of oil mixture, then arrange in air-fryer basket, spaced evenly apart. Place basket into air fryer and set temperature to 400 degrees. Cook until ribs are lightly browned and register 150 degrees, 6 to 10 minutes, flipping ribs halfway through cooking. Transfer ribs to cutting board, tent with aluminum foil, and let rest for 5 minutes.

3 Shred 1 cucumber to yield ¼ cup; slice remaining cucumber thin. Combine shredded cucumber, yogurt, 1 teaspoon lemon juice, dill, remaining garlic, remaining ¼ teaspoon salt, and remaining ¼ teaspoon pepper in separate bowl. Season with salt and pepper to taste.

4 Stack pitas and wrap tightly with foil. Place pita packet in now-empty basket. Return basket to air fryer and cook until pitas are heated through, 2 to 4 minutes. Whisk remaining 2 teaspoons lemon juice into remaining oil mixture. Slice pork thin and toss with lemon-oil mixture. Divide pork evenly among pitas and top with tzatziki, sliced cucumber, kale, and shallot. Serve with lemon wedges.

ITALIAN SAUSAGE AND PEPPER SUBS

Serves 4

COOK TIME 24 minutes   **TOTAL TIME** 50 minutes

why this recipe works Appearing everywhere from ballparks to street fairs, Italian sausage subs stuffed with sweet peppers and onions offer a fun meal—one that's especially easy to make at home in an air fryer. Less fussy than grilling, the air fryer was similarly able to crisp and brown all the ingredients at once, while allowing excess fat to drip away. Since the peppers and onions needed more time to cook, we gave them a jump start, using that time to brush our sausages with a little honey, which improved browning and added pleasant sweetness. We stacked our sausages right on top of our onions and peppers, flipping them after a few minutes to give one side deep browning we thought was achievable only with a grill. For a quick accompaniment, a combination of whole-grain mustard, mayonnaise, and red wine vinegar balanced the richness of the sausage and gave our sandwiches a pop of flavor. Warming the honey makes it easier to brush onto the sausages.

2   red or green bell peppers, stemmed, seeded, and cut into ¼-inch-wide strips

1   onion, halved and sliced ¼ inch thick

2   teaspoons vegetable oil

½   teaspoon pepper, divided

1   pound hot or sweet Italian sausage (6 sausages)

2   teaspoons honey, warmed

2   tablespoons whole-grain mustard

1   tablespoon mayonnaise

1   teaspoon red wine vinegar

½   teaspoon sugar

4   (6-inch) Italian sub rolls, split lengthwise

1 Toss bell peppers and onion with oil and ¼ teaspoon pepper in bowl; transfer to air-fryer basket. Place basket into air fryer, set temperature to 350 degrees, and cook for 8 minutes.

2 Brush sausages with honey. Stir peppers and onion, then arrange sausages on top, spaced evenly apart. Return basket to air fryer and cook until vegetables are tender and sausages are lightly browned and register 160 degrees, 16 to 18 minutes, flipping and rotating sausages and stirring vegetables once after 5 minutes.

3 Transfer sausages to cutting board, tent with aluminum foil, and let rest for 5 minutes. Whisk mustard, mayonnaise, vinegar, sugar, and remaining ¼ teaspoon pepper together in bowl. Halve sausages crosswise on bias. Divide sausages, peppers, and onion evenly among rolls and drizzle with mustard sauce. Serve.

MUSTARD-THYME LAMB CHOPS WITH ROASTED CARROTS

Serves 2

COOK TIME 24 minutes   **TOTAL TIME** 40 minutes

why this recipe works Lamb loin chops are a good fit for the air fryer, which can easily hold four of these "mini T-bones." Taking advantage of the circulated heat, we roasted them atop a side of carrots, coating both with a glaze of mustard, honey, garlic, lemon, and thyme. But while the carrots emerged caramelized, the exterior of the chops lacked color. Brushing the chops with oil and honey before cooking and dabbing on the mustard mixture after gave us browned chops with a flavorful glaze. If your lamb chops are smaller than 6 ounces, you may need to continue cooking the carrots in step 2 after the chops are done. Warming the honey makes it easier to brush onto the lamb. This recipe can be easily doubled (see page 14).

- 1 pound carrots, peeled and cut into 2-inch lengths, thick ends halved lengthwise
- 4 teaspoons extra-virgin olive oil, divided
- ⅜ teaspoon table salt, divided
- ⅜ teaspoon pepper, divided
- 1 tablespoon honey, warmed, divided
- 4 (6-ounce) lamb loin chops, 1¼ inches thick, trimmed
- 1 tablespoon Dijon mustard
- 1½ teaspoons minced fresh thyme
- 1 garlic clove, minced
- 1 teaspoon grated lemon zest plus 1 teaspoon juice
- 1 teaspoon water

1 Toss carrots with 1 teaspoon oil, ⅛ teaspoon salt, and ⅛ teaspoon pepper in bowl; transfer to air-fryer basket. Place basket into air fryer, set temperature to 350 degrees, and cook for 14 minutes, stirring halfway through cooking.

2 Combine 2 teaspoons honey and 2 teaspoons oil in small bowl. Pat chops dry with paper towels, brush with honey-oil mixture, and sprinkle with remaining ½ teaspoon salt and remaining ¼ teaspoon pepper. Stir carrots, then arrange chops on top, spaced evenly apart. Return basket to air fryer and cook until chops are lightly browned and register 120 to 125 degrees (for medium-rare) or 130 to 135 degrees (for medium), 10 to 15 minutes, flipping and rotating chops halfway through cooking.

3 Microwave mustard, thyme, garlic, lemon zest and juice, water, remaining 1 teaspoon oil, and remaining 1 teaspoon honey in medium bowl until fragrant, about 30 seconds, stirring once halfway through. Transfer chops to plate and brush with 1 tablespoon of mustard mixture. Tent with aluminum foil and let rest while finishing carrots.

4 Transfer carrots to bowl with remaining mustard mixture and toss to coat. Season with salt and pepper to taste. Serve lamb with carrots.

LAMB SLIDERS WITH APRICOT CHUTNEY

Serves 2

COOK TIME 9 minutes   **TOTAL TIME** 40 minutes

why this recipe works Sliders should be fun, and part of the fun comes from playing with a variety of flavorings and toppings, as in this supereasy version, which translates the fantastic combo of rich lamb, fragrant rosemary, and sweet-tart apricot chutney into a miniature burger. The lamb patties needed minimal attention when cooked in the air fryer. Meanwhile, we devised a brilliantly simple chutney using dried apricots, a chopped shallot, brown sugar, rosemary, and lemon juice, which cooked in just a minute in the microwave. Goat cheese and baby arugula required zero prep and provided tanginess and a peppery bite to cut the richness of the lamb. Coming together in just 40 minutes, our elegant and attractive sliders make a fun appetizer or an easy and unique weeknight meal for two. You can toast rolls in your air fryer; see page 19. This recipe can be easily doubled (see page 14).

10 ounces ground lamb	2 tablespoons water	1 teaspoon lemon juice
½ teaspoon garlic powder	1 small shallot, chopped fine	1 ounce goat cheese, crumbled (¼ cup)
¼ teaspoon plus pinch table salt, divided	2 teaspoons packed brown sugar	4 soft white dinner rolls or slider buns, toasted, if desired
⅛ teaspoon pepper	1½ teaspoons minced fresh rosemary or ½ teaspoon dried	¾ cup baby arugula
2 tablespoons finely chopped dried apricots		

1 Divide lamb into 4 lightly packed balls, then gently flatten each into ½-inch-thick patties. Press center of each patty with fingertips to create ¼-inch-deep depression. Sprinkle with garlic powder, ¼ teaspoon salt, and pepper.

2 Arrange patties in air-fryer basket, spaced evenly apart. Place basket into air fryer and set temperature to 400 degrees. Cook until sliders are lightly browned and register 160 degrees, about 9 minutes, flipping and rotating sliders halfway through cooking.

3 Meanwhile, microwave apricots, water, shallot, sugar, rosemary, lemon juice, and remaining pinch salt in bowl

until apricots soften, about 1 minute. Using fork, mash apricots against side of bowl to thicken chutney.

4 Transfer sliders to plate and top with goat cheese. Spread 2 teaspoons chutney on each roll bottom, top with sliders and arugula, then cap with roll tops. Serve.

LAMB SLIDERS WITH SMOKY TOMATO RELISH

Omit sugar and lemon juice. Substitute oil-packed sun-dried tomatoes, patted dry and finely chopped, for apricots, ⅛ teaspoon smoked paprika for rosemary, feta cheese for goat cheese, and baby spinach for arugula.

LAMB KOFTE WRAPS

Serves 2

COOK TIME 10 minutes   **TOTAL TIME** 40 minutes

why this recipe works Found throughout the Middle East, North Africa, the eastern Mediterranean, and Asia, kofte come in a variety of shapes—patties, balls, or cigars—and are made from ground lamb or beef flavored with spices and fresh herbs. We were looking to create an easy air-fryer version that mimicked the cigar-shaped lamb kofte that are formed around skewers and grilled, but without the need for skewers and tending to a grill. The kofte's cylindrical shape lent itself to being wrapped in pita bread as a sandwich and also fit well in the confines of the air-fryer basket. A quick mixture of Greek yogurt, fresh mint, lemon juice, and garlic did double duty: it provided moistness and flavor to the ground lamb and served as a base for shredded cucumber to make a cooling and tangy tzatziki sauce to dollop on our sandwiches. At 400 degrees, the kofte cooked quickly in the circulated hot air, staying tender and juicy, but we found that to ensure even cooking without breaking the kofte apart, we needed to rotate them slightly past the halfway point, when they were firmer and more easily handled. Folded in pita breads with minty tzatziki, crisp shredded lettuce, slices of sharp red onion, and juicy tomato, our air-fryer kofte wraps were complete. This recipe can be easily doubled (see page 14).

½ cup plain Greek yogurt	⅜ teaspoon table salt, divided	1 small tomato, cored, halved, and sliced thin
4 teaspoons minced fresh mint	¼ teaspoon pepper, divided	¼ cup thinly sliced red onion
2 teaspoons lemon juice	10 ounces ground lamb	1 cup shredded iceberg lettuce
1 garlic clove, minced	¼ English cucumber, shredded (¼ cup)	2 (8-inch) pita breads

1 Whisk yogurt, mint, lemon juice, garlic, ¼ teaspoon salt, and ⅛ teaspoon pepper in medium bowl until well combined. Transfer 2 tablespoons yogurt mixture to separate medium bowl; set remaining yogurt mixture aside. Break up ground lamb into small pieces over yogurt mixture in bowl and add remaining ⅛ teaspoon salt and remaining ⅛ teaspoon pepper. Lightly knead with hands until well combined. Divide mixture into 4 lightly packed balls, then shape into 5-inch cylinders.

2 Arrange kofte in air-fryer basket, spaced evenly apart. Place basket into air fryer and set temperature to 400 degrees. Cook until kofte are lightly browned and register 160 degrees, about 10 minutes, flipping and rotating kofte after 7 minutes of cooking.

3 Stir cucumber into reserved yogurt sauce and season with salt and pepper to taste. Arrange kofte, tomato, onion, and lettuce evenly over each pita and dollop each wrap with 2 tablespoons tzatziki. Serve, passing remaining tzatziki separately.

LAMB MEATBALLS WITH COUSCOUS

Serves 2

COOK TIME 13 minutes   **TOTAL TIME** 40 minutes

why this recipe works Grain bowls—cooked grains topped with proteins, vegetables, and usually a sauce and garnish—are a go-to weeknight meal. With its hands-off convenience, speed, and easy cleanup, the air fryer promised an easier route to building a bowl. We mixed up some succulent lamb meatballs and popped them in to cook while we pulled together a base of couscous, which we softened in a mixture of water and orange juice for a sweetness and an aroma that paired perfectly with the lamb. A mixture of yogurt, garlic, and fresh dill seasoned the meatballs and added moisture and tang, and a few warm spices rounded out the flavors. The same yogurt mixture doubled as a sauce, so we made plenty to drizzle over our bowls. To bring color and crunch to the dish, we tossed in grated carrots as well as chopped raisins and sprinkled on toasted almonds and additional chopped dill. For more information on toasting nuts in the air fryer, see page 19. This recipe can be easily doubled (see page 14).

⅔ cup plain yogurt	½ teaspoon ground cumin	½ cup couscous
2½ tablespoons minced fresh dill, divided	¼ teaspoon ground cinnamon	2 tablespoons chopped raisins
1 garlic clove, minced	¼ cup water	¼ cup shredded carrot
⅜ teaspoon table salt, divided	¼ teaspoon grated orange zest plus ¼ cup juice	2 tablespoons chopped toasted almonds
⅛ teaspoon pepper		
10 ounces ground lamb		

1 Whisk yogurt, 1 tablespoon dill, garlic, ¼ teaspoon salt, and pepper in bowl until well combined. Transfer 2 tablespoons yogurt sauce to medium bowl; set remaining yogurt sauce aside for serving. Break up ground lamb into small pieces over yogurt mixture in bowl and add cumin, cinnamon, ⅛ teaspoon salt, and ⅛ teaspoon pepper. Lightly knead with hands until well combined. Pinch off and roll mixture into 6 meatballs.

2 Arrange meatballs in air-fryer basket, spaced evenly apart. Place basket into air fryer and set temperature to 400 degrees. Cook meatballs until lightly browned and register 160 degrees, 13 to 14 minutes, rotating meatballs after 10 minutes.

3 Meanwhile, combine water and orange juice in large bowl and microwave until boiling, 3 to 5 minutes. Stir in couscous, raisins, orange zest, and remaining ⅛ teaspoon salt. Cover and let sit until couscous is tender and all liquid has been absorbed, about 7 minutes. Add carrot and 1 tablespoon dill and gently fluff with fork to combine.

4 Divide couscous between individual serving bowls and top with meatballs. Sprinkle with almonds and remaining 1½ teaspoons dill and serve with reserved yogurt sauce.

SEAFOOD

BETTER-THAN-BOXED FISH STICKS

Makes about 20 fish sticks; serves 4

COOK TIME 10 minutes   **TOTAL TIME** 1 hour, plus 1 hour freezing

why this recipe works Making your own fish sticks as a freezer staple guarantees fresh fish and a flavorful coating, and the air fryer can cook a serving fast. Meaty haddock stood up to a crunchy coating and held its shape during cooking. Brining the fish briefly ensured it stayed moist and well seasoned after freezing, and Old Bay seasoning brought classic flavors. You can substitute halibut or cod for the haddock. For the crispiest fish sticks, cook one serving at a time, respraying the basket between batches. You can also cook fish sticks without freezing; reduce the cooking time to 8 to 10 minutes. Serve with Tartar Sauce or Old Bay Dipping Sauce.

¼ cup table salt, for brining

1½ pounds skinless haddock fillets, ¾ inch thick, sliced into 4-inch strips

2 cups panko bread crumbs

1 tablespoon vegetable oil

¼ cup all-purpose flour

¼ cup mayonnaise

2 large eggs

2 tablespoons Dijon mustard

1 tablespoon Old Bay seasoning

⅛ teaspoon table salt

⅛ teaspoon pepper

1 Dissolve ¼ cup salt in 2 quarts cold water in large container. Add haddock, cover, and let sit for 15 minutes.

2 Toss panko with oil in bowl until evenly coated. Microwave, stirring frequently, until light golden brown, 2 to 4 minutes; transfer to shallow dish. Whisk flour, mayonnaise, eggs, mustard, Old Bay, salt, and pepper together in second shallow dish.

3 Set wire rack in rimmed baking sheet and spray with vegetable oil spray. Remove haddock from brine and thoroughly pat dry with paper towels. Working with 1 piece at a time, dredge haddock in egg mixture, letting excess drip off, then coat with panko mixture, pressing gently to adhere. Transfer fish sticks to prepared rack and freeze until firm, about 1 hour. (Frozen fish sticks can be transferred to zipper-lock bag and stored in freezer for up to 1 month; do not thaw before cooking.)

4 to cook fish sticks Lightly spray bottom of air-fryer basket with vegetable oil spray. Arrange up to 5 fish sticks in prepared basket, spaced evenly apart. Place basket into air fryer and set temperature to 400 degrees. Cook until fish sticks are golden and register 140 degrees, 10 to 12 minutes, flipping and rotating fish sticks halfway through cooking. Serve.

TARTAR SAUCE
Whisk ¼ cup plain Greek yogurt, 2 tablespoons mayonnaise, 2 tablespoons dill pickle relish, ¾ teaspoon distilled white vinegar, ¼ teaspoon Worcestershire sauce, ¼ teaspoon pepper, and pinch table salt together in bowl.

OLD BAY DIPPING SAUCE
Whisk ¼ cup plain Greek yogurt, 2 tablespoons mayonnaise, 1½ teaspoons Dijon mustard, and ¾ teaspoon Old Bay seasoning together in bowl. Season with salt and pepper to taste.

CRUNCHY AIR-FRIED COD FILLETS

Serves 2

COOK TIME 12 minutes   **TOTAL TIME** 45 minutes

why this recipe works Rather than try to bread fish fillets all over for a crisp crust, we instead pressed toasted panko crumbs onto the top, which still gave us crunch in every bite. A coating of mayonnaise, egg yolk, and lemon zest boosted flavor and helped the crumbs adhere. But our flaky cod was too delicate to lift from the air fryer without breaking. A foil sling came to the rescue, enabling us to easily remove the fillets in one piece. You can substitute halibut or haddock for the cod. For more information on making a foil sling, see page 13. Serve with Creamy Chipotle Chile Sauce, if desired. This recipe can be easily doubled (see page 14).

- ⅓ cup panko bread crumbs
- 1 teaspoon vegetable oil
- 1 small shallot, minced
- 1 small garlic clove, minced
- ½ teaspoon minced fresh thyme or ⅛ teaspoon dried
- ½ teaspoon table salt, divided
- ⅜ teaspoon pepper, divided
- 1 tablespoon minced fresh parsley
- 1 tablespoon mayonnaise
- 1 large egg yolk
- ¼ teaspoon grated lemon zest, plus lemon wedges for serving
- 2 (8-ounce) skinless cod fillets, 1¼ inches thick

1 Make foil sling for air-fryer basket by folding 1 long sheet of aluminum foil so it is 4 inches wide. Lay sheet of foil widthwise across basket, pressing foil into and up sides of basket. Fold excess foil as needed so that edges of foil are flush with top of basket. Lightly spray foil and basket with vegetable oil spray.

2 Toss panko with oil in bowl until evenly coated. Stir in shallot, garlic, thyme, ¼ teaspoon salt, and ⅛ teaspoon pepper. Microwave, stirring frequently, until panko is light golden brown, 2 to 4 minutes. Transfer to shallow dish and let cool slightly; stir in parsley. Whisk mayonnaise, egg yolk, lemon zest, and ⅛ teaspoon pepper together in bowl.

3 Pat cod dry with paper towels and sprinkle with remaining ¼ teaspoon salt and remaining ⅛ teaspoon pepper. Arrange fillets skinned side down on plate and brush tops

evenly with mayonnaise mixture. (Tuck thinner tail ends of fillets under themselves as needed to create uniform pieces.) Working with 1 fillet at a time, dredge coated side in panko mixture, pressing gently to adhere. Arrange fillets crumb side up on sling in prepared basket, spaced evenly apart. Place basket into air fryer and set temperature to 300 degrees. Cook until cod registers 140 degrees, 12 to 16 minutes, using sling to rotate fillets halfway through cooking. Using sling, carefully remove cod from air fryer. Serve with lemon wedges.

CREAMY CHIPOTLE CHILE SAUCE

Whisk ¼ cup mayonnaise, ¼ cup sour cream, 2 teaspoons minced canned chipotle chile in adobo sauce, 1 small minced garlic clove, 2 teaspoons minced fresh cilantro, and 1 teaspoon lime juice together in bowl.

ROASTED COD WITH LEMON-GARLIC POTATOES

Serves 2

COOK TIME 28 minutes

TOTAL TIME 1 hour

why this recipe works The air fryer excels at cooking both crispy potatoes and moist, flaky fish, and this simple recipe combines both into an elegant dinner. Thin slices of russet potato made an attractive bed for the fish. We tossed the slices with melted butter, garlic, and lemon zest; arranged them in two layers on a foil sling; then roasted them until they turned tender and spotty brown before laying cod fillets on top and letting both cook together. A pat of compound butter and lemon slices basted the fish with flavor as it cooked. You can substitute halibut or haddock for the cod. For more information on making a foil sling, see page 13.

- 3 tablespoons unsalted butter, softened, divided
- 2 garlic cloves, minced
- 1 lemon, grated to yield 2 teaspoons zest, divided, and sliced ¼ inch thick

- ½ teaspoon table salt, divided
- ¼ teaspoon pepper, divided
- 1 large russet potato (12 ounces), unpeeled, sliced ¼ inch thick

- 1 tablespoon minced fresh parsley, chives, or tarragon
- 2 (8-ounce) skinless cod fillets, 1¼ inches thick

1 Make foil sling for air-fryer basket by folding 1 long sheet of aluminum foil so it is 4 inches wide. Lay sheet of foil widthwise across basket, pressing foil into and up sides of basket. Fold excess foil as needed so that edges of foil are flush with top of basket. Lightly spray foil and basket with vegetable oil spray.

2 Microwave 1 tablespoon butter, garlic, 1 teaspoon lemon zest, ¼ teaspoon salt, and ⅛ teaspoon pepper in medium bowl, stirring once, until butter is melted and mixture is fragrant, about 30 seconds. Add potato slices and toss to coat. Shingle potato slices on sling in prepared basket to create 2 even layers. Place basket into air fryer and set temperature to 400 degrees. Cook until potato slices are spotty brown and just tender, 16 to 18 minutes, using sling to rotate potatoes halfway through cooking.

3 Combine remaining 2 tablespoons butter, remaining 1 teaspoon lemon zest, and parsley in small bowl. Pat cod dry with paper towels and sprinkle with remaining ¼ teaspoon salt and remaining ⅛ teaspoon pepper. Place fillets skinned side down on top of potato slices, spaced evenly apart. (Tuck thinner tail ends of fillets under themselves as needed to create uniform pieces.) Dot fillets with butter mixture and top with lemon slices. Return basket to air fryer and cook until cod flakes apart when gently prodded with paring knife and registers 140 degrees, 12 to 15 minutes, using sling to rotate potato slices and cod halfway through cooking.

4 Using sling, carefully remove potatoes and cod from air fryer. Cut potato slices into 2 portions between fillets using fish spatula. Slide spatula along underside of potato slices and transfer with cod to individual plates. Serve.

MOROCCAN SPICED HALIBUT WITH CHICKPEA SALAD

Serves 2

COOK TIME 12 minutes   **TOTAL TIME** 35 minutes

why this recipe works For a delicious fish dinner, we turned to the flavors of North Africa. Rubbing halibut fillets with warm spices gave them a fragrant flavor and aroma, and the air fryer cooked them gently and evenly, producing moist fillets. Meanwhile, we made a quick Moroccan chickpea and carrot salad. Heating the chickpeas helped them absorb the dressing in which honey added sweetness, harissa heat, and mint a cooling note. You can substitute cod or haddock for the halibut. If harissa is unavailable, it can be omitted. For more information on making a foil sling, see page 13. This recipe can be easily doubled (see page 14).

- ¾ teaspoon ground coriander
- ½ teaspoon ground cumin
- ¼ teaspoon ground ginger
- ⅛ teaspoon ground cinnamon
- ¼ teaspoon table salt, divided

- ¼ teaspoon pepper, divided
- 2 (8-ounce) skinless halibut fillets, 1¼ inches thick
- 4 teaspoons extra-virgin olive oil, divided, plus extra for drizzling
- 1 (15-ounce) can chickpeas, rinsed

- 1 tablespoon lemon juice, plus lemon wedges for serving
- 1 teaspoon harissa
- ½ teaspoon honey
- 2 carrots, peeled and shredded
- 2 tablespoons chopped fresh mint, divided

1 Make foil sling for air-fryer basket by folding 1 long sheet of aluminum foil so it is 4 inches wide. Lay sheet of foil widthwise across basket, pressing foil into and up sides of basket. Fold excess foil as needed so that edges of foil are flush with top of basket. Lightly spray foil and basket with vegetable oil spray.

2 Combine coriander, cumin, ginger, cinnamon, ⅛ teaspoon salt, and ⅛ teaspoon pepper in small bowl. Pat halibut dry with paper towels, rub with 1 teaspoon oil, and sprinkle all over with spice mixture. Arrange fillets skinned side down on sling in prepared basket, spaced evenly apart. Place basket in air fryer and set temperature to 300 degrees. Cook until halibut flakes apart when gently prodded with paring knife

and registers 140 degrees, 12 to 16 minutes, using sling to rotate fillets halfway through cooking.

3 Meanwhile, microwave chickpeas in medium bowl until heated through, about 2 minutes. Stir in remaining 1 tablespoon oil, lemon juice, harissa, honey, remaining ⅛ teaspoon salt, and remaining ⅛ teaspoon pepper. Add carrots and 1 tablespoon mint and toss to combine. Season with salt and pepper to taste.

4 Using sling, carefully remove halibut from air fryer and transfer to individual plates. Sprinkle with remaining 1 tablespoon mint and drizzle with extra oil to taste. Serve with salad and lemon wedges.

HARISSA-RUBBED HADDOCK WITH BRUSSELS SPROUTS AND LEEK

Serves 2

COOK TIME 18 minutes   **TOTAL TIME** 35 minutes

why this recipe works For a beautifully pleasing dinner that would be great for a date night, we air-fried a hearty pile of vegetables—earthy brussels sprouts and a tender leek—with halibut. We used harissa, a North African spice paste, to create a zesty crust on the mild-flavored fish. The vegetables got a head start so that they could begin to soften, and then they finished cooking underneath the fish at a hotter temperature to crisp up and char around the edges. Cutting the leek into large pieces, 1-inch thick, helped it cook alongside the hardier sprouts without getting overly charred. Look for small brussels sprouts no bigger than a golf ball, as they're likely to be sweeter and more tender than large sprouts. If you can find only large sprouts, quarter them. Black sea bass, cod, hake, and pollack are good substitutes for the haddock. This recipe can be easily doubled (see page 14).

12 ounces brussels sprouts, trimmed and halved

1 large leek, white and light green parts only, halved lengthwise, sliced 1 inch thick, and washed thoroughly

3 tablespoons extra-virgin olive oil, divided

½ teaspoon table salt, divided

4 teaspoons harissa paste

2 (4- to 6-ounce) skinless haddock fillets, 1 to 1½ inches thick

1 teaspoon grated lemon zest, plus lemon wedges for serving

1 Toss brussels sprouts and leek with 2 tablespoons oil and ¼ teaspoon salt in bowl. Arrange vegetables in even layer in air-fryer basket. Place basket into air fryer; set temperature to 350 degrees; and cook for 10 minutes, stirring vegetables halfway through cooking.

2 Combine harissa paste, remaining 1 tablespoon oil, and remaining ¼ teaspoon salt in small bowl. Pat haddock dry with paper towels and rub with harissa mixture. Stir vegetables, then place fillets, skinned side down, on top, spaced evenly apart. (Tuck thinner tail ends of fillets under themselves as needed to create uniform pieces.) Return basket to air fryer; increase temperature to 400 degrees; and cook until haddock is lightly browned, flakes apart when prodded gently with paring knife, and registers 135 degrees, 8 to 14 minutes.

3 Transfer haddock to serving platter. Stir lemon zest into vegetables and season with salt and pepper to taste. Transfer vegetables to platter with haddock and serve with lemon wedges.

SOLE AND ASPARAGUS BUNDLES WITH TARRAGON BUTTER

Serves 2

COOK TIME 14 minutes   **TOTAL TIME** 40 minutes

why this recipe works Sole can be tricky to cook, as the long, delicate fillets easily fall apart. One solution: sole bundles. Rolled around a filling into a tidy package, the fish is easier to maneuver and is perfectly shaped for the air fryer. For the filling, we chose asparagus, which was easy to prep and made for an attractive presentation. To ensure the spears became tender as the fish finished cooking, we steamed them in the microwave before rolling them in the fillets. Placing the bundles on a foil sling made transferring them easy. To flavor the mild, lean fish, we dotted the bundles with a tarragon compound butter when they came out of the fryer. Served with a salad or grain, this is a light, sophisticated dinner. Look for asparagus spears that are about ½ inch thick. For more information on making a foil sling, see page 13.

8 ounces asparagus, trimmed

1 teaspoon extra-virgin olive oil, divided

   Pinch plus ⅛ teaspoon table salt, divided

2 pinches pepper, divided

4 (3-ounce) skinless sole or flounder fillets, ⅛ to ¼ inch thick

4 tablespoons unsalted butter, softened

1 small shallot, minced

1 tablespoon chopped fresh tarragon

¼ teaspoon lemon zest plus ½ teaspoon juice

1 Toss asparagus with ½ teaspoon oil, pinch salt, and pinch pepper in bowl. Cover and microwave until bright green and just tender, about 3 minutes, tossing halfway through microwaving. Uncover and set aside to cool slightly.

2 Make foil sling for air-fryer basket by folding 1 long sheet of aluminum foil so it is 4 inches wide. Lay sheet of foil widthwise across basket, pressing foil into and up sides of basket. Fold excess foil as needed so that edges of foil are flush with top of basket. Lightly spray foil and basket with vegetable oil spray.

3 Pat sole dry with paper towels and sprinkle with remaining ⅛ teaspoon salt and remaining pinch pepper. Arrange fillets skinned side up on cutting board, with thicker ends closest to you. Arrange asparagus evenly across base of each fillet, then tightly roll fillets away from you around asparagus to form tidy bundles.

4 Rub bundles evenly with remaining ½ teaspoon oil and arrange seam side down on sling in prepared basket. Place basket into air fryer and set temperature to 300 degrees. Cook until asparagus is tender and sole flakes apart when gently prodded with paring knife, 14 to 18 minutes, using sling to rotate bundles halfway through cooking.

5 Combine butter, shallot, tarragon, and lemon zest and juice in bowl. Using sling, carefully remove sole bundles from air fryer and transfer to individual plates. Top evenly with butter mixture and serve.

ROASTED SALMON FILLETS

Serves 2

COOK TIME 10 minutes   **TOTAL TIME** 25 minutes

why this recipe works The air fryer proved to be an excellent way to cook salmon. Testers couldn't stop raving about how the method was easier and less messy than using a skillet, and they loved that they didn't have to closely monitor the fish to avoid overcooking it, thanks to the air fryer's built-in timer and controlled temperature. And the results were great: moist, flaky fish with a beautifully bronzed exterior. Cooking the fish at 400 degrees gave us the best color but also created a problem: smoke, which came from the salmon's delicious fat dripping to the bottom as well as splattering onto the heating element above. Since the fat primarily resides in the skin, we cooked the fillets skin side down, away from the heating element, and used a foil sling, which prevented fat from dripping to the bottom. (Bonus: Our fillets were also now easier to rotate and to remove.) If using wild salmon, cook it until it registers 120 degrees. For more information on making a foil sling, see page 13. Serve with Herb-Yogurt Sauce or Mango-Mint Salsa. This recipe can be easily doubled (see page 14).

2   (8-ounce) skin-on   1   teaspoon   ¼   teaspoon table salt
    salmon fillets,   vegetable oil   ⅛   teaspoon pepper
    1½ inches thick

1 Make foil sling for air-fryer basket by folding 1 long sheet of aluminum foil so it is 4 inches wide. Lay sheet of foil widthwise across basket, pressing foil into and up sides of basket. Fold excess foil as needed so that edges of foil are flush with top of basket.

2 Pat salmon dry with paper towels, rub with oil, and sprinkle with salt and pepper. Arrange fillets skin side down on sling in prepared basket, spaced evenly apart. Place basket in air fryer and set temperature to 400 degrees. Cook salmon until center is still translucent when checked with tip of paring knife and registers 125 degrees (for medium-rare), 10 to 14 minutes, using sling to rotate fillets halfway through cooking.

3 Using sling, carefully remove salmon from air fryer. Slide fish spatula along underside of fillets and transfer to individual serving plates, leaving skin behind. Serve.

HERB-YOGURT SAUCE
Combine ½ cup plain yogurt, 2 tablespoons minced fresh dill or tarragon, ½ teaspoon grated lemon zest plus 2 teaspoons juice, and 1 small minced garlic clove in bowl. Season with salt and pepper to taste. Cover and refrigerate until flavors meld, about 30 minutes. Makes about ½ cup.

MANGO-MINT SALSA
Combine 1 peeled, pitted, and finely chopped mango, 1 small seeded and minced jalapeño chile, 3 tablespoons lime juice (2 limes), 2 tablespoons chopped fresh mint, 1 tablespoon minced shallot, 1 tablespoon extra-virgin olive oil, and ¼ teaspoon table salt in bowl. Makes about 1½ cups.

PISTACHIO-CRUSTED SALMON

Serves 1 to 4

COOK TIME 8 minutes   **TOTAL TIME** 30 minutes

why this recipe works In the air fryer, salmon cooks up silky and moist. Here we enhanced the fish's rich flavor and tender texture with a crunchy nut crust that browned perfectly in the circulated hot air. We placed the nut crust on only the top of the fillet so that the fish didn't need to be turned during air-frying and the crust couldn't get soggy on the bottom. Thick Greek yogurt helped the nuts stick to the fish. We used pistachios here (and hazelnuts and smoked almonds for the variations) and found that chopping them fine (with a knife, spice grinder, or mini food processor) was essential for an even coating. Panko bread crumbs fortified the crust, and patting the salmon dry helped the crust stay on. A foil sling set in the air-fryer basket allowed us to deftly pick up the cooked fish without breakage. We often use oil spray on the foil sling when cooking delicate fish fillets; here the skin adheres to the foil in case you want to remove it. Simply slide a spatula under the fillet and leave the skin behind. If using wild salmon, cook it until it registers 120 degrees. For more information on making a foil sling, see page 13. This recipe is written to serve one but can be easily scaled to serve up to four people (see page 14).

- 1 tablespoon finely chopped toasted pistachios or almonds
- 1 tablespoon panko bread crumbs
- 1 tablespoon minced fresh parsley
- ¼ teaspoon fennel seeds, chopped
- 1 (4- to 6-ounce) skin-on salmon fillet, 1 to 1½ inches thick
- ⅛ teaspoon table salt
- 2 teaspoons plain Greek yogurt
- Olive oil spray

1 Make foil sling for air-fryer basket by folding 1 long sheet of aluminum foil so it is 4 inches wide. Lay sheet of foil widthwise across basket, pressing foil into and up sides of basket. Fold excess foil as needed so that edges of foil are flush with top of basket.

2 Combine pistachios, panko, parsley, and fennel seeds in shallow dish. Pat salmon dry with paper towels and sprinkle with salt. Spread yogurt evenly on flesh side of salmon, then dredge coated side in pistachio mixture, pressing gently to adhere.

3 Arrange salmon, skin side down, on prepared sling and lightly spray top with oil spray. (Space additional fillets evenly apart.) Place basket into air fryer and set temperature to 400 degrees. Cook until salmon is lightly browned and center is still translucent when checked with tip of paring knife and registers 125 degrees (for medium-rare), 8 to 10 minutes.

4 Using sling, carefully remove salmon from air fryer. Slide fish spatula along underside of salmon and transfer to plate, leaving skin behind. Serve.

HAZELNUT-CRUSTED SALMON
Substitute hazelnuts or pecans for pistachios, ½ teaspoon minced fresh oregano for parsley, and ½ teaspoon grated lemon zest for fennel seeds.

SMOKED ALMOND—CRUSTED SALMON
Substitute smoked almonds or smoked peanuts for pistachios, chives for parsley, and ¼ teaspoon paprika and pinch cayenne pepper for fennel seeds.

ORANGE-MUSTARD GLAZED SALMON

Serves 2

COOK TIME 10 minutes	**TOTAL TIME** 30 minutes

why this recipe works A sweet, tangy glaze offers appealing contrast to rich, meaty salmon, but most recipes call for broiling the fish, which can result in unevenly cooked salmon and a burnt glaze. So we were happy to find that the air fryer produced foolproof results: The direct heat from above caramelized the glaze's sugars, while the circulated air cooked the fish from all sides. We liked the idea of an orange glaze, but on their own, orange juice and zest didn't pack enough punch. Adding orange marmalade was just the ticket to boost the flavor, and it helped the glaze cling to the salmon. Some whole-grain mustard gave the glaze pops of mild heat to balance its sweetness and cut the richness of the fish. We brushed the mixture on the fillets before cooking, and after 10 minutes were met with crisp-glazed fish boasting beautiful browned edges and a velvety pink interior. This easy technique lends itself to a variety of flavors, so we also developed a honey-chipotle glaze and one made with hoisin and rice vinegar. If using wild salmon, cook it until it registers 120 degrees. For more information on making a foil sling, see page 13. This recipe can be easily doubled (see page 14).

1 tablespoon orange marmalade

¼ teaspoon grated orange zest plus 1 tablespoon juice

2 teaspoons whole-grain mustard

2 (8-ounce) skin-on salmon fillets, 1½ inches thick

¼ teaspoon table salt

⅛ teaspoon pepper

1 Make foil sling for air-fryer basket by folding 1 long sheet of aluminum foil so it is 4 inches wide. Lay sheet of foil widthwise across basket, pressing foil into and up sides of basket. Fold excess foil as needed so that edges of foil are flush with top of basket.

2 Combine marmalade, orange zest and juice, and mustard in bowl. Pat salmon dry with paper towels and sprinkle with salt and pepper. Brush tops and sides of fillets evenly with glaze. Arrange fillets skin side down on sling in prepared basket, spaced evenly apart. Place basket into air fryer and set temperature to 400 degrees. Cook salmon until center is still translucent when checked with tip of paring knife and registers 125 degrees (for medium-rare), 10 to 14 minutes, using sling to rotate fillets halfway through cooking.

3 Using sling, carefully remove salmon from air fryer. Slide fish spatula along underside of fillets and transfer to individual serving plates, leaving skin behind. Serve.

HONEY-CHIPOTLE GLAZED SALMON
Omit orange zest and juice. Substitute 2 tablespoons honey for marmalade and 2 teaspoons minced canned chipotle chile in adobo sauce for mustard.

HOISIN GLAZED SALMON
Omit orange zest. Substitute 2 tablespoons hoisin sauce for marmalade, 1 tablespoon unseasoned rice vinegar for orange juice, and ⅛ teaspoon ground ginger for mustard.

HONEY GLAZED SALMON WITH SNAP PEAS AND RADISHES

Serves 2

COOK TIME 13 minutes   TOTAL TIME 35 minutes

why this recipe works A glaze coats, flavors, and protects fish from drying out during air-frying. For this glaze, we combined honey, soy sauce, and tahini, which added nuttiness and helped the mixture cling better to the fish. The air fryer's direct heat caramelized the glaze's sugars from above while the circulated air cooked our salmon from all sides. We brushed the glaze on the fish once before cooking and then again halfway through. After about 8 minutes, our glazed fish had browned edges and a tender interior. While the salmon rested, we roasted fresh snap peas and radishes until they were crisp-tender so that they retained their green and pink hues and complemented the orange salmon beautifully for a vivid and appetizing plate. If using wild salmon, cook it until it registers 120 degrees. For more information on using a foil sling, see page 13. This recipe can be easily doubled (see page 14).

- 2 tablespoons honey
- 1 tablespoon tahini
- 1 tablespoon soy sauce
- 1 teaspoon lime juice, plus lime wedges for serving

- 2 (4- to 6-ounce) skin-on salmon fillets, 1 to 1½ inches thick
- 8 ounces sugar snap peas, strings removed
- 8 radishes, trimmed and quartered

- 1 teaspoon toasted sesame oil
- ⅛ teaspoon table salt
- 2 scallions, sliced thin
- 1 tablespoon sesame seeds, toasted

1 Make foil sling for air-fryer basket by folding 1 long sheet of aluminum foil so it is 4 inches wide. Lay sheet of foil widthwise across basket, pressing foil into and up sides of basket. Fold excess foil as needed so that edges of foil are flush with top of basket.

2 Whisk honey, tahini, soy sauce, and lime juice together in bowl. Measure out 2 tablespoons glaze for cooking; set aside remaining glaze for serving. Pat salmon dry with paper towels. Brush flesh side of salmon with 1 tablespoon

glaze for cooking. Arrange salmon, skin side down, on prepared sling. Place basket into air fryer, set temperature to 400 degrees, and cook for 5 minutes.

3 Brush salmon with remaining 1 tablespoon glaze for cooking. Return basket to air fryer and cook until salmon is well browned and center is still translucent when checked with tip of paring knife and registers 125 degrees (for medium-rare), 3 to 5 minutes.

4 Using sling, carefully remove salmon from air fryer. Slide fish spatula along underside of salmon and transfer to serving platter, leaving skin behind. Tent with foil and let rest while preparing peas and radishes.

5 Toss peas and radishes with oil and salt in bowl and arrange in even layer in now-empty basket. Return basket to air fryer and cook until crisp-tender, about 5 minutes. Transfer vegetables to platter with salmon and sprinkle salmon with scallions and sesame seeds. Serve with lime wedges and reserved glaze.

SESAME SALMON WITH ROASTED KIMCHI, BROCCOLI, AND SHIITAKES

Serves 2

COOK TIME 16 minutes	**TOTAL TIME** 35 minutes

why this recipe works We paired spicy cabbage kimchi, the popular Korean condiment, with salmon for this piquant and satisfying one-pan supper. Pan? An air fryer's basket doesn't allow for cooking with juicy ingredients like kimchi, so we placed chopped kimchi, broccoli, and shiitake mushrooms—tossed with fresh ginger, mirin, soy sauce, and sesame oil—in a small cake pan and set that in the basket to cook. Flavorful liquid didn't drip away into the base but collected in the bottom of the pan instead and kept our ingredients moist. Once the vegetables were softened and lightly browned, we placed salmon pieces topped with toasted sesame seeds on them to air-fry. The tartness and gentle heat of the pickled cabbage made a flavorful contrast to the rich sesame-crusted fish. If using wild salmon, cook it until it registers 120 degrees. You will need a 6-inch round nonstick or silicone cake pan for this recipe; before starting this recipe, confirm your air fryer allows enough space for the pan.

1   cup cabbage kimchi, drained and cut into 1-inch pieces

3   ounces 1-inch broccoli florets (1 cup)

4   ounces shiitake mushrooms, stemmed and sliced thin

1   tablespoon mirin

2   teaspoons grated fresh ginger

1   teaspoon soy sauce

1   teaspoon toasted sesame oil, plus extra for drizzling

1   (8- to 12-ounce) skinless salmon fillet, 1-1½ inches thick, cut into 2-inch pieces

1   tablespoon sesame seeds, toasted

1   scallion, sliced thin

1 Combine kimchi, broccoli, mushrooms, mirin, ginger, soy sauce, and oil in bowl. Transfer kimchi mixture to 6-inch round nonstick or silicone cake pan and spread into even layer. Place pan in air-fryer basket and place basket into air fryer. Set temperature to 400 degrees and cook until vegetables are softened and lightly browned, 8 to 14 minutes, stirring halfway through cooking.

2 Pat salmon pieces dry with paper towels and sprinkle tops with sesame seeds, pressing gently to adhere. Arrange salmon on top of kimchi mixture. Return basket to air fryer and cook until salmon is lightly browned and center is still translucent when checked with tip of paring knife and registers 125 degrees (for medium-rare), 8 to 10 minutes. Remove pan from air fryer. Sprinkle salmon with scallion and drizzle with extra oil. Serve.

SALMON BURGERS WITH TOMATO CHUTNEY

Serves 2

COOK TIME 6 minutes	TOTAL TIME 45 minutes

why this recipe works Since salmon prepared in the air fryer consistently turns out well cooked and moist, we tried using the meaty, nutritious fish to make tender burgers. We paired them with a quick, sweet-tangy tomato chutney that is easily made in the microwave. Since the chutney uses pantry ingredients (brown sugar, cider vinegar, and canned tomatoes), you can make it any time and use it instead of ketchup. For our quick-cooking burgers, we preferred to chop the salmon in the food processor for a textured combination of finely minced and coarsely chopped pieces. We bound the patties with crunchy panko (and a little yogurt) so that they held their shape but weren't mushy. We gave the patties some freshness by combining the panko-salmon mixture with cilantro, lemon juice, and scallion whites. The chutney can be made up to three days in advance, making burger night easier. If using wild salmon, cook the burgers until they register 120 degrees. You can use your air fryer to toast the buns; see page 19 for more information. This recipe can be easily doubled (see page 14).

¾ cup canned diced tomatoes, drained and patted dry

1 tablespoon packed light brown sugar

2 teaspoons cider vinegar

¼ teaspoon table salt, divided

¼ teaspoon pepper, divided

2 scallions, white and green parts separated and sliced thin

¼ cup chopped fresh cilantro, divided

12 ounces skinless salmon fillets, cut into 1-inch pieces

3 tablespoons panko bread crumbs

1 tablespoon plain yogurt

2 teaspoons lemon juice

2 hamburger buns, toasted, if desired

2 leaves Bibb lettuce

1 Microwave tomatoes, sugar, vinegar, ⅛ teaspoon salt, and ⅛ teaspoon pepper in bowl until mixture is thickened, about 8 minutes, stirring halfway through microwaving. Let chutney cool completely, then stir in scallion greens and 1 tablespoon cilantro. Season with salt and pepper to taste; set aside for serving. (Chutney can be refrigerated for up to 3 days.)

2 Pulse salmon in food processor until there is even mix of finely minced and coarsely chopped pieces, about 2 pulses, scraping down sides of bowl as needed. Stir panko, yogurt, lemon juice, scallion whites, remaining ⅛ teaspoon salt, remaining ⅛ teaspoon pepper, and remaining 3 tablespoons cilantro together in large bowl. Fold in salmon gently until just combined.

3 Lightly spray bottom of air-fryer basket with vegetable oil spray. Using your lightly moistened hands, divide salmon mixture in half, shape into 2 lightly packed balls, and flatten each ball gently into 1-inch-thick patty. Press center of each patty with your fingertips to create ¼-inch-deep depression.

4 Arrange patties in prepared basket, spaced evenly apart. Place basket into air fryer and set temperature to 350 degrees. Cook until burgers are lightly browned and centers are still translucent when checked with tip of paring knife and register 125 degrees (for medium-rare), 6 to 8 minutes, flipping burgers halfway through cooking. Serve burgers on buns, topped with chutney and lettuce.

SALMON TACOS WITH ROASTED PINEAPPLE SLAW

Serves 2 to 4

COOK TIME 18 minutes   **TOTAL TIME** 50 minutes

why this recipe works California-style fish tacos generally feature deep-fried fish, a tangy cabbage slaw, and a creamy sauce that binds everything together. For a lighter take on this treat, we swapped in salmon for the typical white fish. Since salmon is naturally rich, it wouldn't need to be battered and fried; a spice rub instead gave the fillets a nice crust, and air-frying them skin-on atop a foil sling ensured that they would hold together and emerge perfectly moist inside. For a slaw that stood up to the salmon, we wanted to incorporate a bright, fruity element. Pineapple caught our attention: We could roast pieces in the air fryer, allowing them to caramelize a bit before combining them with crunchy coleslaw mix, cilantro, and lime—a perfect bright complement to the fish. For a creamy topping, in lieu of a heavy sour cream–based sauce, we mashed avocado with lime juice, salt, and pepper. Spread onto warmed corn tortillas, the avocado mash held the moist, flaky fish and tangy slaw in place for a perfect bite. If using wild salmon, cook it until it registers 120 degrees. For more information on making a foil sling, see page 13. You can lightly char the tortillas one at a time over a gas burner or stack tortillas, wrap tightly in aluminum foil, and warm in the air fryer set to 350 degrees for 5 minutes, flipping halfway through cooking.

3 cups (8 ounces) shredded coleslaw mix

¼ cup lime juice (2 limes), divided, plus lime wedges for serving

⅜ teaspoon table salt, divided

¼ teaspoon pepper, divided

1½ cups ½-inch pineapple pieces

2 teaspoons vegetable oil, divided

1 teaspoon smoked paprika

¼ teaspoon ground coriander

⅛ teaspoon cayenne pepper

2 (8-ounce) skin-on salmon fillets, 1½ inches thick

1 avocado, halved and pitted

2 tablespoons minced fresh cilantro

6-12 (6-inch) corn tortillas, warmed

1 Toss coleslaw mix with 3 tablespoons lime juice, ¼ teaspoon salt, and ⅛ teaspoon pepper in bowl; set aside.

2 Toss pineapple with 1 teaspoon oil in separate bowl; transfer to air-fryer basket. Place basket into air fryer and set temperature to 400 degrees. Cook until pineapple is browned at edges, 12 to 16 minutes, tossing halfway through cooking. Transfer to now-empty bowl and set aside; let air-fryer basket cool slightly.

3 Make foil sling for air-fryer basket by folding 1 long sheet of aluminum foil so it is 4 inches wide. Lay sheet of foil widthwise across basket, pressing foil into and up sides of basket. Fold excess foil as needed so that edges of foil are flush with top of basket. Lightly spray foil with vegetable oil spray.

4 Combine paprika, coriander, cayenne, remaining ⅛ teaspoon salt, and remaining ⅛ teaspoon pepper in small bowl. Pat salmon dry with paper towels, rub with remaining 1 teaspoon oil, and sprinkle tops and sides of fillets with spice mixture. Arrange fillets skin side down on sling in prepared basket, spaced evenly apart. Return basket to air fryer and cook salmon until center is still translucent when checked with tip of paring knife and registers 125 degrees (for medium-rare), 6 to 10 minutes, using sling to rotate fillets halfway through cooking.

5 Meanwhile, using fork, mash avocado with remaining 1 tablespoon lime juice in medium bowl. Season with salt and pepper to taste. Drain coleslaw mixture and return to now-empty bowl. Stir in pineapple and cilantro.

6 Using sling, carefully remove salmon from air fryer. Slide fish spatula along underside of fillets and transfer to plate, leaving skin behind. Using 2 forks, flake salmon into rough 1-inch pieces. Serve on tortillas with slaw and mashed avocado, passing lime wedges separately.

CRAB CAKES WITH BIBB LETTUCE AND APPLE SALAD

Serves 2

COOK TIME 13 minutes   **TOTAL TIME** 45 minutes

why this recipe works For an elegant meal (or appetizer), make crab cakes in the air fryer; they turn out well and there's no messy pan frying. Good crab cakes start with sweet, plump crabmeat and minimal binder. Two tablespoons of panko and an egg were all ours needed. Mayonnaise, Dijon mustard, and cayenne added richness, tang, and gentle heat, and scallion contributed subtle aromatics. While the cakes chilled, we air-fried some crispy shallots to garnish a green Bibb and apple salad to serve with our crab cakes. Buy crabmeat (fresh or pasteurized) packed in plastic containers in the refrigerated section of your fish department. We do not recommend canned crabmeat. This recipe can be easily doubled (see page 14).

8 ounces lump crabmeat, picked over for shells	1½ teaspoons Dijon mustard	⅛ teaspoon table salt
	Pinch cayenne pepper	Pinch pepper
2 tablespoons panko bread crumbs	2 shallots, sliced thin	½ small head Bibb lettuce (3 ounces), torn into bite-size pieces
1 scallion, minced	1 tablespoon extra-virgin olive oil, divided	
1 large egg		½ apple, cored and sliced thin
1 tablespoon mayonnaise	1 teaspoon lemon juice, plus lemon wedges for serving	

1 Line large plate with triple layer of paper towels. Transfer crabmeat to prepared plate and pat dry with additional paper towels. Combine panko, scallion, egg, mayonnaise, mustard, and cayenne in bowl. Using rubber spatula, gently fold in crabmeat until combined; discard paper towels. Divide crab mixture into 4 tightly packed balls, then flatten each into 1-inch-thick cake (cakes will be delicate). Transfer cakes to now-empty plate and refrigerate until firm, about 10 minutes.

2 Toss shallots with ½ teaspoon oil in separate bowl; transfer to air-fryer basket. Place basket into air fryer and set temperature to 400 degrees. Cook until shallots are browned, 5 to 7 minutes, tossing once halfway through cooking. Return shallots to now-empty bowl and set aside.

3 Arrange crab cakes in now-empty air-fryer basket, spaced evenly apart. Return basket to air fryer and cook until crab cakes are light golden brown on both sides, 8 to 10 minutes, flipping and rotating cakes halfway through cooking.

4 Meanwhile, whisk remaining 2½ teaspoons oil, lemon juice, salt, and pepper together in large bowl. Add lettuce, apple, and shallots and toss to coat. Serve crab cakes with salad, passing lemon wedges separately.

BACON-WRAPPED SCALLOPS WITH SPINACH, FENNEL, AND RASPBERRY SALAD

Serves 4

COOK TIME 12 minutes   **TOTAL TIME** 50 minutes

why this recipe works Smoky bacon beautifully accents sweet, briny scallops. The pair are often grilled, but the air fryer offered a foolproof, unfussy way to enjoy this combo. Since scallops cook much faster than bacon, we parcooked bacon strips in the microwave before wrapping each strip around two scallops (for an ideal scallop-to-bacon ratio) and skewering them. Served with a bright spinach salad with fennel and juicy berries, this is an easy and elegant dinner for four. We recommend buying "dry" scallops, which don't have chemical additives and taste better than "wet." Do not use thick-cut bacon. We arranged the skewers in the air fryer in two layers like Lincoln Logs (see page 13) to facilitate even cooking.

12	slices bacon
24	large sea scallops, tendons removed
1	teaspoon plus 2 tablespoons extra-virgin olive oil, divided
¼	teaspoon table salt, divided

¼	teaspoon pepper, divided
6	(6-inch) wooden skewers
1	tablespoon cider vinegar
1	teaspoon Dijon mustard

5	ounces (5 cups) baby spinach
1	fennel bulb, stalks discarded, bulb halved, cored, and sliced thin
5	ounces (1 cup) raspberries

1 Line large plate with 4 layers paper towels and arrange 6 slices bacon over towels in single layer. Top with 4 more layers paper towels and remaining 6 slices bacon. Cover with 2 layers of paper towels, place second large plate on top, and press gently to flatten. Microwave until fat begins to render but bacon is still pliable, about 5 minutes.

2 Pat scallops dry with paper towels and toss with 1 teaspoon oil, ⅛ teaspoon salt, and ⅛ teaspoon pepper in bowl until evenly coated. Arrange 2 scallops side to side, flat side down, on cutting board. Starting at narrow end, wrap 1 slice bacon tightly around sides of scallop bundle. (Bacon should overlap slightly; trim excess as needed.) Thread scallop bundle onto skewer through bacon. Repeat with remaining scallops and bacon, threading 2 bundles onto each skewer.

3 Arrange 3 skewers in air-fryer basket, parallel to each other and spaced evenly apart. Arrange remaining 3 skewers on top, perpendicular to bottom layer. Place basket in air fryer and set temperature to 350 degrees. Cook until bacon is crisp and scallops are firm and centers are opaque, 12 to 16 minutes, flipping and rotating skewers halfway through cooking.

4 Meanwhile, whisk remaining 2 tablespoons oil, vinegar, mustard, remaining ⅛ teaspoon salt, and remaining ⅛ teaspoon pepper in large serving bowl until combined. Add spinach, fennel, and raspberries and toss gently to coat. Serve skewers with salad.

SHRIMP SKEWERS WITH PEANUT DIPPING SAUCE

Serves 2

COOK TIME 6 minutes   TOTAL TIME 50 minutes

why this recipe works Shrimp cook very quickly—that's one reason we love them—and they can turn from moist and juicy to rubbery and dry in the blink of an eye. For juicy, boldly seasoned shrimp in the air fryer, we employed a time-honored test kitchen technique: brining. Just 15 minutes in a salty brine helped the shelled and deveined shrimp hang on to their moisture during cooking, and the brine seasoned them evenly throughout. Next, inspired by Thai street food, we coated the brined shrimp in a potent paste of oil, honey, and lime zest and threaded them onto skewers for easy maneuvering in the air fryer and an attractive presentation. After just 6 minutes, they emerged plump, juicy, and deeply flavored, and with a burnished sheen. We then whipped up a simple but classic peanut dipping sauce to serve with our Thai-style shrimp skewers. We whisked together creamy peanut butter, lime juice, cilantro, and a touch of pungent fish sauce, thinning out the sauce with hot water. Dipped in this sauce, our shrimp skewers offered a perfect balance of sweet, salty, and vibrant flavors. We arranged the skewers in the air fryer in two layers like Lincoln Logs (see page 13) to facilitate even cooking. Serve with rice or steamed vegetables.

2 tablespoons table salt, for brining	1 teaspoon honey	3 tablespoons creamy peanut butter
12 ounces extra-large shrimp (21 to 25 per pound), peeled and deveined	½ teaspoon grated lime zest plus 1 tablespoon juice, plus lime wedges for serving	3 tablespoons hot tap water
1 tablespoon vegetable oil	¼ teaspoon pepper	1 tablespoon chopped fresh cilantro
	6 (6-inch) wooden skewers	1 teaspoon fish sauce

1 Dissolve 2 tablespoons salt in 1 quart cold water in large container. Add shrimp, cover, and refrigerate for 15 minutes.

2 Remove shrimp from brine and pat dry with paper towels. Whisk oil, honey, lime zest, and pepper together in large bowl. Add shrimp and toss to coat. Thread shrimp onto skewers, leaving about ¼ inch between each shrimp (3 or 4 shrimp per skewer).

3 Arrange 3 skewers in air-fryer basket, parallel to each other and spaced evenly apart. Arrange remaining 3 skewers on top, perpendicular to bottom layer. Place basket into air fryer and set temperature to 400 degrees. Cook until shrimp are opaque throughout, 6 to 8 minutes, flipping and rotating skewers halfway through cooking.

4 Whisk peanut butter, hot tap water, lime juice, cilantro, and fish sauce together in bowl until smooth. Serve skewers with peanut dipping sauce and lime wedges.

SOUTH CAROLINA–STYLE SHRIMP BAKE

Serves 2

COOK TIME 18 minutes   **TOTAL TIME** 30 minutes

why this recipe works South Carolina's seafood boil features shell-on shrimp, smoked sausage, corn on the cob, and potatoes simmered in an Old Bay–spiked broth. Translating a stew meant for large gatherings to the air fryer might sound curious, but we had a hunch that it would prove ideal for two people, speeding up the process (no need to boil water!) and concentrating the flavors in the hot-air environment. Just like the boiled original, the dish would be a one-"pot" meal, which is a big part of its charm but can also be its downfall. Cooks often throw everything into the pot at once, resulting in mushy potatoes, mealy corn, and rubbery shrimp. The same proved true in the air fryer. We found that staggering the cooking times of the components permitted each to cook just right. We started by seasoning cubes of potatoes and 2-inch rounds of corn with Old Bay and giving them a head start in the air fryer. Meanwhile, we tossed andouille sausage and shrimp (with the shells snipped for easy peeling but left on to protect the delicate meat) with more Old Bay and a liberal dose of minced garlic. Adding them to the basket on top of the vegetables brought them close to the heating element for better browning; they cooked through in almost no time. In just 30 minutes we were able to produce tender potatoes and corn, juicy shrimp, and smoky sausage, perhaps the easiest-ever take on the South Carolina classic.

8 ounces red potatoes, unpeeled, cut into 1-inch pieces	2 teaspoons Old Bay seasoning, divided	6 ounces andouille or chorizo sausage, cut into 1-inch pieces
1 ear corn, husk and silk removed, cut into 2-inch rounds	¼ teaspoon pepper	2 garlic cloves, minced
	8 ounces extra-large shrimp (21 to 25 per pound)	1 tablespoon chopped fresh parsley
2 teaspoons vegetable oil, divided		

1 Toss potatoes and corn with 1 teaspoon oil, 1 teaspoon Old Bay, and pepper in bowl; transfer to air-fryer basket. Place basket into air fryer, set temperature to 400 degrees, and cook for 12 minutes, tossing halfway through cooking.

2 Using kitchen shears or sharp paring knife, cut through shell of shrimp and devein but do not remove shell. Using paring knife, continue to cut shrimp ½ inch deep, taking care not to cut in half completely.

3 Toss shrimp and sausage with garlic, remaining 1 teaspoon oil, and remaining 1 teaspoon Old Bay in now-empty bowl. Arrange shrimp and sausage on top of vegetables. Return basket to air fryer and cook until shrimp are opaque throughout, 6 to 8 minutes, tossing halfway through cooking. Transfer to serving platter and sprinkle with parsley. Serve.

SPICY ROASTED SHRIMP AND FENNEL SALAD WITH CANNELLINI BEANS AND WATERCRESS

Serves 2

COOK TIME 16 minutes

TOTAL TIME 45 minutes

why this recipe works This sumptuous main course salad bursting with spice, sweetness, and color brings together an unlikely combination of ingredients. But why do we use the air fryer for a quick-cooking protein like shrimp? It makes the process hands-off and easy. We tossed fennel and shrimp in a spicy, sharp mixture of extra-virgin olive oil, tart tomato paste, oregano, pepper flakes, and fresh garlic. Then we softened and lightly browned the fennel. Now it was just a matter of placing our shrimp on the vegetable and cooking them until they were tender. We used the remaining oil mixture to toss the fennel and shrimp with cannellini beans, sun-dried tomatoes, watercress, and pepperoncini. Large shrimp (26 to 30 per pound) will also work here; adjust the cooking time as needed. If your fennel doesn't have fronds, omit them. For a spicier dish, use the larger amount of pepper flakes. This recipe can be easily doubled (see page 14).

3 tablespoons extra-virgin olive oil

1 tablespoon tomato paste

2 garlic cloves, minced

¼ teaspoon dried oregano

¼–½ teaspoon red pepper flakes

1 large fennel bulb (1 pound), fronds minced, stalks discarded, bulb halved, cored, and sliced thin

12 ounces extra-large shrimp (21 to 25 per pound), peeled, deveined, and tails removed

1 (15-ounce) can cannellini beans, rinsed

2 ounces (2 cups) watercress, cut into 2-inch lengths

2 tablespoons oil-packed sun-dried tomatoes, rinsed, patted dry, and chopped

2 tablespoons sliced pepperoncini plus 1 tablespoon brine

1 Whisk oil, tomato paste, garlic, oregano, and pepper flakes together in large bowl. Microwave until fragrant, about 30 seconds.

2 Toss sliced fennel with 1 teaspoon oil mixture in separate bowl. Arrange fennel in even layer in air-fryer basket. Place basket into air fryer and set temperature to 400 degrees. Cook until fennel is softened and lightly browned at the edges, 10 to 15 minutes, tossing halfway through cooking.

3 Toss shrimp with 1 teaspoon oil mixture in now-empty bowl. Arrange shrimp in even layer on top of fennel. Return basket to air fryer and cook until shrimp are opaque throughout, 6 to 8 minutes, flipping shrimp halfway through cooking.

4 Add fennel and shrimp mixture, beans, watercress, tomatoes, pepperoncini and brine, and fennel fronds to remaining oil mixture and toss gently to combine. Season with salt and pepper to taste. Serve.

CHIPOTLE SHRIMP TACOS

Serves 2

COOK TIME 6 minutes   **TOTAL TIME** 45 minutes

why this recipe works Shrimp cook quickly, but with the air fryer we could set the timer and not worry about them overcooking and getting chewy. For these tacos, we paired them with fresh, crunchy cabbage; cilantro; and a light lime yogurt. Flavor also came from smoky canned chipotles, with which we coated the shrimp after cutting them in half lengthwise to coat more surface area. We quickly pickled thinly sliced onion in brine and used the pickling liquid to dress the shredded cabbage and cilantro. Large shrimp (26 to 30 per pound) will also work here; adjust the cooking time as needed. You can lightly char the tortillas, one at a time, over a gas burner or stack tortillas, wrap tightly in aluminum foil, and warm in the air fryer set to 350 degrees for 5 minutes, flipping halfway through cooking. Serve with queso fresco and diced avocado. This recipe can be easily doubled (see page 14).

½ cup distilled white vinegar

2 tablespoons packed light brown sugar, divided

½ teaspoon table salt, divided

½ small red onion, sliced thin

12 ounces extra-large shrimp (21 to 25 per pound), peeled, deveined, and tails removed

2 tablespoons minced canned chipotle chile in adobo sauce

1 tablespoon extra-virgin olive oil

½ teaspoon chili powder

¼ cup plain Greek yogurt

1 tablespoon lime juice, plus lime wedges for serving

1½ cups shredded napa cabbage

¼ cup chopped fresh cilantro, plus extra leaves for serving

6 (6-inch) corn tortillas, warmed

1 Microwave vinegar, 1½ tablespoons sugar, and ¼ teaspoon salt in medium bowl until steaming, 2 to 3 minutes; whisk to dissolve sugar and salt. Add onion to hot brine and press to submerge completely. Let sit for 45 minutes. Drain, reserving 2 tablespoons brine. (Drained onion and reserved brine can be refrigerated for up to 1 week.)

2 Lightly spray air-fryer basket with vegetable oil spray. Halve shrimp lengthwise. Combine chipotle, oil, chili powder, remaining 1½ teaspoons sugar, and remaining

¼ teaspoon salt in large bowl. Add shrimp and toss to coat. Arrange shrimp in even layer in prepared basket. Place basket into air fryer and set temperature to 400 degrees. Cook until shrimp are opaque throughout, 6 to 10 minutes, tossing halfway through cooking.

3 Whisk yogurt and lime juice together in small bowl. Toss cabbage with cilantro and reserved brine in separate bowl. Serve shrimp with warmed tortillas, cabbage, pickled onion, yogurt, lime wedges, and extra cilantro leaves.

VEGETABLE SIDES AND MAINS

ROASTED ASPARAGUS

Serves 4

COOK TIME 6 minutes   **TOTAL TIME** 15 minutes

why this recipe works There are many reasons to cook vegetables in your air fryer, and not just fried renditions of them. The air fryer's convection heat ably cooks vegetables of all kinds—without hogging valuable oven space. While we loved using it to roast sturdy root vegetables, perhaps its simplest application was to cook a bunch of asparagus. Because of asparagus's high water content, we found it best to avoid taking the spears to the point of crispness, which dried them out. Instead, we let the air fryer's circulated heat cook the asparagus until vibrant green and crisp-tender, akin to what we might produce through boiling but without the risk of a waterlogged, mushy outcome. The asparagus needed just a teaspoon of oil and in 6 minutes they emerged perfectly cooked. We love asparagus served simply with lemon wedges, but for more bright flavor, pair it with a gremolata topping. This recipe can be easily doubled (see page 14).

1 pound asparagus, trimmed and halved crosswise

1 teaspoon extra-virgin olive oil

⅛ teaspoon table salt

⅛ teaspoon pepper

Lemon wedges

Toss asparagus with oil, salt, and pepper in bowl; transfer to air-fryer basket. Place basket into air fryer and set temperature to 400 degrees. Cook asparagus until tender and bright green, 6 to 8 minutes, tossing halfway through cooking. Season with salt and pepper to taste. Serve with lemon wedges.

MINT-ORANGE GREMOLATA
Combine 2 tablespoons minced fresh mint, 2 tablespoons minced fresh parsley, 2 teaspoons grated orange zest, 1 minced garlic clove, and pinch cayenne pepper in bowl.

TARRAGON-LEMON GREMOLATA
Combine 2 tablespoons minced fresh tarragon, 2 tablespoons minced fresh parsley, 2 teaspoons grated lemon zest, and 1 minced garlic clove in bowl.

ROASTED BROCCOLI

Serves 2

COOK TIME 8 minutes   **TOTAL TIME** 20 minutes

why this recipe works The nutty crispness of roasted broccoli is irresistible. For a side you can't stop eating, we air-fried the vegetable quickly. We cut broccoli florets into 2-inch pieces. To cook, flavor, and crisp up vegetables such as broccoli in the air fryer, we learned that tossing them with water and oil does the trick. Oil and water together might seem counterintuitive, but here's what happens: The water steams the vegetable initially to soften it, and when the water evaporates, the oil provides optimal heat transfer and browning. We drizzled the cooked broccoli with a little more oil before serving. To preserve the crispness in our variations, we sprinkled the roasted broccoli with toppings that added flavor and texture rather than a liquid finish that would make the broccoli soggy. This recipe can be easily doubled (see page 14).

1 tablespoon water

1 tablespoon extra-virgin olive oil, plus extra for drizzling

¼ teaspoon table salt

1 pound broccoli florets, cut into 2-inch pieces

Lemon wedges

Whisk water, oil, and salt in large bowl until salt has dissolved. Add broccoli and toss to coat; transfer to air-fryer basket and spread into even layer. Place basket into air fryer and set temperature to 350 degrees. Cook until broccoli is well browned and tender, 8 to 12 minutes, tossing halfway through cooking. Transfer broccoli to serving platter and drizzle with extra oil. Serve with lemon wedges.

ROASTED BROCCOLI WITH PARMESAN, LEMON, AND BLACK PEPPER TOPPING

Omit lemon wedges. Using your fingers, mix ½ teaspoon pepper and ½ teaspoon grated lemon zest in small bowl until evenly combined. Add ½ cup grated Parmesan and toss with your fingers or fork until pepper and lemon zest are evenly distributed. Transfer roasted broccoli to serving platter and sprinkle with topping before serving.

ROASTED BROCCOLI WITH SESAME AND LIME TOPPING

Omit lemon wedges. Substitute toasted sesame oil for extra-virgin olive oil. Using your fingers, mix 2 tablespoons toasted sesame seeds, ½ teaspoon grated lime zest, and pinch table salt in small bowl until evenly combined. Transfer roasted broccoli to serving platter and sprinkle with topping before serving.

AIR-FRIED BRUSSELS SPROUTS

Serves 4

COOK TIME 20 minutes   **TOTAL TIME** 25 minutes

why this recipe works Fried brussels sprouts have become a menu staple—and for good reason. The tiny cabbages caramelize and crisp while maintaining enough structure to work as a dipping vessel. Of course, deep-frying them is something of a project and doesn't yield the healthiest results. We wanted to see if we could use the air fryer to make "fried" brussels sprouts that kept their virtuous qualities but tasted as decadent as their deep-fried counterparts. Our first attempts were promising but not perfect. Since we usually achieve crispiness (when not frying) by using a very hot oven, we tossed the brussels sprouts in a little oil and roasted them in the air fryer at 400 degrees. They crisped up but tasted raw inside: The air fryer was doing too good a job at browning. We tried adding a splash of water before cooking the sprouts, hoping the resulting steam might soften them faster, but no luck. The solution turned out to be more obvious: Lowering the heat to 350 gave the sprouts time to soften on the inside while crisping. The results mimicked the deep-fried sprouts so well that we were inspired to create a version with another beloved fried vegetable: crispy shallots. Both versions were delicious with a squeeze of lemon, but irresistible with Lemon-Chive Dipping Sauce. If you are buying loose brussels sprouts, select those that are about 1½ inches long. Quarter brussels sprouts longer than 2½ inches. This recipe can be easily doubled (see page 14).

1 pound brussels sprouts, trimmed and halved

1 tablespoon extra-virgin olive oil

¼ teaspoon table salt

⅛ teaspoon pepper

Lemon wedges

Toss brussels sprouts with oil, salt, and pepper in bowl; transfer to air-fryer basket. Place basket into air fryer and set temperature to 350 degrees. Cook brussels sprouts until tender, well browned, and crisp, 20 to 25 minutes, tossing halfway through cooking. Season with salt and pepper to taste. Serve with lemon wedges.

AIR-FRIED BRUSSELS SPROUTS WITH CRISPY SHALLOTS

Add 3 thinly sliced shallots to bowl with brussels sprouts along with oil, salt, and pepper.

LEMON-CHIVE DIPPING SAUCE

Whisk together ¼ cup mayonnaise, 1 tablespoon minced fresh chives, ½ teaspoon grated lemon zest plus 2 teaspoons juice, ½ teaspoon Worcestershire sauce, ½ teaspoon Dijon mustard, and ¼ teaspoon garlic powder in bowl.

ORANGE-CARDAMOM ROASTED CARROTS

Serves 4

COOK TIME 30 minutes　　　　　**TOTAL TIME** 45 minutes

why this recipe works Crunchy and fairly bland when raw, carrots become sweet and buttery when roasted, with chewy caramelized edges. We had those edges in mind when we set out to roast carrots in the air fryer, initially cutting them into coins to create plenty of surface area that we hoped would produce maximum browning. Disappointingly, the carrots came out shriveled. Such small pieces were no match for the intense hot air. We realized we needed bigger pieces, which would have more time to brown before overcooking. Indeed, this improved the carrots' texture, but we still wanted more browning and found our solution in the coating: Switching from oil to butter (which contains milk solids that brown quickly) and adding honey (which caramelizes quickly) gave us deep roasted color and flavor. For even more flavor, we bloomed cardamom and orange zest in the butter as it melted, reserving a portion for a satiny glaze—adding a splash of juice for acidity. Now we had beautifully roasted carrots draped in a luscious glaze; with just a sprinkle of fresh chives, this side dish was complete. If the carrots have very narrow tips, trim the thin ends; they scorch easily.

- 2 tablespoons unsalted butter
- 1 tablespoon honey
- ½ teaspoon grated orange zest plus 1 tablespoon juice
- ½ teaspoon ground cardamom
- ¼ teaspoon table salt
- 2 pounds carrots, peeled and cut into 2-inch lengths, thick ends halved lengthwise
- 1 tablespoon minced fresh chives

1 Microwave butter, honey, orange zest, cardamom, and salt in large bowl at 50 percent power, stirring occasionally, until butter is melted, about 1 minute. Whisk to combine. Combine 1 tablespoon butter mixture and orange juice in small bowl; set aside. Add carrots to remaining butter mixture and toss to coat; transfer to air-fryer basket.

2 Place basket into air fryer and set temperature to 400 degrees. Cook carrots until tender and browned, about 30 minutes, tossing every 10 minutes.

3 Transfer carrots to now-empty bowl and toss with reserved butter mixture. Season with salt and pepper to taste and sprinkle with chives. Serve.

CUMIN-LIME ROASTED CARROTS
Substitute lime zest for orange zest, 1 teaspoon lime juice for orange juice, cumin for cardamom, and cilantro for chives.

SMOKED PAPRIKA–LEMON ROASTED CARROTS
Substitute lemon zest for orange zest, 1 teaspoon lemon juice for orange juice, smoked paprika for cardamom, and mint for chives.

CURRIED ROASTED CAULIFLOWER AND CHICKPEA SALAD

Serves 4

COOK TIME 23 minutes   **TOTAL TIME** 45 minutes

why this recipe works Roasting brings out the best in cauliflower, giving the otherwise plain vegetable a nutty sweetness. Given our love of roasted cauliflower, we were excited to discover that we could roast an entire head's worth of florets in the air fryer at once, and in less time than it takes in an oven. We just had to ensure that the pieces cooked evenly, which was easily achieved by tossing the florets halfway through cooking to redistribute them. A bit of curry powder and olive oil tossed on the florets before roasting enhanced their golden hue. While the cauliflower cooked and cooled, we assembled other components to turn it into a flavorful salad: a tangy cilantro-lime yogurt dressing, chickpeas for substance, red grapes for sweetness, and chopped cashews for crunch. We mixed everything up, and with an extra sprinkle of cilantro, our roasted cauliflower salad was done, easy enough to be a simple side or a light lunch any day.

3½ tablespoons extra-virgin olive oil, divided

1½ teaspoons curry powder

¼ teaspoon table salt, divided

¼ teaspoon pepper, divided

1 head cauliflower (2 pounds), cored and cut into 1½-inch florets

¼ cup plain yogurt

2 tablespoons chopped fresh cilantro, divided

1½ teaspoons lime juice

1 garlic clove, minced

1 (15-ounce) can chickpeas, rinsed

3 ounces seedless red grapes, halved (½ cup)

¼ cup roasted cashews, chopped

1 Whisk 1½ tablespoons oil, curry powder, ⅛ teaspoon salt, and ⅛ teaspoon pepper together in medium bowl. Add cauliflower and toss to coat; transfer to air-fryer basket. Place basket into air fryer and set temperature to 400 degrees. Cook cauliflower until tender and golden at edges, 23 to 25 minutes, tossing halfway through cooking.

2 Set cauliflower aside to cool slightly. Meanwhile, whisk yogurt, 1 tablespoon cilantro, lime juice, garlic, remaining ⅛ teaspoon salt, remaining ⅛ teaspoon pepper, and remaining 2 tablespoons oil together in serving bowl. Add cooled cauliflower and chickpeas and toss to coat. Season with salt and pepper to taste. Sprinkle with grapes, cashews, and remaining 1 tablespoon cilantro. Serve.

ROASTED EGGPLANT WITH CAPERS, OREGANO, AND GARLIC

Serves 2

COOK TIME 16 minutes   **TOTAL TIME** 30 minutes

why this recipe works Marinated eggplant is a classic Middle Eastern dish that's great as an appetizer or a side with summery main dishes. To keep the eggplant in the spotlight and reduce the amount of oil used for frying and marinating it, we roasted it instead and replaced the marinade with a brightly flavored dressing. We chose baby eggplants, which are smaller than the standard supermarket size, are more readily available in the summer months, and cook quickly. Roasting helped us achieve flavorful browning on the eggplant. To keep the dressing delicate, a Greek-inspired combination of just a tablespoon of extra-virgin olive oil, fragrant lemon zest and juice, capers, oregano, and garlic worked perfectly. If baby eggplant is unavailable, one 1-pound eggplant can be substituted; halve it lengthwise before slicing it crosswise. This recipe can be easily doubled (see page 14).

2   baby eggplants (8 to 10 ounces each), sliced into 1-inch-thick rounds

Olive oil spray

¼   teaspoon table salt

⅛   teaspoon pepper

1   tablespoon extra-virgin olive oil

1   teaspoon capers, rinsed and minced

1   teaspoon minced fresh oregano

1   small garlic clove, minced

½   teaspoon grated lemon zest plus 2 teaspoons juice

1 Lightly spray both sides of eggplant with oil spray and sprinkle with salt and pepper. Arrange eggplant in even layer in air-fryer basket (pieces may overlap). Place basket into air fryer and set temperature to 350 degrees. Cook until eggplant is deep golden brown, 16 to 20 minutes, flipping eggplant halfway through cooking.

2 Whisk oil, capers, oregano, garlic, and lemon zest and juice together in large bowl. Add eggplant and toss gently to combine. Serve warm or at room temperature. (Eggplant can be refrigerated for up to 3 days. Let come to room temperature before serving.)

ROASTED FENNEL WITH ORANGE-HONEY DRESSING

Serves 2

COOK TIME 12 minutes   **TOTAL TIME** 30 minutes

why this recipe works The short roasting time needed for fennel in the air fryer helps retain its anise flavor. We began by cutting the bulb into wedges, which had two benefits: It provided good surface area for browning, and the attached core kept the pieces intact. Tossing the wedges with salted water and oil allowed them to steam and turn creamy during the first part of cooking; it also allowed seasoning to get between their layers. Once the water evaporated, the oil helped turn the wedges golden and deliciously caramelized. The orange and honey in the dressing enhanced the sweetness of the roasted fennel. Look for a fennel bulb that measures 3½ to 4 inches in diameter and weighs around 1 pound with the stalks; trim the base very lightly so that the bulb remains intact. If your fennel does not have fronds, omit them. This recipe can be easily doubled (see page 14).

- 1 fennel bulb, base lightly trimmed, 2 tablespoons fronds chopped coarse, stalks discarded
- 2 tablespoons extra-virgin olive oil, divided
- 1 tablespoon water
- ¼ teaspoon table salt
- ¼ teaspoon pepper
- 2 teaspoons honey
- 1½ teaspoons white wine vinegar
- ⅛ teaspoon grated orange zest plus 1 tablespoon juice

1 Cut fennel bulb lengthwise through core into 8 wedges (do not remove core). Whisk 1 tablespoon oil, water, salt, and pepper in large bowl until salt has dissolved. Add fennel wedges and toss gently to coat.

2 Arrange fennel wedges cut side down in air-fryer basket (wedges may overlap). Place basket into air fryer and set temperature to 350 degrees. Cook until fennel is tender and well browned, 12 to 20 minutes, flipping wedges halfway through cooking.

3 Whisk fennel fronds, honey, vinegar, orange zest and juice, and remaining 1 tablespoon oil together in bowl. Season with salt and pepper to taste. Transfer fennel to serving platter and drizzle with dressing. Serve.

ROASTED GREEN BEANS WITH SUN-DRIED TOMATOES AND SUNFLOWER SEEDS

Serves 4

COOK TIME 12 minutes   **TOTAL TIME** 30 minutes

why this recipe works There may be no sadder side dish than the pile of army-green, bland, spoon-soft green beans many of us recall from childhood. On the flip side, green beans can be the most vibrant of vegetables and a wonderful base for a salad bursting with flavors, textures, and colors. The air fryer made the job easy: Just 12 minutes at a high temperature gave us bright, crisp-tender green beans that retained all of their grassy, sweet flavor. Now we had to do them justice with additions. Umami-rich sun-dried tomatoes and fresh basil gave the salad contrasting flavors: briny, sweet, and herbal. Goat cheese added creamy richness. In lieu of the almonds often paired with green beans, we turned to earthy sunflower seeds to finish the dish with a nutty crunch. Lemon juice brought clean acidity, and olive oil rounded out the punch for a simple dressing. With little work we had a green bean salad overflowing with flavors and redolent of a summer garden, a perfect match for all kinds of main dishes. For more information on toasting sunflower seeds in the air fryer, see page 19. This recipe can be easily doubled (see page 14).

- 1 pound green beans, trimmed and halved
- 2 teaspoons extra-virgin olive oil, divided
- ⅛ teaspoon table salt
- ⅛ teaspoon pepper
- ½ cup torn fresh basil
- ⅓ cup oil-packed sun-dried tomatoes, rinsed, patted dry, and chopped
- 1 tablespoon lemon juice
- 2 ounces goat cheese, crumbled (½ cup)
- ¼ cup roasted sunflower seeds

1 Toss green beans with 1 teaspoon oil, salt, and pepper in bowl; transfer to air-fryer basket. Place basket into air fryer and set temperature to 400 degrees. Cook green beans until crisp-tender, 12 to 15 minutes, tossing halfway through cooking.

2 Toss green beans with remaining 1 teaspoon oil, basil, sun-dried tomatoes, and lemon juice in large bowl. Season with salt and pepper to taste. Transfer to serving dish and sprinkle with goat cheese and sunflower seeds. Serve.

ROASTED MUSHROOMS WITH SHALLOT AND THYME

Serves 2

COOK TIME 10 minutes   **TOTAL TIME** 25 minutes

why this recipe works We started with the classic combination of woodsy mushrooms, aromatic shallot, and earthy thyme. Air-frying allowed us to use less oil and prevented the mushrooms from losing too much liquid, as they might in a skillet. These tender roasted mushrooms pair beautifully with beef, fish, and tofu; can be served with other sides such as potatoes; and make a great topping for salads or bruschetta. To prevent the shallot from burning, we gave the mushrooms a head start, roasting them until they were softened and then adding the shallot for the final few minutes, until the mushrooms were well browned (but still juicy) and the shallot was softened and lightly browned. Meanwhile, we made an aromatic dressing to toss the cooked mushroom mixture in. Use a single variety of mush-room or a combination. Stem and halve portobello mushrooms and cut into ½-inch pieces. Trim white or cremini mushrooms; quarter them if they're large or medium or halve them if they're small. Tear trimmed oyster mushrooms into 1- to 1½-inch pieces. Stem shiitake mushrooms; quarter large caps and halve small caps. Cut trimmed maitake (hen of the woods) mush-rooms into 1- to 1½-inch pieces. This recipe can be easily doubled (see page 14).

1   pound mushrooms

2   tablespoons extra-virgin olive oil, divided

¼   teaspoon table salt, divided

⅛   teaspoon pepper

1   shallot, sliced thin

2   teaspoons lemon juice

2   teaspoons minced fresh thyme, rosemary, oregano, marjoram, or sage

1 Toss mushrooms with 1 tablespoon oil, ⅛ teaspoon salt, and pepper in large bowl; arrange in even layer in air-fryer basket. Place basket into air fryer and set temperature to 400 degrees. Cook until mushrooms are softened, 8 to 12 minutes, tossing halfway through cooking.

2 Stir shallot into mushrooms. Return basket to air fryer and cook until mushrooms are well browned, 2 to 4 minutes.

3 Whisk lemon juice, thyme, remaining 1 tablespoon oil, and remaining ⅛ teaspoon salt together in now-empty bowl. Add mushroom mixture and toss to coat. Season with salt and pepper to taste. Serve.

ROASTED BELL PEPPER SALAD WITH MOZZARELLA AND BASIL

Serves 2

COOK TIME 25 minutes   **TOTAL TIME** 1 hour

why this recipe works Roasting bell peppers on the grill or over a direct flame can be a pain: Unevenly charred, black skin sticks to everything and can be frustrating to peel off. But jarred roasted peppers, despite their convenience, don't have the same fresh flavor or meaty texture. So we were thrilled to find that the air fryer does a beautiful job of roasting bell peppers. Twenty-five minutes after tucking four small bell peppers snugly on their sides in the air-fryer basket, we had well-browned, wrinkled skin and tender flesh. After a quick steam, the skin peeled off cleanly. To showcase our sweet, meaty roasted peppers, we paired them with a balsamic dressing, creamy fresh mozzarella, fragrant basil, and toasted pine nuts for a deeply flavored salad. Choose a mix of red, yellow, and orange bell peppers for the most attractive presentation. Be sure to buy peppers that will fit comfortably on their sides in your air fryer. For more information on toasting nuts in the air fryer, see page 19.

- 4 small bell peppers (red, orange, and/or yellow)
- 2 tablespoons extra-virgin olive oil
- 1 tablespoon balsamic vinegar
- 1 garlic clove, minced
- ⅛ teaspoon table salt
- ⅛ teaspoon pepper
- 2 ounces fresh mozzarella cheese, torn into 1-inch pieces
- 2 tablespoons torn fresh basil
- 1 tablespoon pine nuts, toasted

1 Trim ½ inch from top and bottom of bell peppers. Using paring knife, remove ribs, core, and seeds and discard. Arrange bell peppers in air-fryer basket on their sides. (Bell peppers will fit snugly.) Place basket into air fryer and set temperature to 400 degrees. Cook bell peppers until skins are brown and wrinkled and have collapsed, about 25 minutes, flipping and rotating bell peppers halfway through cooking. Transfer bell peppers to bowl, cover tightly with plastic wrap, and let steam for 10 minutes.

2 Whisk oil, vinegar, garlic, salt, and pepper together in serving dish. Uncover bowl to let bell peppers cool slightly. When cool enough to handle, peel bell peppers and discard skin, then cut bell peppers into 1-inch-wide strips. Add bell peppers and mozzarella to bowl with dressing and toss to coat; season with salt and pepper to taste. Sprinkle with basil and pine nuts. Serve.

ROASTED BELL PEPPER SALAD WITH MANCHEGO AND OLIVES

Substitute sherry vinegar for balsamic vinegar and add 2 teaspoons minced fresh marjoram (or oregano) to dressing in step 2. Substitute 1 ounce shaved Manchego for mozzarella. Substitute ¼ cup sliced pitted green olives for basil. Substitute 2 tablespoons toasted slivered almonds for pine nuts.

BAKED POTATOES

Serves 2

COOK TIME 40 minutes   **TOTAL TIME** 55 minutes

why this recipe works One great advantage of an air fryer is how it untethers you from your oven—no more heating up the house for a small project. Enter baked potatoes: Typically requiring at least an hour of oven time at high heat, simple baked potatoes can become a nuisance on a hot day, or when trying to bake another dish at a different temperature. The air fryer handily solved that problem. With no need to preheat, it took just 40 minutes to bake two fluffy, tender potatoes. Our foolproof method of lightly oiling and salting the outside of the potatoes produced crisp, tasty, well-seasoned skins, and poking holes for steam to escape ensured the centers became fluffy. Top the potatoes as desired or with one of our compound butters. This recipe can be easily doubled (see page 14).

2 russet potatoes (8 ounces each), unpeeled

¼ teaspoon vegetable oil

⅛ teaspoon table salt

1 Lightly prick each potato several times with fork. Rub potatoes with oil and sprinkle with salt. Arrange potatoes in air-fryer basket, spaced evenly apart. Place basket into air fryer and set temperature to 400 degrees. Cook until paring knife inserted into potatoes meets little resistance, 40 to 45 minutes.

2 Transfer potatoes to large plate and, using paring knife, cut 2 slits, forming X, in each potato. Press in at ends of potatoes to push flesh up and out. Season with salt and pepper to taste. Serve.

BLUE CHEESE–PEPPER BUTTER
Mash 1½ tablespoons softened unsalted butter, 1 tablespoon crumbled blue cheese, and ¼ teaspoon pepper together in bowl.

LEMON-THYME BUTTER
Mash 2 tablespoons softened unsalted butter, 1 teaspoon minced fresh thyme, and ¼ teaspoon grated lemon zest and ¼ teaspoon juice together in bowl.

CRISPY BAKED POTATO FANS

Serves 2

COOK TIME 25 minutes　　　　　**TOTAL TIME** 45 minutes

why this recipe works Hasselback potatoes are whole potatoes that are sliced thin almost all the way through to create a cool-looking fanned effect. This impressive potato dish—believed to have originated in Sweden at the Hasselbacken restaurant—is surprisingly easy to prepare. Our air-fried potato fans become extra-crispy on the outside while their interiors remain fluffy and moist. For a lighter take on a classic often loaded with butter, sour cream, cheese, or other rich toppings, we turned to olive oil to help crisp the segments, and we added flavor with aromatic smoked paprika and garlic powder instead. We found that using the right kind of potato was key. The russet, or Idaho, potato was the best choice because of its starchy flesh and creamy texture. Taking the time to rinse the potatoes of surface starch after they were sliced prevented them from sticking together, and trimming off the ends of each potato gave the slices room to fan out. To prevent overcooking or burning our spuds in the heat of the air fryer, we precooked them briefly in the microwave. To ensure that the potatoes fan out evenly, look for uniformly shaped potatoes. Chopsticks or thick skewers provide a foolproof guide for slicing the potato petals without cutting all the way through the potato in step 1.

2 russet potatoes, unpeeled

2 tablespoons extra-virgin olive oil

¼ teaspoon smoked paprika

¼ teaspoon garlic powder

¼ teaspoon table salt

⅛ teaspoon pepper

2 tablespoons minced scallions, fresh chives, fresh dill, and/or fresh parsley

Lemon wedges

1 Cut ¼ inch from bottoms and ends of potatoes. Place 1 chopstick or thick skewer lengthwise on each side of 1 potato, then slice potato crosswise at ¼-inch intervals, stopping ¼ inch from bottom of potato. Repeat with second potato. Rinse potatoes gently under running water, let drain, and transfer to plate. Microwave until slightly tender when squeezed gently, 6 to 12 minutes, flipping potatoes halfway through cooking.

2 Combine oil, paprika, garlic powder, salt, and pepper in bowl. Brush potatoes with portion of oil mixture, then drizzle remaining oil in between slices. Arrange potatoes cut side up in air-fryer basket, spaced evenly apart. Place basket into air fryer and set temperature to 400 degrees. Cook until potato skins are crisp and golden brown and potato interiors register 205 degrees, 25 to 30 minutes. Sprinkle potatoes with scallions and serve with lemon wedges.

CRISPY SMASHED POTATOES

Serves 2 to 4

COOK TIME 40 minutes   **TOTAL TIME** 1 hour

why this recipe works Smashed potatoes offer the best of both worlds: the crackling crust of roast potatoes and a creamy mashed potato–like interior. Traditionally, the potatoes are boiled and then flattened and crisped in a hot pan of oil. However, the air fryer crisped the smashed potatoes even more thoroughly, as the hot air made its way into the broken potatoes' many cracks and crevices to produce an intensely crackly exterior (the air fryer also required less oil). Better still, we could skip the boiling and steam the potatoes in a foil packet in the air fryer, which not only simplified the process but intensified the potatoes' earthy flavor. We chose red potatoes for their moist texture and thin skin. After steaming them until soft, we used a baking sheet to press on all of the potatoes at once, cracking and flattening them to ½ inch. (A potato masher can also be used.) After tossing them with olive oil, salt, pepper, and fresh thyme, we returned them to the air fryer, where they crisped to perfection. We found that not stirring or shaking the basket during the final 15 minutes helped produce an even more pronounced crunchy outer layer. Use small red potatoes measuring no larger than 1½ inches in diameter.

1½ pounds small red potatoes, unpeeled

2 tablespoons extra-virgin olive oil

1 teaspoon chopped fresh thyme

½ teaspoon table salt

⅛ teaspoon pepper

1 Arrange potatoes in center of large sheet of aluminum foil and lift sides to form bowl. Pour ¾ cup water over potatoes and crimp foil tightly to seal. Place foil packet in air-fryer basket, place basket into air fryer, and set temperature to 400 degrees. Cook until paring knife inserted into potatoes meets little resistance (poke through foil to test), 25 to 30 minutes.

2 Carefully open foil packet, allowing steam to escape away from you, and let cool slightly. Arrange potatoes in single layer on cutting board; discard foil. Place baking sheet on top of potatoes and press down firmly on baking sheet, flattening potatoes to ½-inch thickness. Transfer smashed potatoes to large bowl; drizzle with oil and sprinkle with thyme, salt, and pepper. Toss until well combined and most potatoes have broken apart into chunks.

3 Return potatoes to air fryer and cook until well browned and crispy (do not stir or shake during cooking), 15 to 20 minutes. Season with salt and pepper to taste. Serve.

CRISPY SMASHED POTATOES WITH GARLIC AND DILL

Substitute chopped fresh dill for thyme. Add ½ teaspoon garlic powder to potatoes with oil in step 2.

FRENCH FRIES

Serves 2 to 4

COOK TIME 28 minutes   **TOTAL TIME** 1 hour

why this recipe works After years of turning out fries of every stripe, we know a good fry when we taste one: the browned, crisp exterior, the fluffy center. And we know that achieving this ideal requires a few tricks, typically a presoak and a two-part frying. But who can argue with the promise of fries cooked with minimal effort or oil? So, we set out to create the ideal air-fryer french fry. Some recipes called for hours of prework. Others had you throw the potatoes in the basket and cross your fingers. Seventy pounds of potatoes later, we learned that air-fryer fries require the same tricks as their deep-fried cousins: soaking, a low-temp fry to par-cook the spuds, and a high-temp fry to crisp them. But we found shortcuts: A rinse and a 10-minute soak in hot water was sufficient. Cutting thick fries prevented hollow centers and yielded a great crispy-fluffy ratio. Still, our fries tasted lean. A second toss in a bit of oil and salt in between fryings proved the solution, producing crisp, perfectly seasoned results. Excellent homemade fries had never been easier. Frequently tossing the potatoes ensured the most even cooking and the best browning. We found tossing the fries in a bowl, rather than in the basket, yielded the best results and the fewest broken fries. Do not clean out the tossing bowl while you are cooking; the residual oil helps the crisping process. Serve with Sriracha Dipping Sauce.

1½   pounds russet   2 tablespoons   ½   teaspoon table salt
     potatoes, peeled   vegetable oil,
                            divided

1 Cut potatoes lengthwise into ½-inch-thick planks. Stack 3 or 4 planks and cut into ½-inch-thick sticks; repeat with remaining planks.

2 Submerge potatoes in large bowl of water and rinse to remove excess starch. Drain potatoes and repeat process as needed until water remains clear. Cover potatoes with hot tap water and let sit for 10 minutes. Drain potatoes, transfer to paper towel–lined rimmed baking sheet, and thoroughly pat dry.

3 Toss potatoes with 1 tablespoon oil in clean, dry bowl, then transfer to air-fryer basket. Place basket into air fryer, set temperature to 350 degrees, and cook for 8 minutes. Transfer potatoes to now-empty bowl and toss gently to redistribute. Return potatoes to air fryer and cook until softened and potatoes have turned from white to blond (potatoes may be spotty brown at tips), 5 to 10 minutes.

4 Transfer potatoes to now-empty bowl and toss with remaining 1 tablespoon oil and salt. Return potatoes to air fryer, increase temperature to 400 degrees, and cook until golden brown and crisp, 15 to 20 minutes, tossing gently in bowl to redistribute every 5 minutes. Transfer fries to large plate and season with salt and pepper to taste. Serve immediately.

SRIRACHA DIPPING SAUCE
Whisk ¼ cup mayonnaise, 1 tablespoon sriracha, 1 tablespoon lime juice, 1½ teaspoons grated fresh ginger, and ⅛ teaspoon soy sauce together in bowl.

SHOESTRING FRIES

Serves 2

COOK TIME 15 minutes   **TOTAL TIME** 45 minutes

why this recipe works In the realm of fries, the flavor of shoestring fries is hard to beat. Their thinner shape allows for more of our favorite part—the crunch. Instead of cutting them by hand, we used a spiralizer to quickly cut potatoes into thin, even strings. Then we cut them into manageable 4-inch lengths. This was followed by rinsing to remove excess starch and a thorough drying with paper towels. We coated the fries with just 2 tablespoons of oil, which made them perfectly golden while still maintaining a dry, crisp exterior. To mix up the flavor, try one of our seasoning variations. Serve these fries with your favorite dipping sauce. We found that frequently tossing the potatoes ensured the most even cooking and the best browning. You will need a spiralizer with a ¼-inch (6mm) noodle attachment for this recipe.

1 pound russet potatoes, unpeeled	2 tablespoons vegetable oil	¼ teaspoon table salt ⅛ teaspoon pepper

1 Use chef's knife to trim off ends of potatoes. Using spiralizer fitted with ¼-inch (6mm) noodle attachment, cut potatoes into ribbons, cutting ribbons into 4-inch lengths with kitchen shears as you spiralize. Submerge potatoes in large bowl of water and rinse to remove excess starch. Drain potatoes and repeat process as needed until water remains clear. Drain potatoes, transfer to paper towel–lined rimmed baking sheet, and thoroughly pat dry.

2 Toss potatoes with oil, salt, and pepper. Arrange potatoes in even layer in air-fryer basket. Place basket into air fryer and set temperature to 350 degrees. Cook for 15 to 20 minutes, using tongs to toss gently and separate potatoes every 5 minutes to prevent sticking. Season with salt and pepper to taste, and serve.

SHOESTRING FRIES WITH ROSEMARY AND LEMON ZEST

Sprinkle 1 teaspoon minced fresh rosemary over potatoes and toss to combine before final 5 minutes of cooking. Before serving, toss fries with 1 teaspoon grated lemon zest.

SHOESTRING FRIES WITH CORIANDER AND DILL

Sprinkle 1 teaspoon ground coriander and ½ teaspoon pepper over potatoes and toss to combine before final 5 minutes of cooking. Before serving, toss fries with 1 teaspoon minced fresh dill.

ROASTED SWEET POTATO WEDGES

Serves 2

COOK TIME 20 minutes   **TOTAL TIME** 30 minutes

why this recipe works These sweet potato wedges are as indulgent to eat as sweet potato fries but a healthier option because they're made in the air fryer with only a little oil and no deep frying. Sweet potatoes release a sweet, syrupy liquid as they cook, and this turned the wedges mushy. The key was to leave the sweet potatoes unpeeled and cut them into wide wedges so that they would hold their shape while roasting. This worked well because the skins are delicious, and they're also rich in vitamins and fiber. Cut thinner, the wedges burned before their interiors had the chance to cook through. Since sweet potatoes have plenty of flavor on their own, we limited the seasoning to salt, pepper, and a little olive oil to encourage browning. After about 20 minutes in the air fryer, the sweet potatoes were perfectly creamy and sweet on the inside, with plenty of crunch on the outside. We prefer to use small potatoes, about 8 ounces each, because this ensures that the wedges fit more uniformly in the air-fryer basket; they should be of similar size so that they cook at the same rate. Be sure to scrub and dry the whole potatoes thoroughly before cutting them into wedges and tossing them with the oil, salt, and pepper.

1 pound small sweet potatoes (8 ounces each), unpeeled, cut lengthwise into 1½-inch wedges

1 tablespoon extra-virgin olive oil

¼ teaspoon table salt

¼ teaspoon pepper

Toss all ingredients together in bowl and arrange in even layer in air-fryer basket. Place basket into air fryer and set temperature to 350 degrees. Cook until lightly browned and tender, 20 to 25 minutes, tossing halfway through cooking. Serve.

MAPLE-GLAZED ACORN SQUASH

Serves 2 to 4

COOK TIME 19 minutes   **TOTAL TIME** 35 minutes

why this recipe works Acorn squash and the air fryer are a winning combination: The squash's petite size makes it easy to fit an entire squash inside the basket. To add to its appeal, the squash doesn't need to be peeled—its dark-green skin is edible and provides a visually stunning contrast to its bright orange flesh—and it slices easily into attractive uniform wedges. The squash takes well to roasting, and in the air fryer it became tender and caramelized. To dress it up, we turned to another winning combination: a glaze of maple syrup and butter, which complemented the drier, savory flesh of the squash. We brushed the mixture, spiced with black pepper and cayenne, on squash wedges before roasting them in the air fryer flesh side up to capture the glaze. Because they overlapped slightly, we rotated the wedges halfway through cooking to ensure evenly browned flesh, then brushed on additional glaze before serving. The wedges were done in just over half an hour, ready to complement a variety of main courses.

- 2 tablespoons maple syrup
- 2 tablespoons unsalted butter
- ½ teaspoon table salt
- ¼ teaspoon pepper
- Pinch cayenne pepper
- 1 acorn squash (1½ pounds), halved pole to pole and seeded
- 2 teaspoons fresh thyme leaves

1 Microwave maple syrup, butter, salt, pepper, and cayenne in bowl at 50 percent power until butter is melted, about 1 minute, stirring occasionally.

2 Cut each squash half into 4 wedges. Brush flesh of squash wedges with half of syrup mixture. Arrange squash flesh side up in air-fryer basket (squash may overlap slightly). Place basket into air fryer and set temperature to 400 degrees. Cook squash until deep golden brown and tender, 19 to 24 minutes, rotating wedges halfway through cooking.

3 Transfer squash to serving platter, drizzle with remaining syrup mixture, and sprinkle with thyme. Season with salt and pepper to taste. Serve.

ROASTED DELICATA SQUASH

Serves 2

COOK TIME 18 minutes	**TOTAL TIME** 30 minutes

why this recipe works To have another squash side dish in your back pocket, consider delicata. The air fryer enhanced its natural sweetness and also added toastiness. The air fryer sped up the cooking process, too, and tossing the unpeeled squash with a little oil aided in browning. Two sauces—a spicy maple syrup and a goat cheese and chive sauce—bring heat or add richness to the roasted squash. Delicata have thin, edible skin that needn't be removed; simply use a vegetable peeler to pare away any tough brown blemishes.

1 delicata squash (12 to 16 ounces), ends trimmed, halved lengthwise, seeded, and sliced crosswise ½ inch thick

1 tablespoon extra-virgin olive oil

¼ teaspoon table salt

1 tablespoon minced fresh parsley

Toss squash with oil and salt in bowl; arrange in even layer in air-fryer basket. Place basket into air fryer and set temperature to 350 degrees. Cook until squash is tender and golden brown, 18 to 20 minutes, tossing halfway through cooking. Transfer squash to serving platter, sprinkle with parsley, and serve.

SPICY MAPLE SYRUP

We prefer vinegary Frank's RedHot Original Cayenne Pepper Sauce here. Do not substitute a thick hot sauce, such as sriracha; it will make the syrup too thick to drizzle.

Reduce salt to ⅛ teaspoon. Stir 2 tablespoons maple syrup and 1 tablespoon hot sauce together in medium bowl. Microwave until mixture comes to boil, about 30 seconds. Continue to microwave in 20-second intervals until mixture is reduced to 2 tablespoons, about 1 minute. Let cool for 10 minutes. Drizzle syrup over squash before serving.

GOAT CHEESE AND CHIVE SAUCE

Whisk ¼ cup crumbled goat cheese, 2 tablespoons milk, 2 teaspoons minced fresh chives, ¼ teaspoon grated lemon zest, and ½ teaspoon lemon juice in bowl until smooth. Add up to 1 tablespoon more milk, 1 teaspoon at a time, as needed to create sauce that is thick but pourable. Season with salt and pepper to taste. Let sit for 10 minutes. Drizzle sauce over squash before serving.

ZUCCHINI FRIES

Serves 2 to 4

COOK TIME 10 minutes   **TOTAL TIME** 45 minutes

why this recipe works As summer's bounty of zucchini rolls in, being able to whip up a quick batch of these crispy, salty zucchini fries—a refreshing alternative to their starchier cousins—may be reason enough to keep your air fryer within arm's reach. A combination of toasted panko bread crumbs and grated Parmesan gave us a delightfully crackly and delicate exterior. To adhere the panko mixture to the zucchini, we used a combination of flour and egg seasoned with oregano, salt, and pepper. Zucchini is notoriously watery, so preventing moisture from sogging out the crust was key. Our solution: We cut the zucchini into spears and used a vegetable peeler to quickly remove the watery inner seed pulp. Arranging the fries in a "Lincoln Log" pattern in the basket (see page 13) allowed for maximum air circulation. We love these zucchini fries with a simple, bright sauce of yogurt and lemon, but feel free to substitute your favorite marinara sauce. This recipe works best with a single medium zucchini, but larger or smaller zucchini can be used; simply cut the zucchini into ½ by 4-inch sticks (after removing the seeds).

- 1 zucchini (8 ounces), quartered lengthwise
- ¾ cup panko bread crumbs
- 2 tablespoons extra-virgin olive oil
- 1 ounce Parmesan cheese, grated (½ cup)
- 1 large egg
- 1 tablespoon all-purpose flour
- ½ teaspoon dried oregano
- ½ teaspoon table salt, divided
- ¼ teaspoon pepper, divided
- ½ cup plain yogurt
- ½ teaspoon grated lemon zest plus 1 tablespoon juice

1 Using vegetable peeler, shave seeds from inner portion of each zucchini quarter. Halve each quarter lengthwise, then cut in half crosswise. (You should have 16 pieces.)

2 Toss panko with oil in bowl until evenly coated. Microwave, stirring frequently, until light golden brown, 1 to 3 minutes. Transfer to shallow dish, let cool slightly, then stir in Parmesan. Whisk egg, flour, oregano, ¼ teaspoon salt, and ⅛ teaspoon pepper together in second shallow dish. Working with several pieces of zucchini at a time, dredge in egg mixture, letting excess drip off, then coat with panko mixture, pressing gently to adhere; transfer to large plate.

3 Lightly spray bottom of air-fryer basket with vegetable oil spray. Arrange half of zucchini pieces in prepared basket, spaced evenly apart. Arrange remaining zucchini pieces on top, perpendicular to first layer. Place basket into air fryer and set temperature to 400 degrees. Cook until zucchini is tender and crisp, 10 to 12 minutes, gently shaking basket to loosen pieces halfway through cooking.

4 Meanwhile, whisk yogurt, lemon zest and juice, remaining ¼ teaspoon salt, and remaining ⅛ teaspoon pepper together in small bowl. Transfer zucchini to serving platter and season with salt and pepper to taste. Serve with yogurt sauce.

STUFFED PORTOBELLO MUSHROOMS WITH KALE, CORN, AND PICKLED JALAPEÑOS

Serves 2

COOK TIME 13 minutes	**TOTAL TIME** 45 minutes

why this recipe works For a vegetable main that meat eaters and vegetarians alike would enjoy, we packed meaty portobellos with a combination of earthy kale, smoky fire-roasted corn, spicy jalapeños, and creamy yogurt. We started by using a spoon to gently scrape off the feathery dark gills from the underside of each portobello cap, which resulted in a pleasant, smooth texture. Next, we roasted the mushrooms until they were tender and then filled them with the vegetable goodness that complemented their savoriness. Finally, we topped them with crunchy panko bread crumbs and heated the dish through. These mushrooms are satisfying and flavorful, especially when served with the sauce that echoes the ingredients in the filling. If fire-roasted corn is unavailable, substitute traditional frozen corn; avoid canned corn here. For a spicier filling, use the greater amount of jalapeños.

7 tablespoons plain Greek yogurt, divided

2 teaspoons lime juice, plus lime wedges for serving

1 teaspoon chili powder, divided

¼ teaspoon honey

⅜ teaspoon table salt, divided

4 portobello mushroom caps (4 to 5 inches in diameter), gills removed

Olive oil spray

¼ cup panko bread crumbs

1 teaspoon plus 2 tablespoons extra-virgin olive oil, divided

2 cups frozen chopped kale or spinach, thawed and squeezed dry

1 cup frozen fire-roasted corn, thawed

2–4 tablespoons minced jarred jalapeños

1 Whisk ¼ cup yogurt, lime juice, ½ teaspoon chili powder, honey, and ⅛ teaspoon salt together in bowl. Season with salt and pepper to taste; set aside for serving.

2 Lightly spray mushrooms with oil spray and arrange gill side down in air-fryer basket. (Mushrooms will overlap and basket will seem quite full at first; mushrooms will shrink down substantially while cooking.) Place basket into air fryer and set temperature to 400 degrees. Cook until mushrooms are tender, 8 to 10 minutes.

3 Toss panko with 1 teaspoon oil in small bowl until evenly coated. Microwave, stirring frequently, until light golden brown, 1 to 3 minutes. Whisk remaining 3 tablespoons yogurt, remaining ½ teaspoon chili powder, remaining ¼ teaspoon salt, and remaining 2 tablespoons oil together in large bowl. Stir in kale, corn, and jalapeños.

4 Transfer mushrooms to cutting board, gill side up; pat dry with paper towels. Distribute filling evenly among mushrooms and sprinkle with panko, pressing gently to adhere. Arrange mushrooms in now-empty basket; place basket into air fryer; and cook until mushrooms are heated through, 5 to 7 minutes. Serve with sauce and lime wedges.

WHITE BEAN AND MUSHROOM GRATIN

Serves 2

COOK TIME 23 minutes	TOTAL TIME 45 minutes

why this recipe works A gratin is a dish of seasoned potatoes or other vegetables topped with bread crumbs or cheese and baked until the crust is crisp and golden. For our sumptuous gratin sized for two, we used creamy white beans, meaty cremini mushrooms, and zucchini flavored with savory tomato paste, soy sauce, and thyme. To make our vegetable gratin hearty, we opted to use bread cubes instead of bread crumbs. The larger chunks made the topping a blend of chewy and toasty. We used a pan to hold the ingredients so that the liquid could flavor the vegetables and create a sauce, which we thickened with a combination of flour and the starchy canned bean liquid. The sauce's flavor came from browning the mushrooms and shallot before assembling the gratin. We topped the gratin with lightly seasoned and oiled bread cubes and baked it at a low temperature. The lower portion of the bread merged with the vegetables, creating a pleasantly soft texture, while the upper portion became golden brown and crisp. You will need a 6-inch round nonstick or silicone cake pan for this recipe; before starting this recipe, confirm your air fryer allows enough space for the pan.

- 8 ounces cremini mushrooms, trimmed and sliced ½ inch thick
- 1 large shallot, sliced thin
- 2 tablespoons extra-virgin olive oil, divided, plus extra for drizzling
- 1 tablespoon tomato paste
- 1½ teaspoons all-purpose flour
- 1 (15-ounce) can cannellini or great northern beans, undrained
- 1 small zucchini, cut into ½-inch pieces
- 2 tablespoons water
- 1 teaspoon soy sauce
- 1 teaspoon minced fresh thyme or ¼ teaspoon dried
- ¼ teaspoon pepper
- 1 slice rustic whole-grain bread, cut into ½-inch pieces (1 cup)
- 1 tablespoon minced fresh parsley

1 Toss mushrooms, shallot, 1 tablespoon oil, tomato paste, and flour together in large bowl; transfer to air-fryer basket. Place basket into air fryer and set temperature to 400 degrees. Cook until mushrooms are tender and lightly browned, 8 to 10 minutes, tossing halfway through cooking.

2 Transfer vegetables to now-empty bowl. Add beans and their liquid, zucchini, water, soy sauce, thyme, and pepper and toss to combine. Transfer vegetable mixture to 6-inch round nonstick or silicone cake pan and spread into even layer. Toss bread with remaining 1 tablespoon oil in now-empty bowl; spread evenly over vegetable mixture.

3 Place pan in air-fryer basket and place basket into air fryer. Set temperature to 300 degrees and cook until sauce is bubbling around edges and topping is golden brown, 15 to 20 minutes. Remove pan from basket and let cool slightly. Sprinkle with parsley and drizzle with extra oil. Serve.

ROASTED BUTTERNUT SQUASH SALAD WITH ZA'ATAR AND HALLOUMI

Serves 2

COOK TIME 20 minutes   **TOTAL TIME** 45 minutes

why this recipe works For a main-dish vegetarian salad, we air-fried butternut squash, making it golden brown and tender in less than half the time it would take in a conventional oven. Roasting enhanced the squash's sweetness; za'atar, a Middle Eastern blend that often contains dried thyme, sumac, and sesame seeds, added woodsy notes. We paired the squash with halloumi, a firm, salty Cypriot cheese that's traditionally grilled but crisps up beautifully in the air fryer. If you can't find halloumi, you can finish the dish with crumbled feta (but skip cooking the cheese in step 2). A lemon-honey dressing gave the salad brightness, and pepitas added protein and crunch. This recipe can be easily doubled (see page 14).

1 small shallot, minced	4 teaspoons extra-virgin olive oil, divided	2 teaspoons honey
1 teaspoon grated lemon zest plus 2 tablespoons juice	2 teaspoons za'atar	¼ teaspoon pepper
2 pounds butternut squash, peeled, seeded, and cut into 1-inch pieces (6 cups)	½ teaspoon table salt	2 ounces (2 cups) baby arugula
	Olive oil spray	¼ cup roasted, unsalted pepitas
	2 ounces halloumi cheese, cut into ½-inch pieces and patted dry	2 tablespoons chopped fresh dill

1 Combine shallot and lemon juice in small bowl; set aside. Toss squash with 1 teaspoon oil, za'atar, and salt in large bowl. Arrange squash in even layer in air-fryer basket. Place basket into air fryer; set temperature to 400 degrees; and cook until squash is just tender and browned in spots, 16 to 22 minutes, tossing twice during cooking.

2 Return squash to large bowl; set aside. Lightly spray bottom of now-empty basket with oil spray, scatter halloumi in basket, and lightly spray halloumi with oil spray. Return basket to fryer and cook until halloumi is browned around edges, 4 to 6 minutes.

3 Whisk honey, pepper, lemon zest, and remaining 1 tablespoon oil into shallot mixture. Add to squash and toss to coat. Add arugula, pepitas, and dill and toss to combine. Season with salt and pepper to taste. Transfer to serving platter, top with halloumi, and serve.

RAMEN NOODLE BOWL WITH EGGPLANT AND FIVE-SPICE TOFU

Serves 2

COOK TIME 20 minutes   **TOTAL TIME** 45 minutes

why this recipe works Inspired by ramen, we wanted to develop a satisfying vegetarian noodle bowl mounded high with eggplant and crispy tofu. This was not a dish that screamed air fryer, but we used it to perfectly cook the eggplant and fry the tofu, leaving our hands free to whisk together a dressing and soak dried ramen noodles in boiling water. Eggplant batons coated with soy sauce, mirin, and toasted sesame oil became appetizingly silky in the air fryer. Draining our tofu on paper towels removed excess moisture so that the exterior of the cubes could crisp up, and tossing them with cornmeal (instead of cornstarch) gave them added crunch. Five-spice powder and soy sauce brought flavor to the dish, as did the rice vinegar, mirin, and ginger dressing. Despite the package instructions, the noodles need only a quick soak in boiling water to become tender. The large bowl in step 2 is reused several times in this recipe; there is no need to clean it. This recipe can be easily doubled (see page 14).

7 ounces firm or extra-firm tofu, cut into 1-inch pieces

1 eggplant (1 pound)

2 tablespoons mirin, divided

1 tablespoon soy sauce, divided

1 tablespoon toasted sesame oil, divided

2 teaspoons cornmeal

¾ teaspoon five-spice powder

¼ teaspoon table salt

4 teaspoons unseasoned rice vinegar

2 scallions, white parts minced, green parts sliced thin on bias

1 teaspoon grated fresh ginger

2 (3-ounce) packages ramen noodles, seasoning packets discarded

2 radishes, sliced thin

1 Spread tofu on paper towel–lined plate, let drain for 20 minutes, then press dry gently with paper towels.

2 Meanwhile, slice eggplant lengthwise into ¾-inch-thick planks. Halve each plank crosswise, then cut lengthwise into ¾-inch-wide strips. Whisk 1 tablespoon mirin, 1 teaspoon soy sauce, and 1 teaspoon oil together in large bowl. Add eggplant and toss to coat; transfer to air-fryer basket. Place basket into air fryer and set temperature to 400 degrees. Cook until eggplant is softened and lightly browned, 10 to 15 minutes, tossing halfway through cooking.

3 Transfer eggplant to plate; set aside. Toss tofu with cornmeal, five-spice powder, salt, and 1 teaspoon oil in now-empty bowl until evenly coated. Arrange tofu in even layer in now-empty basket. Return basket to air fryer and cook until tofu is crisp and lightly browned, 10 to 15 minutes, tossing halfway through cooking.

4 Meanwhile, whisk vinegar, 1 tablespoon water, scallion whites, ginger, remaining 1 tablespoon mirin, remaining 2 teaspoons soy sauce, and remaining 1 teaspoon oil together in small bowl. Place ramen in again-empty large bowl; cover with boiling water; and let sit until softened, about 5 minutes, stirring occasionally to separate noodles.

5 Drain noodles thoroughly and return to large bowl. Add dressing and toss to coat. Divide noodles between 2 serving bowls and top with any remaining dressing in bowl, eggplant, tofu, and radishes. Sprinkle with scallion greens and serve.

MAKE-AHEAD LENTIL AND MUSHROOM BURGERS

Makes 6 patties

COOK TIME 10 minutes   **TOTAL TIME** 45 minutes

why this recipe works The complex flavor and satisfying texture of this vegetarian burger is well worth the prep. Using the air fryer to cook the patties meant that they were ready from fresh or frozen in just 10 minutes. An earthy mix of canned lentils, bulgur, and panko paired with shallot and celery gave our burgers a flavorful, hearty meat-free base. Cremini mushrooms and a surprising addition—chopped cashews—created rich meatiness. Chopping everything in the food processor made for a cohesive and even-textured mix, and olive oil provided fat to bind the patties. Microwaving the mixture helped soften the bulgur and allowed the flavors to meld. Look for medium-grind bulgur (labeled "#2"), which is roughly the size of mustard seeds. Avoid coarsely ground bulgur; it will not cook through in time. The number of patties you can cook at one time will depend on the size of your air fryer. Serve with your favorite toppings and Roasted Sweet Potato Wedges (page 228), if desired. You can use your air fryer to toast the buns; see page 19 for more information.

8 ounces cremini or white mushrooms, trimmed and quartered

½ cup raw cashews

1 celery rib, cut into 1-inch pieces

1 shallot, quartered

½ cup medium-grind bulgur

¼ cup water

3 tablespoons extra-virgin olive oil

½ teaspoon table salt

1 (15-ounce) can brown lentils, rinsed

½ cup panko bread crumbs

1–6 slices deli cheese (optional)

1–6 hamburger buns, toasted, if desired

1 Pulse mushrooms, cashews, celery, and shallot in food processor until finely chopped, about 10 pulses, scraping down sides of bowl as needed. Transfer vegetables to large bowl and stir in bulgur, water, oil, and salt. Microwave, stirring occasionally, until bulgur is softened and most of liquid has been absorbed, about 6 minutes. Let cool slightly.

2 Lightly spray bottom of air-fryer basket with vegetable oil spray. Vigorously stir lentils and panko into vegetable-bulgur mixture until well combined and mixture forms cohesive mass. Using your lightly moistened hands, divide mixture into 6 equal portions (about ½ cup each), then tightly pack each portion into ½-inch-thick patty.

3 Space up to 4 patties at least ½ inch apart in prepared basket. Place basket into air fryer and set temperature to 400 degrees. Cook until patties are golden brown and crisp, 10 to 15 minutes. Turn off air fryer. Top each burger with 1 slice cheese, if using; let sit in warm air fryer until melted, about 1 minute. Serve burgers on buns.

4 Evenly space any remaining patties on parchment paper–lined rimmed baking sheet and freeze until firm, about 1 hour. Stack patties between pieces of parchment, wrap in plastic wrap, and place in zipper-lock freezer bag. Patties can be frozen for up to 1 month. Cook frozen patties as directed; do not thaw.

MAKE-AHEAD LENTIL AND MUSHROOM BURGERS WITH RADICCHIO AND PEAR SALAD

The radicchio and pear salad makes enough for two burgers; it can be easily doubled or tripled.

Whisk 2 teaspoons oil, 1 teaspoon Dijon mustard, 1 teaspoon honey, ⅛ teaspoon table salt, and ⅛ teaspoon pepper in separate large bowl. Add 1 cup shredded radicchio and ½ ripe but firm pear, cored and cut into 2-inch-long matchsticks, and toss until evenly coated. Omit deli cheese. Spread 2 tablespoons softened goat cheese on each bun top. Serve burgers on buns, topped with radicchio and pear salad.

MAKE-AHEAD PHYLLO HAND PIES WITH FENNEL, OLIVE, AND GOAT CHEESE FILLING

Makes 15 hand pies

COOK TIME 13 minutes (10 minutes from frozen)	**TOTAL TIME** 1 hour

why this recipe works While testing making baked goods in the air fryer, we discovered that even finicky phyllo dough, the paper-thin dough used throughout the eastern Mediterranean, is suited to the air fryer's dry heat. Phyllo made the perfect parcel for little savory hand pies. Baking in a conventional oven tends to yield blond results, but our pies took on a deep golden color and turned supercrisp in the air fryer. Store-bought phyllo made it dead simple to fill, fold, and bake these triangles packed with browned fennel, meaty olives, and tangy goat cheese. Phyllo dough is also available in larger 18 by 14-inch sheets; if using, cut them in half to make 14 by 9-inch sheets. Don't thaw the phyllo in the microwave; let it sit in the refrigerator overnight or on the counter for 4 to 5 hours. The number of hand pies you can cook at one time will depend on the size of your air fryer. This recipe can be easily doubled (see page 14).

Filling

- 1 fennel bulb, stalks discarded, bulb halved, cored, and sliced thin
- 1 tablespoon extra-virgin olive oil
- ⅛ teaspoon table salt
- ¼ teaspoon pepper
- ¼ cup pitted kalamata olives, chopped fine
- 2 teaspoons grated lemon zest plus 1 tablespoon juice
- ½ teaspoon dried oregano
- 4 ounces goat cheese, crumbled (1 cup)

Hand Pies

- 10 (14 by 9-inch) phyllo sheets, thawed

  Olive oil spray

1 for the filling Toss fennel with oil, salt, and pepper and arrange in even layer in air-fryer basket. Set temperature to 350 degrees and cook until softened and lightly browned, 6 to 8 minutes. Transfer fennel to large bowl and stir in olives, lemon zest and juice, and oregano. Let cool completely, about 10 minutes. Stir in goat cheese gently. (Filling can be refrigerated for up to 24 hours.)

2 for the hand pies Place one phyllo sheet on counter with long side parallel to counter edge, lightly spray with oil spray, then top with second phyllo sheet and lightly spray with oil spray again. Cut phyllo vertically into three 9 by 4⅔-inch strips. Place rounded 1 tablespoon of filling on bottom left-hand corner of each strip. Fold up phyllo to form right-angle triangle, pressing gently on filling as needed to create even layer. Continue folding up and over, as if folding a flag, to end of strip. Press to adhere edges.

3 Lightly spray triangle with oil spray and place seam side down on parchment paper–lined rimmed baking sheet. Repeat with remaining phyllo sheets and filling to make 15 triangles. (Hand pies can be refrigerated for up to 12 hours or frozen and stored in zipper-lock bag for up to 1 month. Do not thaw frozen hand pies before cooking; increase cooking time to 10 to 12 minutes.)

4 Arrange desired number of hand pies in air-fryer basket, spaced at least ½ inch apart. Place basket into air fryer and set temperature to 350 degrees. Bake until hand pies are golden brown, 7 to 9 minutes, flipping halfway through cooking. Serve.

MAKE-AHEAD PHYLLO HAND PIES WITH APPLE, WALNUT, AND BLUE CHEESE FILLING

Combine 1 Granny Smith apple, peeled, cored, halved, and sliced thin; 3 tablespoons raisins; 1 tablespoon extra-virgin olive oil; 1½ teaspoons apple cider vinegar; 1 tablespoon water; ¼ teaspoon table salt; and ¼ teaspoon pepper in bowl. Microwave until apples begin to turn translucent and raisins are plump, about 5 minutes, stirring halfway through microwaving; let cool completely. Fold in ¼ cup chopped toasted walnuts and ½ cup crumbled blue cheese. Substitute apple filling for fennel filling.

HEARTY VEGETABLE HASH WITH GOLDEN YOGURT

Serves 2

| **COOK TIME** 18 minutes | **TOTAL TIME** 35 minutes |

why this recipe works Magic happens when you cook vegetables in an air fryer. In minutes, you have the crisped exteriors, tender interiors, and caramelized deliciousness you usually associate with oven roasting. We transformed that roasted veggie concept into a quick, flavorful hash you can eat for dinner (or breakfast or lunch). We used hearty sweet potatoes and meaty mushrooms along with shallots, which crisp up nicely in the air fryer. To add some fresh greens, we also incorporated raw baby kale. We tried air frying the kale with the other vegetables, but it burned long before the sweet potatoes and mushrooms were done. Instead, we tossed the warm vegetables with the kale to wilt it. We drizzled a silky-smooth yogurt sauce, flavored with cumin, turmeric, and cilantro, over the hash. A sprinkling of pistachios added some protein and a finishing crunch. For more information on toasting nuts in the air fryer, see page 19. This recipe can be easily doubled (see page 14); if cooking as one batch, increase cooking time to about 45 minutes, stirring twice during cooking.

- 4 teaspoons extra-virgin olive oil, divided
- ¼ teaspoon ground cumin
- ¼ teaspoon ground turmeric
- ¼ cup plain yogurt
- 1 tablespoon minced fresh cilantro
- ½ teaspoon table salt, divided
- 1 pound sweet potatoes, peeled and cut into ½-inch pieces
- 12 ounces cremini mushrooms, trimmed and quartered
- 2 shallots, sliced thin
- ¼ teaspoon pepper
- 2 ounces (2 cups) baby kale
- ¼ cup shelled pistachios, toasted and chopped

1 Combine 1 teaspoon oil, cumin, and turmeric in small bowl and microwave until fragrant, about 1 minute. Stir in yogurt, cilantro, and ¼ teaspoon salt; set aside for serving.

2 Toss potatoes, mushrooms, and shallots with pepper, remaining 1 tablespoon oil, and remaining ¼ teaspoon salt in large bowl; transfer to air-fryer basket. Place basket into air fryer and set temperature to 400 degrees. Cook until vegetables are tender and golden brown, 18 to 20 minutes, stirring halfway through cooking.

3 Return vegetables to now-empty bowl. Add kale and toss gently to combine. Drizzle individual portions with yogurt sauce and sprinkle with pistachios before serving.

SMALL BATCH BAKING

APPLE CRISP

Serves 2

COOK TIME **35 minutes**   TOTAL TIME **1 hour**

why this recipe works Apple crisp is an easy fruit dessert that is made even easier in the air fryer. It marries almost fall-apart fruit with a rich, crisp topping. To start, we tossed pieces of apple with the familiar flavors of cinnamon, sugar, and lemon juice. We like to use Golden Delicous apples for this crisp because they are on the sweeter side and break down to a lush texture. We placed the seasoned apples in a covered ovensafe bowl and cooked them until tender. While the apples cooked, we made a hearty oat topping with chewy rolled oats bringing depth and crunch. After sprinkling the oats over the softened apples and popping the crisp back into the air fryer for 5 minutes, our homey dessert emerged evenly browned and just bubbling. You will need a 3-cup ovensafe bowl for this recipe. Before starting, confirm your air fryer allows enough space for the dish. This recipe can be easily doubled; use a 1½-quart soufflé dish (see page 14) and bake for the same amount of time.

2 **Golden Delicious apples, peeled, cored, and cut into ¾-inch pieces**	2 **teaspoons lemon juice**	2 **tablespoons all-purpose flour**
5 **teaspoons packed brown sugar, divided**	⅛ **teaspoon plus pinch table salt, divided**	1 **tablespoon old-fashioned rolled oats**
	⅛ **teaspoon ground cinnamon**	1 **tablespoon unsalted butter**

1 Toss apples with 2 teaspoons sugar, lemon juice, ⅛ teaspoon salt, and cinnamon in large bowl. Transfer to 3-cup ovensafe bowl and cover tightly with aluminum foil. Place bowl in air-fryer basket. Place basket into air fryer; set temperature to 400 degrees; and bake until apples are tender and begin to collapse, 30 to 35 minutes.

2 Meanwhile, mix flour, oats, remaining 1 tablespoon sugar, and remaining pinch salt together in second bowl. Using your fingers, rub butter into flour mixture until mixture has texture of coarse crumbs. Remove basket from air fryer. Discard foil and scatter topping evenly over apples. Return basket to air fryer and bake until topping is evenly browned and filling is just bubbling at edges, 5 to 7 minutes. Let crisp cool for 5 minutes before serving.

WARM CHOCOLATE FUDGE CAKES

Serves 2

COOK TIME **8 minutes**	TOTAL TIME **35 minutes**

why this recipe works Dense chocolate cakes are a perennial favorite. To create a super-fudgey cake recipe for the air fryer, we started by building a rich, brownie-like batter with an intense chocolate flavor courtesy of bittersweet chocolate. An egg contributed to the cakes' moisture and richness, and a small amount of flour gave the cakes structure and lift. Once we melted the chocolate in the microwave, we whisked all of the other ingredients into the same bowl. It couldn't be easier. You will need two 6-ounce ramekins for this recipe. This recipe can be easily doubled (see page 14).

3 ounces bittersweet chocolate, chopped

¼ cup milk

1 large egg

2 tablespoons canola oil

2 tablespoons packed brown sugar

¼ teaspoon vanilla extract

¼ teaspoon baking powder

⅛ teaspoon baking soda

⅛ teaspoon table salt

6 tablespoons (1¾ ounces) all-purpose flour

1 Microwave chocolate and milk in medium bowl at 50 percent power, stirring occasionally, until mixture is smooth, about 2 minutes. Whisk in egg, oil, sugar, vanilla, baking powder, baking soda, and salt. Gently whisk in flour until combined.

2 Grease two 6-ounce ramekins. Divide batter between prepared ramekins. Place ramekins in air-fryer basket, then place basket into air fryer. Set temperature to 325 degrees and bake until cakes have risen above rim of ramekins and tops are just firm to touch, 8 to 10 minutes. Let cool for 5 minutes before serving.

CHEESECAKE

Serves 8 (makes one 6-inch cake)

COOK TIME 1¼ hours

TOTAL TIME 1¾ hours, plus 4½ hours
cooling, chilling, and standing

why this recipe works With an air fryer, you can cook this fantastic cheesecake in much less time than in an oven. Between the prep, baking, cooling, and chilling steps, most cheesecake recipes require over 8 hours from start to finish. It takes less than half that time in the air fryer; the overall cooking time is less than an hour. Another advantage? There's no water bath to balance precariously while transferring the cheesecake into and out of a hot oven With the air fryer's heat coming directly from above, you can achieve a rich and creamy interior with the golden-brown top that's the mark of a great New York–style cheesecake. Turning off the air fryer and letting the cheesecake sit in there for half an hour ensures a cooked but creamy and rich cheesecake, as the carryover heat is super gentle and mimics a water bath. Running a knife around the edge of the pan before chilling helps to ensure that no cracks appear down the center. It is also important to chill the cheesecake in the pan until fully cool before removing it to ensure that it stays intact. You will need a 6-inch round nonstick or silicone cake pan for this recipe; before starting this recipe, confirm your air fryer allows enough space for the pan.

6 whole graham crackers, broken into 1-inch pieces

3 tablespoons unsalted butter, melted and cooled

1 tablespoon plus ⅔ cup (4⅔ ounces) sugar, divided

½ teaspoon ground cinnamon

Pinch plus ¼ teaspoon table salt, divided

18 ounces cream cheese, softened (use 2 whole packages of cream cheese, plus 2 ounces from a third)

1 teaspoon vanilla extract

¼ cup sour cream

2 large eggs, room temperature

1 Pulse cracker pieces in food processor to fine crumbs, about 20 pulses. Add melted butter, 1 tablespoon sugar, cinnamon, and pinch salt and pulse to combine, about 4 pulses. Sprinkle crumbs into 6-inch springform pan and press into even layer using bottom of dry measuring cup. Place pan into air-fryer basket and place basket into air fryer. Set temperature to 350 degrees and cook until crust sets and turns light golden brown, 2 to 4 minutes. Let cool on wire rack while making filling.

2 Wipe out processor bowl. Process cream cheese, vanilla, remaining ⅔ cup sugar, and remaining ¼ teaspoon salt in now-empty processor until combined, about 15 seconds, scraping down sides of bowl as needed. Add sour cream and eggs and process until just incorporated, about 15 seconds; do not overmix. Pour filling over crust in pan, smooth top, and cover tightly with aluminum foil.

3 Place pan into air-fryer basket and place basket into air fryer. Set temperature to 300 degrees and cook until tiny bubbles form and edges begin to set, 30 to 35 minutes. Remove foil and continue to cook until top is golden brown, edges begin to crack, and center of cake is slightly wobbly when shaken, 15 to 20 minutes. Turn off air fryer and allow cake to continue to sit inside basket for 30 minutes.

4 Transfer pan to wire rack, run small knife around edge of cake, and let cheesecake cool completely in pan, about 1 hour. Cover with plastic wrap and refrigerate until well chilled, at least 3 hours or up to 3 days.

5 About 30 minutes before serving, run small knife around edge of cheesecake and then remove sides of pan and slide cake onto serving platter. Let cheesecake stand at room temperature for about 30 minutes, then cut into wedges and serve.

MAKE-AHEAD FRUIT, NUT, AND OAT SCONES

Makes 10

COOK TIME **10 minutes** (20 minutes from frozen)	TOTAL TIME **45 minutes**

why this recipe works Our tender oat-based scones can be easily baked in the air fryer, even from frozen. We toasted both oats and nuts to enhance their flavor and then added sweet dried fruit. The challenge was temperature: At 400 degrees, the exterior became too dark before the scone baked all the way through, but at 350 degrees the exterior and interior finished cooking at the same time. We developed this recipe with raisins and walnuts, but any dried fruit and nuts will work. The number of scones you can cook at one time will depend on the size of your air fryer. For the variations, extra glaze can be stored in an airtight container for up to a week. For more information on toasting nuts in the air fryer, see page 19.

½ cup whole milk

1 large egg

1½ cups (7½ ounces) all-purpose flour

¼ cup (1¾ ounces) plus 1 tablespoon sugar, divided

2 teaspoons baking powder

½ teaspoon table salt

8 tablespoons unsalted butter, chilled, cut into ½-inch pieces

1¼ cups (3¾ ounces) old-fashioned rolled oats, toasted

½ cup raisins

¼ cup walnuts, toasted and chopped

1 Whisk milk and egg together in bowl; measure out and reserve 1 tablespoon milk mixture. Pulse flour, ¼ cup sugar, baking powder, and salt in food processor until combined, about 4 pulses. Scatter butter over top and pulse until mixture resembles coarse cornmeal, 12 to 14 pulses. Transfer mixture to large bowl and stir in oats, raisins, and walnuts. Stir in remaining milk mixture until large clumps form. Continue to mix dough by hand in bowl until dough forms cohesive mass.

2 Turn dough and any floury bits onto lightly floured counter; pat gently into 7-inch circle. Cut dough into 10 wedges. Brush tops with reserved 1 tablespoon milk mixture and sprinkle with remaining 1 tablespoon sugar.

3 Lightly spray bottom of air-fryer basket with vegetable oil spray. Space desired number of scones at least ½ inch apart in prepared basket; evenly space remaining scones on parchment paper–lined rimmed baking sheet. Place basket into air fryer and set temperature to 350 degrees. Bake until scones are golden brown, 10 to 15 minutes. Transfer scones to wire rack and let cool for at least 5 minutes before serving.

4 Freeze remaining sheet of scones until firm, about 1 hour. Transfer scones to 1-gallon zipper-lock bag and freeze for up to 1 month. To bake from frozen, place scones into air-fryer basket. Place basket into air fryer, set temperature to 250 degrees, and bake for 10 minutes. Increase temperature to 350 degrees and continue to bake until golden brown, about 10 minutes.

CURRANT, ALMOND, AND OAT SCONES WITH EARL GREY GLAZE

Substitute currants for raisins and almonds for walnuts. Microwave 1 tablespoon milk and ½ teaspoon crumbled Earl Grey tea leaves in medium bowl until steaming, about 30 seconds. Let cool completely, about 10 minutes. Whisk in ½ cup confectioners' sugar until smooth and let sit until thick but pourable, about 10 minutes. Omit sugar for sprinkling. Let scones cool to room temperature, about 20 minutes, then drizzle with glaze. Let glaze set for 10 minutes before serving.

APRICOT, PISTACHIO, AND OAT SCONES WITH GARAM MASALA GLAZE

Substitute chopped dried apricots for raisins and pistachios for walnuts. Microwave 1 tablespoon milk and ½ teaspoon garam masala in medium bowl until steaming, about 30 seconds. Let cool completely, about 10 minutes. Whisk in ½ cup confectioners' sugar until smooth and let sit until thick but pourable, about 10 minutes. Omit sugar for sprinkling. Let scones cool to room temperature, about 20 minutes, then drizzle with glaze. Let glaze set for 10 minutes before serving.

WHOLE-WHEAT BLUEBERRY-ALMOND MUFFINS

Makes 4 muffins

COOK TIME **12 minutes**   TOTAL TIME **45 minutes**

why this recipe works We wanted to build a whole-wheat blueberry muffin (scaled to make four quick, one-bowl muffins) that would be a breeze to bake in the air fryer. The problem is, most whole-wheat muffins are dense and heavy. Could we create an air-fried version that was tender and delicious? First, we addressed the cardboard-like flavor of many whole-wheat muffins. We replaced part of the whole-wheat flour with finely chopped almonds and loved how their rich nuttiness complemented the wheat's own earthy, toasty flavor. But the muffins were still squat and dense. We tried combining two leaveners—baking soda and baking powder—and were surprised to find that the muffins became too tender, lacking the structure to even come out of the muffin tins. Incorporating just a little all-purpose flour into the mix brought structural integrity and tenderness to our muffins. Both aluminum foil and silicone muffin-tin liners work equally well in the air fryer.

3 tablespoons sugar

¾ teaspoon baking powder

⅛ teaspoon baking soda

¼ teaspoon table salt

¼ teaspoon ground cinnamon

⅓ cup plain yogurt

1 large egg

2 tablespoons canola oil

½ teaspoon vanilla extract

⅓ cup (1¾ ounces) whole-wheat flour

¼ cup (1¼ ounces) all-purpose flour

¼ cup finely chopped almonds, divided

⅓ cup fresh or frozen blueberries

1 Spray 4 aluminum foil or silicone muffin-tin liners with vegetable oil spray. Whisk sugar, baking powder, baking soda, salt, and cinnamon together in medium bowl. Whisk in yogurt, egg, oil, and vanilla until smooth. Using rubber spatula, stir whole-wheat flour, all-purpose flour, and 2 tablespoons almonds into yogurt mixture until just combined (do not overmix). Fold in blueberries gently until incorporated.

2 Divide batter evenly among prepared muffin-tin liners (liners will be filled to rim) and sprinkle with remaining 2 tablespoons almonds. Place muffin-tin liners in air-fryer basket. Place basket into air fryer; set temperature to 350 degrees; and bake until muffins are golden brown and toothpick inserted in center comes out with few crumbs attached, 12 to 14 minutes.

3 Transfer muffins to wire rack and let cool for at least 10 minutes before serving.

DATE-ALMOND SNACK BARS

Makes 8 bars

COOK TIME **17 minutes**	TOTAL TIME **1 hour, plus 1¼ hours cooling**

why this recipe works To make a delicious and nutritious snack (or breakfast) bar packed with protein and fiber, we first toasted a collection of nuts and seeds in a cake pan. A blitzed mix of dates and a touch of maple syrup helped hold everything together when we pressed the mixture back into the same cake pan. Lining the pan with foil made it easy to get the bars in and out. The result was evenly toasted wedges with good crunch and a slight chew. Use pure maple syrup, not pancake syrup, here. You will need a 6-inch round nonstick or silicone cake pan for this recipe; before starting this recipe, confirm your air fryer allows enough space for the pan.

⅔ cup whole raw almonds, cashews, pecans, and/or walnuts

5 tablespoons raw pepitas and/or sunflower seeds

2 tablespoons whole flax seeds and/or sesame seeds

3 ounces pitted dates

2 tablespoons warm water

1 tablespoon maple syrup

1 teaspoon grated orange zest

¼ teaspoon table salt

⅛ teaspoon ground cinnamon

1 Combine almonds, pepitas, and flax seeds in 6-inch nonstick round cake pan. Place pan in air-fryer basket. Place basket into air fryer; set temperature to 350 degrees; and cook until nuts and seeds are toasted and fragrant, 3 to 5 minutes, stirring halfway through cooking.

2 Transfer nut mixture to food processor and let cool slightly; reserve pan. Process nut mixture until ground medium-fine, 15 to 20 seconds; transfer to large bowl. Process dates, warm water, maple syrup, orange zest, salt, and cinnamon in now-empty processor until finely chopped, scraping down sides of bowl as needed, about 30 seconds. Stir date mixture into nut mixture, folding and pressing with rubber spatula, until well combined.

3 Line now-empty pan with aluminum foil, pressing foil into corners of pan, and lightly spray with vegetable oil spray. Transfer mixture to prepared pan and press firmly into even layer with greased spatula. Return pan to air-fryer basket and return basket to air fryer. Set temperature to 300 degrees and cook until bars are evenly browned, 14 to 20 minutes.

4 Let bars cool in pan for 15 minutes. Using foil liner, remove bars from pan and transfer to wire rack. Discard foil and let bars cool completely, about 1 hour. Cut bars into 8 wedges and serve. (Bars can be stored in airtight container for up to 1 week.)

OLIVE OIL CAKE

Serves 4

COOK TIME **30 minutes**

TOTAL TIME **50 minutes, plus 1¼ hours cooling**

why this recipe works Olive oil cake is simple yet sophisticated. It has a light and plush crumb with a subtle but noticeable olive oil flavor. To pare down a full-size cake to a daintier 6-inch round that will fit in an air fryer, we simply reduced the ingredients by one-third (and in some cases by half for more straightforward measuring). Instead of a springform pan, we lined the bottom and sides of a 6-inch cake pan with parchment, which allowed the cake to release easily when inverted, so its crackly sugar top remained beautifully intact. For the best flavor, use a fresh, high-quality extra-virgin olive oil. You'll need a handheld electric mixer and a 6-inch round nonstick or silicone cake pan for this recipe; before starting this recipe, confirm your air fryer allows enough space for the pan.

- ⅔ cup (3⅓ ounces) all-purpose flour
- ½ teaspoon baking powder
- ¼ teaspoon table salt
- ½ cup (3½ ounces) plus 1 teaspoon sugar, divided
- 1 large egg
- ⅛ teaspoon grated lemon zest
- ¼ cup extra-virgin olive oil
- ¼ cup milk

1 Lightly grease 6-inch round cake pan, line with parchment paper, and grease parchment. Whisk flour, baking powder, and salt together in bowl.

2 Using handheld electric mixer, mix ½ cup sugar, egg, and lemon zest in bowl on low speed until combined. Increase speed to high and whip until mixture is fluffy and pale yellow, about 2 minutes. Reduce speed to medium and, with mixer running, slowly pour in oil. Mix until oil is fully incorporated, about 30 seconds. Add half of flour mixture and mix on low speed until incorporated, about 30 seconds. Add milk and mix until combined, about 30 seconds. Add remaining flour mixture and mix until just incorporated, about 30 seconds, scraping down bowl as needed.

3 Transfer batter to prepared pan and sprinkle remaining 1 teaspoon sugar over surface. Place pan in air-fryer basket. Place basket into air-fryer and set temperature to 275 degrees. Bake until skewer inserted diagonally into crack and aimed toward center of cake comes out with few crumbs attached, 30 to 35 minutes.

4 Transfer pan to wire rack and let cool for 15 minutes. Gently invert pan onto rack; remove parchment and reinvert. Let cake cool completely, about 1 hour. Cut into wedges and serve. (Cake can be wrapped in plastic wrap and stored at room temperature for up to 3 days.)

MAKE-AHEAD CHOCOLATE CHIP COOKIES

Makes 24 cookies

COOK TIME **10 minutes**

TOTAL TIME **45 minutes**
(10 minutes from frozen)

why this recipe works Most cookie recipes leave the baker with a yield that's larger than what can be eaten before they go stale. We wanted a recipe for the perfect chocolate chip cookie that would enable us to bake a mini batch, perfect for eating fresh and warm, right out of our air fryer. To keep the recipe quick, we wanted to eliminate the need to lug out an electric mixer. Rather than creaming the butter and sugar, we melted the butter so that we could stir everything together in one bowl. Furthermore, the liquid fat in the melted butter encouraged a bit of gluten development, making our cookies chewier. Folding the dry ingredients into the wet ingredients ensured that our cookies were tender, and using more brown sugar than granulated, plus a dash of vanilla extract, gave the cookies a subtle caramelized flavor. Bake as many as you want hot and ready for eating and freeze the rest for later—anytime you want a freshly baked treat. The number of cookies you can bake at one time will depend on the size of your air-fryer basket.

2⅛ cups (10⅔ ounces) all-purpose flour

½ teaspoon baking soda

½ teaspoon table salt

1 cup packed (7 ounces) light brown sugar

½ cup (3½ ounces) granulated sugar

12 tablespoons unsalted butter, melted and cooled

1 large egg plus 1 large yolk

2 teaspoons vanilla extract

1 cup (6 ounces) semisweet chocolate chips

1 Line air-fryer basket with aluminum foil, crimping edges to prevent foil from flapping. Line large rimmed baking sheet with parchment paper. Whisk flour, baking soda, and salt together in bowl.

2 Whisk brown sugar and granulated sugar together in medium bowl. Whisk in melted butter until combined. Whisk in egg and yolk and vanilla until smooth. Gently stir in flour mixture with rubber spatula until soft dough forms. Fold in chocolate chips.

3 Working with 2 tablespoons dough at a time, roll into balls. Space desired number of dough balls at least 1½ inches apart in prepared basket; space remaining dough balls evenly on prepared sheet. Using bottom of greased drinking glass, press each ball until 2 inches in diameter.

4 Place basket into air fryer and set temperature to 350 degrees. Bake cookies until light golden brown and centers are soft and puffy, 10 to 12 minutes. Let cookies cool slightly in basket. Serve warm or at room temperature.

5 Freeze remaining sheet of cookies until firm, about 1 hour. Transfer cookies to 1-gallon zipper-lock bag and freeze for up to 1 month. Bake frozen cookies as directed; do not thaw.

NUTRITIONAL INFORMATION FOR OUR RECIPES

To calculate the nutritional values of our recipes per serving, we used The Food Processor SQL by ESHA Research. When using this program, we entered all the ingredients, using weights for important ingredients such as most vegetables. We also used our preferred brands in these analyses. When the recipe called for seasoning with an unspecified amount of salt and pepper, we added ½ teaspoon of salt and ¼ teaspoon of pepper to the analysis. We did not include additional salt or pepper for food that's "seasoned to taste." If there is a range in the serving size, we used the highest number of servings to calculate the nutritional values.

	CALORIES	TOTAL FAT (G)	SAT FAT (G)	CHOL (MG)	TOTAL CARB (G)	TOTAL SUGAR (G)	ADDED SUGAR (G)	PROTEIN (G)	DIETARY FIBER (G)	SODIUM (MG)
Snacks and Toppings										
Whole-Wheat Pita Chips with Salt and Pepper	70	1	0	0	14	1	0	4	0	260
Buttermilk-Ranch Whole-Wheat Pita Chips	70	1	0	0	15	1	0	4	0	250
Crispy Barbecue Chickpeas (per ¼ cup)	110	6	1	0	11	1	1	4	3	230
Crispy Coriander-Cumin Chickpeas (per ¼ cup)	210	12	1.5	0	20	1	1	7	7	470
Crispy Smoked Paprika Chickpeas (per ¼ cup)	220	12	1.5	0	21	1	1	7	7	470
Jalapeño Poppers	405	37	17	89	5	2	0	14	1	575
Pigs in Blankets	150	10	5	10	8	0	0	4	0	290
Roasted Garlic	30	0	0	0	5	0	0	1	0	25
Roasted Plum Tomatoes	60	3.5	0.5	0	6	4	1	1	1	150
Roasted Peppers	30	0	0	0	5	4	0	1	2	0
Croutons	35	2.5	0	0	3	0	0	1	0	60
Crispy Shallots	25	0.5	0	0	5	2	0	1	1	0
Roasted Fruit Topping	45	0	0	0	13	9	0	0	2	35
Toasted Nuts	210	18	1.5	0	8	2	0	8	4	0
Smoked Paprika–Spiced Almonds	240	21	2	0	8	2	0	8	5	580
Orange-Fennel Toasted Walnuts	200	20	2	0	4	1	0	4	2	580
Warm-Spiced Pecans	220	21	2	0	7	4	3	2	3	0
Almond, Cherry, and Chocolate Trail Mix (per ½ cup)	240	14	5	0	26	7	4	5	4	65
Toasted Burger or Sandwich Buns	120	1.5	0	0	22	3	0	4	0	220

	CALORIES	TOTAL FAT (G)	SAT FAT (G)	CHOL (MG)	TOTAL CARB (G)	TOTAL SUGAR (G)	ADDED SUGAR (G)	PROTEIN (G)	DIETARY FIBER (G)	SODIUM (MG)
Breakfast										
Egg in a Hole with Tomato, Avocado, and Herb Salad	450	27	5	185	39	7	0	17	9	580
Baked Eggs with Smoky Zucchini, Red Pepper, and Bread Hash	430	22	5	370	36	11	0	23	2	810
Baked Eggs with Spinach, Artichokes, and Feta	340	23	7	385	14	3	0	22	6	740
Kale, Roasted Red Pepper, and Goat Cheese Frittata	230	14	6	355	5	2	0	18	2	460
Ham, Pea, and Swiss Cheese Frittata	260	15	6	400	7	3	0	24	2	680
Broccoli, Sun-Dried Tomato, and Cheddar Frittata	250	16	6	390	7	2	0	18	2	420
Make-Ahead Breakfast Burritos	420	16	4	250	45	2	0	21	4	940
Roasted Fruit and Almond Butter Toast	390	20	2.5	0	42	13	3	15	4	290
Overnight Breakfast Grain Bowl	480	18	2.5	0	73	30	6	10	9	310
Overnight Breakfast Three-Grain Bowl	420	18	2.5	5	56	11	6	10	9	320
Chicken and Turkey										
Chicken Parmesan	700	32	9	285	30	4	0	67	2	1100
Chicken Nuggets	690	24	4.5	305	51	2	0	63	2	910
Sweet-and-Sour Dipping Sauce	150	0	0	0	39	36	0	0	0	40
Honey-Dijon Dipping Sauce	90	0	0	0	17	16	16	0	0	720
Crispy Breaded Chicken Breasts with Creamy Apple-Fennel Salad	540	17	3.5	195	46	15	0	46	6	740
Spicy Fried-Chicken Sandwich	520	23	4	135	42	5	0	34	2	1210
Apricot-Thyme Glazed Boneless Chicken Breasts	340	8	1.5	165	13	9	0	51	0	400
Pineapple-Ginger Glazed Boneless Chicken Breasts	340	8	1.5	165	13	12	0	51	0	390
Unstuffed Chicken Breasts with Dijon Mayonnaise	550	27	9	220	1	1	0	70	0	1500
Brown Sugar–Balsamic Glazed Bone-In Chicken Breast (with skin/without skin)	550/420	20/10	5/2.5	165/135	30	28	27	59/50	0	440/420
Peach-Jalapeño Glazed Bone-In Chicken Breast (with skin/without skin)	490/360	20/10	5/2.5	165/135	14	12	0	59/49	0	430/410
Honey-Miso Glazed Bone-In Chicken Breast (with skin/without skin)	520/390	20/11	5/2.5	165/135	21	18	16	60/50	0	750/720
Spiced Chicken Breasts with Asparagus, Arugula, and Cannellini Bean Salad	550	20	3.5	165	29	6	0	63	10	1180
Roasted Bone-In Chicken Breasts (with skin/without skin)	410/280	18/8	4.5/2	165/135	0	0	0	59/49	0	430/410
Peach-Ginger Chutney	140	2.5	0	0	30	27	13	1	2	150
Lemon-Basil Salsa Verde	200	21	3	0	2	0	0	1	1	320

	CALORIES	TOTAL FAT (G)	SAT FAT (G)	CHOL (MG)	TOTAL CARB (G)	TOTAL SUGAR (G)	ADDED SUGAR (G)	PROTEIN (G)	DIETARY FIBER (G)	SODIUM (MG)
Chicken and Turkey (cont.)										
Roasted Bone-In Chicken Breasts and Fingerling Potatoes with Sun-Dried Tomato Relish (with skin/without skin)	650/520	22/12	5/2.5	165/135	46	2	0	55	7	1020/1000
Barbecued Bone-In Chicken Breasts with Creamy Coleslaw (with skin/without skin)	600/480	30/21	8/5	180/150	17	11	1	61/51	3	1340/1320
Spicy Peanut Chicken with Charred Green Beans and Tomatoes (with skin/without skin)	620/520	29/21	6/4	140/115	33	18	0	60/52	8	970/950
Red Curry Chicken Kebabs with Peanut Dipping Sauce	230	11	2	60	10	5	3	23	1	460
Spiced Chicken Kebabs with Vegetable and Bulgur Salad	590	24	4.5	130	42	8	0	52	8	700
Air-Fried Chicken	670	28	8	175	39	5	0	62	2	1330
Chipotle-Honey-Fried Chicken with Brussels Sprout and Citrus Salad	510	13	2.5	115	48	20	8	49	6	780
Coriander Chicken Thighs with Roasted Cauliflower and Shallots (with skin/without skin)	410/340	27/21	6/4	110/90	19	8	0	25/23	7	740/730
Chicken-Tomatillo Tacos with Roasted Pineapple Salsa	640	22	5	170	69	23	0	44	5	720
Hoisin-Ginger Chicken Salad with Napa Cabbage, Shiitakes, and Bell Pepper	540	29	5	160	26	13	0	43	6	890
Thai-Style Chicken Lettuce Wraps	290	11	2	105	22	15	2	27	4	290
Jerk Chicken Leg Quarters	500	31	8	230	11	7	7	43	1	800
Buffalo Chicken Drumsticks	480	33	13	210	7	5	5	36	1	1420
Lemon-Pepper Chicken Wings	170	11	3.5	95	0	0	0	16	0	140
Parmesan-Garlic Chicken Wings	210	14	4	115	1	0	0	19	0	200
Cilantro-Lime Chicken Wings	200	13	3.5	115	1	0	0	18	0	160
Roasted Chicken Sausages with Butternut Squash and Radicchio	510	29	5	135	50	13	5	18	8	770
Whole Roast Chicken with Lemon, Dill, and Garlic (with skin/without skin)	600/280	43/13	12/3	195/115	1	0	0	49/37	0	450/400
Whole Roast Chicken with Orange, Aleppo, and Cinnamon (with skin/without skin)	600/280	43/13	12/3	195/115	1	0	0	49/37	1	470/400
Whole Roast Chicken with Ginger, Cumin, and Cardamom (with skin/without skin)	600/280	43/13	12/3	195/115	1	0	0	49/37	0	480/400
California Turkey Burgers	460	19	8	70	36	8	1	42	4	710
Mini Glazed Turkey Meatloaves	580	29	6	260	31	18	7	48	1	980
Turkey-Zucchini Meatballs with Orzo, Spiced Tomato Sauce, and Feta	410	13	5	60	40	7	0	37	2	880

	CALORIES	TOTAL FAT (G)	SAT FAT (G)	CHOL (MG)	TOTAL CARB (G)	TOTAL SUGAR (G)	ADDED SUGAR (G)	PROTEIN (G)	DIETARY FIBER (G)	SODIUM (MG)
Beef, Pork, and Lamb										
Spice-Rubbed Steak with Snap Pea and Cucumber Salad	530	39	12	135	8	3	0	36	3	990
Lemon-Sage Top Sirloin Steak with Roasted Carrots and Shallots	350	13	3	60	34	16	0	26	9	780
Top Sirloin Steak with Roasted Mushrooms and Blue Cheese Sauce	450	25	10	135	10	6	0	43	1	860
Steak Frites	570	27	6	90	43	2	0	39	3	810
Flank Steak with Corn and Black Bean Salad	510	19	6	70	49	6	0	36	8	810
Beef Satay with Red Curry Noodles	680	27	15	105	64	11	7	44	5	840
Steak Tacos	530	24	7	85	48	7	1	32	10	520
Gochujang-Sesame Steak Tips with Napa Slaw	470	26	7	115	19	13	8	39	3	600
Roasted Steak Tips with Tomatoes and Gorgonzola	380	23	7	95	10	6	0	34	3	780
Ginger-Soy Beef and Vegetable Kebabs	560	38	8	115	15	10	4	40	2	1310
Coffee- and Fennel-Rubbed Boneless Short Ribs with Celery Root Salad	650	34	10	100	49	15	2	40	10	950
Roasted Boneless Short Ribs with Red Pepper Relish	400	27	9	100	5	3	2	33	1	510
Big Italian Meatballs with Zucchini Noodles	650	31	11	250	28	13	0	63	5	1540
Beef-and-Bulgur Meatballs with Tahini-Yogurt Dipping Sauce	180	9	3.5	45	10	2	0	15	2	350
Juicy Well-Done Cheeseburgers	580	32	13	130	28	5	0	41	1	900
Juicy Well-Done Green Chile Cheeseburgers	640	37	15	140	29	5	0	44	2	940
Juicy Well-Done Burgers with Caramelized Onions and Blue Cheese	620	35	14	130	31	6	0	41	2	850
Southwestern Beef Hand Pies	480	29	13	115	34	0	0	23	1	760
Southwestern Bean and Corn Hand Pies	510	29	12	80	52	3	0	15	5	1020
Roasted Bone-In Pork Chop	210	9	2.5	75	0	0	0	30	0	370
Peach-Mustard Sauce	50	0	0	0	13	12	6	1	1	40
Chermoula	340	37	5	0	2	0	0	0	1	0
Roasted Bone-In Pork Chop with Sweet Potatoes and Maple-Rosemary Sauce	610	21	5	105	66	28	18	36	7	780
Crispy Pork Chops with Roasted Peach, Blackberry, and Arugula Salad	580	26	5	130	55	24	8	32	6	720
Lemon-Oregano Roasted Pork Chops with Tomato-Feta Salad	620	34	10	175	20	14	5	58	3	970
Sweet and Spicy Glazed Pork Chops with Sesame Bok Choy	360	22	4.5	60	16	13	0	23	2	730

	CALORIES	TOTAL FAT (G)	SAT FAT (G)	CHOL (MG)	TOTAL CARB (G)	TOTAL SUGAR (G)	ADDED SUGAR (G)	PROTEIN (G)	DIETARY FIBER (G)	SODIUM (MG)
Beef, Pork, and Lamb (cont.)										
Fennel-Rubbed Pork Tenderloin with Zucchini Ribbon Salad	500	27	14	230	0	0	0	60	0	900
Pork Tenderloin with Prosciutto and Sage	500	24	6	160	13	8	4	56	3	830
Lemon-Thyme Pork Tenderloin with Green Beans and Hazelnuts	490	27	4	105	23	12	3	40	7	770
Marinated Pork Gyros	510	21	7	95	44	4	0	37	3	930
Italian Sausage and Pepper Subs	440	18	5	35	45	12	3	25	7	1160
Mustard-Thyme Lamb Chops with Roasted Carrots	430	19	4.5	100	29	18	8	34	6	860
Lamb Sliders with Apricot Chutney	670	36	16	110	58	21	4	36	4	760
Lamb Sliders with Smoky Tomato Relish	630	37	16	115	45	7	0	35	3	850
Lamb Kofte Wraps	550	37	19	115	24	5	0	33	2	720
Lamb Meatballs with Couscous	670	35	16	115	54	16	0	35	5	760
Seafood										
Better-Than-Boxed Fish Sticks	430	17	2.5	195	29	1	0	35	1	990
Tartar Sauce (per tablespoon)	70	7	2	5	1	1	0	1	0	210
Old Bay Dipping Sauce (per tablespoon)	70	7	2	5	1	1	0	1	0	110
Crunchy Air-Fried Cod Fillets	340	12	2	190	12	1	0	43	1	490
Creamy Chipotle Chile Sauce	230	25	5	25	2	1	0	1	0	190
Roasted Cod with Lemon-Garlic Potatoes	490	19	11	145	33	1	0	44	3	710
Moroccan Spiced Halibut with Chickpea Salad	470	17	2.5	110	30	5	1	50	9	910
Harissa-Rubbed Haddock with Brussels Sprouts and Leek	330	22	3	30	21	6	0	15	7	830
Sole and Asparagus Bundles with Tarragon Butter	380	29	15	135	6	3	0	24	2	500
Roasted Salmon Fillets	500	34	7	125	0	0	0	46	0	430
Herb-Yogurt Sauce (per tablespoon)	40	2	1.5	10	4	3	0	2	0	30
Mango-Mint Salsa (per tablespoon)	150	8	1	0	20	3	0	0	1	360
Pistachio-Crusted Salmon	320	20	5	65	7	1	0	26	1	370
Hazelnut-Crusted Salmon	310	21	4.5	65	6	1	0	26	1	370
Smoked Almond–Crusted Salmon	320	20	4.5	65	6	1	0	26	1	410
Orange-Mustard Glazed Salmon	520	32	7	125	8	7	0	46	0	550
Honey-Chipotle Glazed Salmon	550	32	7	125	18	16	16	47	0	430
Hoisin Glazed Salmon	520	32	7	125	8	4	0	47	1	680

	CALORIES	TOTAL FAT (G)	SAT FAT (G)	CHOL (MG)	TOTAL CARB (G)	TOTAL SUGAR (G)	ADDED SUGAR (G)	PROTEIN (G)	DIETARY FIBER (G)	SODIUM (MG)
Seafood (cont.)										
Honey Glazed Salmon with Snap Peas and Radishes	330	16	3	30	30	21	16	18	5	660
Sesame Salmon with Roasted Kimchi, Broccoli, and Shiitakes	350	21	4	60	11	5	0	28	3	620
Salmon Burgers with Tomato Chutney	570	25	6	95	41	13	7	41	2	840
Salmon Tacos with Roasted Pineapple Slaw	600	29	4.5	60	59	13	0	30	12	330
Crab Cakes with Bibb Lettuce and Apple Salad	350	16	2.5	225	17	8	0	32	3	780
Bacon-Wrapped Scallops with Spinach, Fennel, and Raspberry Salad	540	42	12	75	16	6	1	24	6	950
Shrimp Skewers with Peanut Dipping Sauce	340	21	3	215	10	5	3	29	2	770
South Carolina–Style Shrimp Bake	410	18	5	200	31	4	0	34	3	880
Spicy Roasted Shrimp and Fennel Salad with Cannellini Beans and Watercress	470	24	3.5	145	40	10	0	27	12	1060
Chipotle Shrimp Tacos	420	14	3.5	165	47	10	7	24	5	670
Vegetable Sides and Mains										
Roasted Asparagus	30	1.5	0	0	3	2	0	2	2	75
Mint-Orange Gremolata (per tablespoon)	30	1.5	0	0	4	2	0	2	2	75
Tarragon-Lemon Gremolata (per tablespoon)	30	1.5	0	0	4	2	0	2	2	75
Roasted Broccoli	130	8	1	0	11	3	0	7	5	350
Roasted Broccoli with Parmesan, Lemon, and Black Pepper Topping	250	16	5	20	12	3	0	19	5	850
Roasted Broccoli with Sesame and Lime Topping	190	13	1	0	13	3	0	9	6	440
Air-Fried Brussels Sprouts	80	4	0.5	0	9	2	0	3	4	170
Air-Fried Brussels Sprouts with Crispy Shallots	90	4	0.5	0	13	4	0	4	5	170
Lemon-Chive Dipping Sauce	90	10	1.5	5	1	0	0	0	0	115
Orange-Cardamom Roasted Carrots	150	6	3.5	15	24	14	4	2	6	280
Cumin-Lime Roasted Carrots	150	6	3.5	15	24	14	4	2	6	290
Smoked Paprika–Lemon Roasted Carrots	150	6	3.5	15	24	14	4	2	6	290
Curried Roasted Cauliflower and Chickpea Salad	290	19	2.5	0	29	9	0	10	9	420
Roasted Eggplant with Capers, Oregano, and Garlic	120	7	1	0	15	7	0	2	6	330

	CALORIES	TOTAL FAT (G)	SAT FAT (G)	CHOL (MG)	TOTAL CARB (G)	TOTAL SUGAR (G)	ADDED SUGAR (G)	PROTEIN (G)	DIETARY FIBER (G)	SODIUM (MG)
Vegetable Sides and Mains (cont.)										
Roasted Fennel with Orange-Honey Dressing	190	14	2	0	15	11	5	2	4	350
Roasted Green Beans with Sun-Dried Tomatoes and Sunflower Seeds	160	11	3	5	11	4	0	7	4	170
Roasted Mushrooms with Shallot and Thyme	190	14	2	0	10	7	0	4	1	310
Roasted Bell Pepper Salad with Mozzarella and Basil	300	23	6	20	13	9	0	7	3	230
Roasted Bell Pepper Salad with Manchego and Olives	300	26	6	10	12	6	0	7	4	510
Baked Potatoes	180	1	0	0	41	1	0	5	3	160
Blue Cheese–Pepper Butter (per tablespoon)	90	9	6	25	0	0	0	1	0	50
Lemon-Thyme Butter (per tablespoon)	100	11	7	30	0	0	0	0	0	0
Crispy Baked Potato Fans	300	14	2	0	40	2	0	5	3	300
Crispy Smashed Potatoes	180	7	1	0	27	2	0	3	3	320
Crispy Smashed Potatoes with Garlic and Dill	180	7	1	0	27	2	0	3	3	320
French Fries	200	7	0.5	0	31	1	0	4	2	300
Sriracha Dipping Sauce (per teaspoon)	100	10	1.5	5	1	1	0	0	0	170
Shoestring Fries	150	7	1	0	20	1	0	2	1	150
Shoestring Fries with Rosemary and Lemon Zest	150	7	1	0	21	1	0	2	2	150
Shoestring Fries with Coriander and Dill	160	7	1	0	21	1	0	2	3	150
Roasted Sweet Potato Wedges	200	7	1	0	33	7	0	3	5	380
Maple-Glazed Acorn Squash	130	6	3.5	15	20	9	6	1	2	300
Roasted Delicata Squash	120	7	1	0	14	3	0	1	2	300
Spicy Maple Syrup	50	0	0	0	13	12	12	0	0	290
Goat Cheese and Chive Sauce	60	4.5	3	15	1	1	0	4	0	65
Zucchini Fries	210	12	3	55	16	3	0	8	1	480
Stuffed Portobello Mushrooms with Kale, Corn, and Pickled Jalapeños	400	24	7	10	38	9	1	13	5	740
White Bean and Mushroom Gratin	450	16	2.5	0	59	11	0	22	12	900
Roasted Butternut Squash Salad with Za'atar and Halloumi	400	25	8	20	57	16	5	15	10	910
Ramen Noodle Bowl with Eggplant and Five-Spice Tofu	540	15	2	0	86	11	0	23	6	760

	CALORIES	TOTAL FAT (G)	SAT FAT (G)	CHOL (MG)	TOTAL CARB (G)	TOTAL SUGAR (G)	ADDED SUGAR (G)	PROTEIN (G)	DIETARY FIBER (G)	SODIUM (MG)
Vegetable Sides and Mains (cont.)										
Make-Ahead Lentil and Mushroom Burgers	350	14	2	0	47	6	0	12	6	490
Make-Ahead Lentil and Mushroom Burgers with Radicchio and Pear Salad	480	22	5	5	59	14	3	15	8	770
Make-Ahead Phyllo Hand Pies with Fennel, Olive, and Goat Cheese Filling (per hand pie)	70	3.5	1.5	5	8	1	0	3	1	130
Make-Ahead Phyllo Hand Pies with Apple, Walnut, and Blue Cheese Filling (per hand pie)	90	4	1	5	10	3	0	2	0	140
Hearty Vegetable Hash with Golden Yogurt	400	18	3	5	52	15	0	13	10	720
Small Batch Baking										
Apple Crisp	210	6	3.5	15	39	26	7	2	5	220
Warm Chocolate Fudge Cakes	340	17	8	95	42	8	7	9	2	330
Cheesecake	380	29	17	125	25	22	18	6	0	330
Make-Ahead Fruit, Nut, and Oat Scones	320	12	6	45	30	24	6	5	1	230
Currant, Almond, and Oat Scones with Earl Grey Glaze	290	12	6	45	40	17	11	6	2	220
Apricot, Pistachio, and Oat Scones with Garam Masala Glaze	280	12	6	45	39	15	11	5	2	220
Whole-Wheat Blueberry-Almond Muffins	240	12	1.5	50	29	12	9	6	2	290
Date-Almond Snack Bars	140	9	1	0	13	9	2	5	3	40
Olive Oil Cake	340	16	2.5	50	44	27	26	4	0	220
Make-Ahead Chocolate Chip Cookies	180	8	5	30	26	16	16	2	0	80

CONVERSIONS AND EQUIVALENTS

Some say cooking is a science and an art. We would say that geography has a hand in it, too. Flours and sugars manufactured in the United Kingdom and elsewhere will feel and taste different from those manufactured in the United States. So we cannot promise that the loaf of bread you bake in Canada or England will taste the same as a loaf baked in the States, but we can offer guidelines for converting weights and measures. We also recommend that you rely on your instincts when making our recipes. Refer to the visual cues provided. If the dough hasn't "come together in a ball" as described, you may need to add more flour—even if the recipe doesn't tell you to. You be the judge.

The recipes in this book were developed using standard U.S. measures following U.S. government guidelines. The charts below offer equivalents for U.S. and metric measures. All conversions are approximate and have been rounded up or down to the nearest whole number.

Example

1 teaspoon	=	4.9292 milliliters, rounded up to 5 milliliters
1 ounce	=	28.3495 grams, rounded down to 28 grams

Volume Conversions

U.S.	METRIC
1 teaspoon	5 milliliters
2 teaspoons	10 milliliters
1 tablespoon	15 milliliters
2 tablespoons	30 milliliters
¼ cup	59 milliliters
⅓ cup	79 milliliters
½ cup	118 milliliters
¾ cup	177 milliliters
1 cup	237 milliliters
1¼ cups	296 milliliters
1½ cups	355 milliliters
2 cups (1 pint)	473 milliliters
2½ cups	591 milliliters
3 cups	710 milliliters
4 cups (1 quart)	0.946 liter
1.06 quarts	1 liter
4 quarts (1 gallon)	3.8 liters

Weight Conversions

OUNCES	GRAMS
½	14
¾	21
1	28
1½	43
2	57
2½	71
3	85
3½	99
4	113
4½	128
5	142
6	170
7	198
8	227
9	255
10	283
12	340
16 (1 pound)	454

Conversions for Common Baking Ingredients

Baking is an exacting science. Because measuring by weight is far more accurate than measuring by volume, and thus more likely to produce reliable results, in our recipes we provide ounce measures in addition to cup measures for many ingredients. Refer to the chart below to convert these measures into grams.

INGREDIENT	OUNCES	GRAMS
flour		
1 cup all-purpose flour*	5	142
1 cup cake flour	4	113
1 cup whole-wheat flour	5½	156
sugar		
1 cup granulated (white) sugar	7	198
1 cup packed brown sugar (light or dark)	7	198
1 cup confectioners' sugar	4	113
cocoa powder		
1 cup cocoa powder	3	85
butter†		
4 tablespoons (½ stick or ¼ cup)	2	57
8 tablespoons (1 stick or ½ cup)	4	113
16 tablespoons (2 sticks or 1 cup)	8	227

* U.S. all-purpose flour, the most frequently used flour in this book, does not contain leaveners, as some European flours do. These leavened flours are called self-rising or self-raising. If you are using self-rising flour, take this into consideration before adding leaveners to a recipe.

† In the United States, butter is sold both salted and unsalted. We generally recommend unsalted butter. If you are using salted butter, take this into consideration before adding salt to a recipe.

Oven Temperatures

FAHRENHEIT	CELSIUS	GAS MARK
225	105	¼
250	120	½
275	135	1
300	150	2
325	165	3
350	180	4
375	190	5
400	200	6
425	220	7
450	230	8
475	245	9

Converting Temperatures from an Instant-Read Thermometer

We include doneness temperatures in many of the recipes in this book. We recommend an instant-read thermometer for the job. Refer to the table above to convert Fahrenheit degrees to Celsius. Or, for temperatures not represented in the chart, use this simple formula:

Subtract 32 degrees from the Fahrenheit reading, then divide the result by 1.8 to find the Celsius reading.

Example:
"Roast chicken until thighs register 175 degrees."
To convert:

$$175°F - 32 = 143°$$
$$143° \div 1.8 = 79.44°C, \text{ rounded down to } 79°C$$

INDEX

Note: Page references in *italics* indicate photographs.